Will Africa Feed China?

Will Africa Feed China?

Deborah Brautigam

OXFORD
UNIVERSITY PRESS

Oxford University Press is a department of the University of
Oxford. It furthers the University's objective of excellence in research,
scholarship, and education by publishing worldwide.

Oxford   New York
Auckland   Cape Town   Dar es Salaam   Hong Kong   Karachi
Kuala Lumpur   Madrid   Melbourne   Mexico City   Nairobi
New Delhi   Shanghai   Taipei   Toronto

With offices in
Argentina   Austria   Brazil   Chile   Czech Republic   France   Greece
Guatemala   Hungary   Italy   Japan   Poland   Portugal   Singapore
South Korea   Switzerland   Thailand   Turkey   Ukraine   Vietnam

Oxford is a registered trademark of Oxford University Press
in the UK and certain other countries.

Published in the United States of America by
Oxford University Press
198 Madison Avenue, New York, NY 10016

© Oxford University Press 2015

Cataloging-in-Publication Data is on file with the Library of Congress.
ISBN: 978-0-19-939685-6

9 8 7 6 5 4 3 2 1
Printed in the United States of America
on acid-free paper

For Amalie, Carrie, Jenna, Jeremy, Jesse, Lisa, Matthew,
Max, Miles, and Oscar

CONTENTS

ACKNOWLEDGMENTS

An official in China's Ministry of Agriculture once said to me: "It is difficult to study this topic, even for us." I couldn't agree more. Hunger and food security, land grabbing, the fate of small farmers in faraway African villages, Chinese migration: all important topics, all with inadequate data, all covered by the international media with TV, radio, and newspaper stories of sharply varying accuracy. Over the past decade, fact and fiction have merged into a conventional wisdom on China's agricultural engagement in Africa that does not match the realities on the ground. Peeling away the layers of myths required extensive fieldwork, grounded in an appreciation of the long, complex history and evolution of Africa's experience with China. The result is, I hope, a more balanced and realistic account that can provide a baseline for current and future analyses of China's rise and the impact this is likely to have in Africa.

This book had its origin in research I did during a year as a visiting senior research fellow in the Development Strategy and Governance Division at the International Food Policy Research Institute (IFPRI), in Washington, DC. I thank Margaret McMillan, Paul Dorosh, Xinshen Diao, Xiaobo Zhang, Kevin Chen, and Shenggen Fan for their help and support. I acknowledge with appreciation Johns Hopkins University School of Advanced International Studies, the Bill and Melinda Gates Foundation, Carnegie Corporation of New York, and the Smith Richardson Foundation, who all funded parts of this research.

For their encouragement in urging me to dig further into the issue of Chinese "land grabs," I thank Tony Allan, Martin Keulertz, Suvi Sojamo, Jeroen Warner, Philipp Baumgartner, and Carlos Oya. Participants at a May 2014 conference we organized at Johns Hopkins University on Chinese agricultural investment in Africa provided a terrific way to share early findings from our fieldwork and compare notes. I am grateful to the participants: Lila Buckley, Solange Guo Chatelard, Chen Xiaochen, Jessica Chu, Sérgio Chichava, Josh Maiyo, Margaret Myers, Nama Ouattara, Louis Putzel, Henry Tugendhat, Eckart Woertz, Xu Xuili, Yang Jiao and Zhou Jinyan. For their perceptive comments at our conference, I thank Peter

Lewis, M. David Lampton, Yoon Jung Park, and Robert Thompson. Tang Xiaoyang and Janet Eom organized a very helpful workshop on the draft book manuscript at Tsinghua University in March 2015, for which I am grateful.

For repeated patience in answering so many questions, I thank Sérgio Chichava, Aaron de Grassi, George Schoneveld, officials in China's Ministry of Agriculture, the China Africa Agricultural Investment Corporation, Ministry of Agriculture officials in every country I visited in Africa, the Chinese and African investors, and the workers and villagers who gave so generously of their time. Sigrid-Marianella Stensrud Ekman, Zhang Haisen, and Tang Xiaoyang deserve special thanks as coauthors, friends, and intrepid companions in fieldwork.

Many people have read and commented on various chapters, including Pieter Botellier, Anne Brautigam, Richard Brautigam, Carla Freeman, Solange Guo Chatelard, Sérgio Chichava, Sigrid-Marianella Stensrud Ekman, Lin Hai, Elizabeth Holmes, Shubo Li, Mima Nedelcovych, Bruce Parrott, Helge Rønning, Tang Xiaoyang, Robert Thompson, Xu Xiuli, and Zhang Haisen. Their suggestions are much appreciated.

I have been blessed with the most amazing research assistants. Tang Xiaoyang has worked with me since 2007 and is now himself a professor at Tsinghua University. The talented, multilingual Bonnie Brodsky, Yunnan Chen, Nicollette Maunganidze, Ilaria Mazzocco, Noah Schlosser, and Yuanli Zhu all helped in the research for this book at various times, but Hanning Bi and Jyhjong Hwang were the heavy lifters. They tracked down impossibly difficult sources, made cold calls to Chinese businesses, improved my translations, answered e-mails at ridiculous hours, and generally made this a much better, more accurate, book. Their assistance is very gratefully acknowledged. Of course, I am responsible for any mistakes.

Parts of this book have been presented at seminars or conferences sponsored by the Center for Global Development, the University of Cape Town, the World Bank, the University of Wisconsin Land Tenure Center, the University of Pennsylvania, the International Food Policy Research Institute, and Johns Hopkins University. I thank the participants for their questions and comments. My editor at Oxford University Press, David McBride, encouraged me to write this book, shepherding it from idea to completion with just the right amount of judicious attention. Two anonymous reviewers added constructive suggestions. Ada Ho, Robin Washington, Alma Alcaraz and Shirley Raymundo helped keep me organized with humor and care, while Katie Weaver, Janet Eom and Molly Morrison skillfully brought the book through the last stages of production.

My husband and dearest companion, David Hirschmann, is my most insightful reader, gentlest critic, and most helpful editor. He brings the warm heart of Africa into my life on a daily basis. The youngest members of my family have done their best to distract me: on the shores of Moosehead Lake, in the snows of Vermont, splashing on the Potomac, or exploring the forests of Rambouillet. They are a continual reminder that there is so much more to life than conferences, books, and fieldwork. I dedicate this book to them.

ACRONYMS

ADM	Archer Daniels Midland
AfDB	African Development Bank
ARDA	Agricultural and Rural Development Authority (Zimbabwe)
ATDC	agro-technology demonstration center
CAADP	Comprehensive Africa Agriculture Development Program
CAAIC	China-Africa Agriculture Investment Corporation
CAD-Fund	China Africa Development Fund
CALF	Chinese International Cooperation Company for Agriculture, Livestock and Fisheries
CARI	China Africa Research Initiative
CCECC	China Civil Engineering and Construction Company
CCPIT	China Council for the Promotion of International Trade
CDB	China Development Bank (National Development Bank)
CEIEC	China Electronics Import and Export Corporation
CGC	China Geo-engineering Corporation
CGCOC	China Geo-engineering Construction Overseas Corporation (a subsidiary of Sinopec and CGC)
CGOC	China Grains and Oils Group
China Eximbank	Export-Import Bank of China
CIC	China Investment Corporation
CIFOR	Center for International Forestry Research
CIWEC	China International Water and Electricity Corporation
CITIC	China International Trust and Investment Corporation
CLETC	China Light Industrial Corporation for Foreign Economic and Technical Co-operation
CNADC	China National Agricultural Development Corporation Group

CNHRRDC	China National Hybrid Rice Research and Development Center
CNPC	China National Petroleum Corporation
COFCO	China National Cereals, Oils, and Foodstuffs Corporation
Complant	China Complete Plant Import and Export Corporation
COVEC	China Overseas Engineering Corporation
CPC	Communist Party of China
CSFAC	China State Farm Agribusiness Corporation (China *Nongken*)
CSIS	Center for Strategic and International Studies
CSR	corporate social responsibility
DRC	Democratic Republic of Congo
DWM	December Women's Movement (Ghana)
FAC	Future Agricultures Consortium
FAO	Food and Agriculture Organization
FCFA	CFA Franc
FDI	foreign direct investment
FETC	foreign economic and technical cooperation
FOCAC	Forum on China Africa Cooperation
Frelimo	Frente de Libertação de Moçambique (Mozambique Liberation Front)
FT	*Financial Times*
GATT	General Agreement on Tariffs and Trade
GDP	gross domestic product
GPZ	Zambezi Valley Planning Office (Mozambique)
GSFF	Global Solidarity Forest Fund
IFAD	International Fund for Agriculture
IFC	International Finance Corporation
IFPRI	International Food Policy Research Institute
IIED	International Institute for Environment and Development
IISD	International Institute for Sustainable Development
IMF	International Monetary Fund
IPRCC	International Poverty Reduction Center of China
IRRI	International Rice Research Institute
LPHT	Longping High-Tech Agriculture Corporation
MOA	Ministry of Agriculture (China)
MOFA	Ministry of Foreign Affairs (China)
MOFCOM	Ministry of Commerce (China)
MOU	Memorandum of Understanding

NAFCO	National Food and Agricultural Corporation (Tanzania)
NDRC	National Development and Reform Commission (China)
OECD	Organisation for Economic Cooperation and Development
Renamo	Resistência Nacional Moçambicana (Mozambican National Resistance)
SASAC	State-owned Assets Supervision and Administration Commission (China)
Sucobe	Complant Sugar Complex of Benin
Sucoma	Complant Sugar Complex of Madagascar
Sukala	Upper Kala Sugar Complex
USAID	US Agency for International Development
USTDA	US Trade and Development Agency
WTO	World Trade Organization
ZANU-PF	Zimbabwe African National Union—Patriotic Front

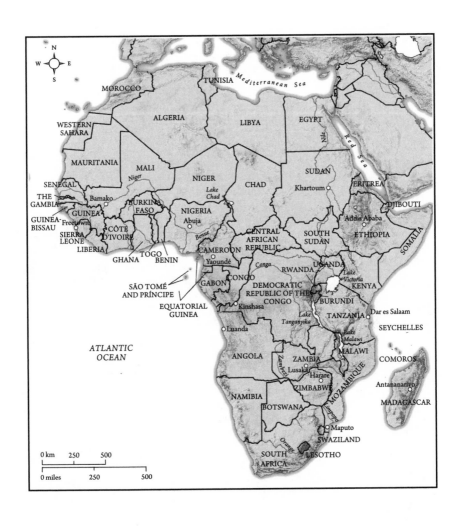

Will Africa Feed China?

INTRODUCTION

In August 2012, the chief economist of the African Development Bank published an article on the risks and opportunities associated with China's rise. China, he wrote, was "the biggest 'land grabber' in the world *and in Africa*."[1] China's meteoric economic rise and emergence as an investor country coincided with global price increases in food, oil, and many other commodities between 2007 and 2008. Alarm about what was perceived to be a huge, state-sponsored program of African land grabbing swept through the press, governments, and civil society. Sustained interest in China's role as an overseas agricultural investor in Africa has generated hundreds of newspaper articles and editorials, sensational statements and robust myths—but surprisingly little investigative reporting.

This book challenges four widespread beliefs about Chinese agricultural engagement in Africa that have shaped the conventional wisdom, circulating through influential policy circles and popular culture, where they have been readily absorbed by pundits, researchers, intellectuals, and even writers of fiction. It draws on my own field research and that of others who have explored what the Chinese are actually doing in the rice paddies, maize fields, and sugar plantations of rural Africa. In doing so, it seeks to fill the gap between the conventional wisdom and a paucity of evidence on a topic that has clearly fascinated many who are concerned with food security and development in the world's poorest region.

The first belief, echoed in the chief economist's statement, is that the Chinese have actually acquired very large areas of farmland in Africa. Many media stories have featured Chinese companies (or, more commonly, simply "China" or "the Chinese") as central players in African land acquisitions. "China . . . now has extensive holdings in Africa, including pending or attempted deals for millions of hectares in the Democratic Republic of

Congo, Zambia, Zimbabwe, Uganda, and Tanzania, with many thousands of Chinese workers brought in to work on these lands," a reporter wrote for Inter Press Service.[2] We read on an Israeli news website: "Chinese farms control most of Zambia's agriculture." CBS News published an article stating that "China recently purchased half the farm land under cultivation in the Congo."

Second, it is widely believed that the Chinese government is leading the effort to acquire land in Africa as part of a grand plan, using its state-owned enterprises and sovereign wealth funds.[3] "The strategy has been carefully devised by officials in Beijing," a British journalist wrote in the *Daily Mail*. An article in a prominent American magazine, the *Atlantic*, claimed that the Chinese government had set up a $5 billion fund just to invest in agriculture in Africa. Echoing this, a researcher at a major Washington, DC–based think tank wrote, "China has invested immense sums in African agriculture."

Third, across Europe and the United States, the conventional wisdom holds that the Chinese have developed a voracious appetite for African grain.[4] The Rockefeller Foundation warned that "the growing Chinese desire for African-produced food" could mean that "poor people in African countries may no longer have the resources they need to survive." In a French newspaper, we read: "What they [the Chinese] do is invest in Africa to feed the Chinese people." In Benin, the head of a civil society organization told a television crew that the Chinese were growing vegetables in his country and sending them back to China.

Finally, many believe that the Chinese government has sent (or plans to send) large numbers of Chinese peasants to settle in Africa. For example, the *Economist* repeated (without endorsing) a report that more than a million Chinese farmers were cultivating crops in Africa. A French television station predicted that the "Chinese conquest of African farmland" would provide a solution for millions of Chinese peasants deprived of their land. The Swedish crime novelist, Henning Mankell, told a journalist, "I read just the other day that China has rented land in Kenya to move some one million peasants to Africa." An American reporter wrote that China's National People's Congress had debated a proposal to send 100 million unemployed Chinese to Africa to grow food.

This book explains why *none* of these stories turned out to be true. In examining the evidence, we will see that surprisingly few of the Chinese investments headlined in media stories have actually taken place. No one has yet identified a village full of Chinese farmers anywhere on the continent. A careful review of Chinese policy shifts shows steadily rising support for outward investment of all kinds but no pattern of sponsoring the migration of Chinese peasants, funding large-scale land acquisitions in Africa, or investing "immense sums" in African agriculture. Finally, according to the United Nations Commodity Trade database, it is *China* that has been sending food to Africa.[5] While this could (and should) change, so far, the only significant food exports from Africa to China have been sesame seeds and cocoa, produced by African farmers.

Nevertheless, the headlines and media reports turned into "data" that became the foundation for analysis by researchers in NGOs, universities, and think tanks. In October 2008, for example, GRAIN, a nongovernmental organization (NGO) based in Barcelona, published an attention-getting analysis of "land grabbing" based on media reports. The words "China" or "Chinese" were mentioned 47 times in the paper, mainly as one of a group of countries whose main goal was to "outsource their domestic food production by gaining control of farms in other countries."[6] Although it is now clear that firms from wealthier countries were also eagerly seeking to acquire land, the report did not mention the United States or "American" at all, and the UK was featured as an investor country only once. These reports underpinned a general, if erroneous, sense among public policy specialists, civil society, and intellectuals that the Chinese were not only very active players in this arena but also almost alone among the major countries.

This conventional wisdom percolated into the realm of foreign policy. For example, in the summer of 2011, a widely circulated European media story led with this sentence: "Germany's Africa policy coordinator on Thursday blamed China's practice of buying up land in the Horn of Africa for contributing to the devastating drought ravaging the region."[7] I read this with some surprise, having just returned from extensive fieldwork in the Horn of Africa, where we and two other teams of researchers had identified *no* Chinese land acquisitions beyond a handful of Chinese-run vegetable farms growing *bok choy* and eggplants for Chinese restaurants. When I met him later, the policy coordinator explained that he had been misunderstood by the reporter, yet the statement still created an unnecessary diplomatic incident for the German government.

Most public fears about Chinese agricultural investment in Africa have been expressed in the West. On the other hand, unsurprisingly, the Chinese press and African governments have often failed to reveal the very real problems faced by Chinese projects under negotiation or those that have gone into implementation over the past 50 years, including many originally funded by China's aid program. Chinese journalists writing about farming investments predictably fail to cover tense labor relations, complaints from villagers about compensation and resettlement, violent protests, higher than expected costs, or the surprising disparity between predicted and actual yields. African governments have courted foreign investment, sought to commercialize their rural areas, and often discounted the social costs of their modernization plans.

WHO WILL FEED CHINA?

The production and control of food is an emotive as well as a practical issue. "The battle to feed all of humanity is over," Stanford University biologist Paul Ehrlich wrote in a bestselling 1968 book *The Population Bomb*.[8] "In the 1970s and 1980s hundreds of millions of people will starve to death in spite of any crash programs embarked upon now." Although the green revolution helped ensure that this did not happen, pessimists have continued to sound the alarm, while optimists have pointed to continued, steady increases in global production and yields.

With their histories of food insecurity and periodic famine, China and Africa have long occupied a central place in the global concern for food security. In 1995, Lester Brown, environmental activist and founder of the Washington DC–based Worldwatch Institute, published a short book entitled *Who Will Feed China?* Brown noted how industrialization in China's densely populated neighbors Japan and South Korea had quickly led to heavy dependence on food imports. A growing population, shrinking farmland, and a slowing of yield increases would force China to rely on imports, which could quickly outrun the supplies available from food-exporting nations. Brown intended his book to be a wake-up call for China's leaders on the environmental and social implications of its likely emergence as a "massive grain importer." If not carefully managed, China's food demands would soon rock world grain markets. "China's rising food prices will become the world's rising food prices," Brown's book argued. "China's land scarcity will become everyone's land scarcity."[9]

Brown's argument generated enormous coverage, including a *Washington Post* article with the headline "How China Could Starve the World." A year later, in a review of Brown's book in *Foreign Affairs*, Robert Paarlberg, a professor at Wellesley and an expert on the political economy of agriculture, wrote that Brown's Malthusian pessimism about production increases was unjustified.[10] For example, Brazil's acidic *cerrado* contained more than 150 million acres of arable land. Advances in science could make the *cerrado* into a grain basket (as Paarlberg predicted, this transformation of the *cerrado* has indeed happened). Furthermore, if China did come to depend more on world markets, this would be a positive development. "Grain imports make economic and environmental sense for China," he wrote. The challenges to the world food system, Paarlberg argued, were most likely to come from Africa, where low levels of irrigation, corruption, desertification, poverty, and poor infrastructure were already a threat to food security.

As we will see in chapter 3, China commenced opening its own agricultural sector to foreign investment and agricultural imports as part of its gradual policy of reform. In 2003, less than a decade after the publication of *Who Will Feed China?*, the *Financial Times* (*FT*) wrote that foreign investors were eyeing *Chinese* farmland. In the fertile alluvial plains of landlocked Shanxi province, Swiss agribusiness giant Syngenta was growing sweet-corn and iceberg lettuce. Strong foreign markets for Chinese exports of high-value peppers, mushrooms, and leeks led an Australian foreign investor to predict: "China can be Asia's farm and kitchen."[11] A 2009 study by the US Department of Agriculture estimated that although demand for animal feed (soybeans, maize/corn) was rising, Chinese per capita demand for rice and wheat would fall. With total demand already starting to decline, "future imports of [these] food grains will likely remain small."[12]

The geopolitics of food security for a country with 1.3 billion people are very complicated. For example, outside experts have urged China to import more grain. In 2014, the head of the Washington DC–based International Food Policy Research Institute (IFPRI), Shenggen Fan, wrote in *China Daily* that "food security does not equal grain self-sufficiency."[13] The *Economist* concurred: China's "obsession with food self-sufficiency" was outdated and wasteful: "It is time for China to abandon autarkic thinking and import more food." Yet Chinese president Xi Jinping has repeatedly emphasized: "We must fill our bowls with grain we grow ourselves."[14] For historic reasons, including a 21-year trade embargo imposed by the United States in 1950, the Chinese have been hesitant to become dependent on outside supplies of critical staple foods. Yet these hesitations are not shared by all Chinese experts. In a reflection on the debates inside China, economist Mao Yushi wrote in 2009 that if China were now to face a global grain embargo "certainly it would be because we ourselves had committed some huge and dreadful crime against heaven. Even if there were grain to eat, it would not be good times for the Chinese people."[15]

The Chinese have worked hard to modernize their agriculture and ease the rapid transition to a predominately urban nation. Agriculture has been growing at around 5 percent annually for the past three decades, far above the rate of population growth. The government has invested heavily in irrigation, technology, and machinery. In 2013, Professor Jikun Huang, director of the Center for Chinese Agricultural Policy at the Chinese Academy of Sciences in Beijing, predicted that China would experience large increases in the import of animal feeds, including soybeans and maize, and smaller increases for dairy products, but would continue to be a net exporter of rice, fruits, and vegetables.[16]

FEEDING AFRICA

Concern about Chinese farming investment in Africa coincides with intense debates about foreign investment and the future of the many small subsistence farms across the continent, as commercial agriculture continues to grow. Worries about private and state-sponsored "land grabbing" are well justified. Throughout history and around the globe, governments and powerful elites have colluded to enclose and privatize land originally held in common. The era of European colonialism sponsored official land grabbing on an epic scale. Today, in countries with a weak rule of law (and this includes China), traditional landholders, subsistence farmers, and others without secure title continue to be pushed off of their land, displaced by commercial real estate developers, large-scale commercial farms, and plantations.

Although there are exceptions, in most of Africa agriculture remains overwhelmingly small scale and oriented toward subsistence. In Nigeria, Africa's most populous country, a 2014 World Bank study reported that "most farming . . . is still done at the subsistence level with minimal commercialization."[17] With so many farmers focused on survival and not on the market, Africa remains dependent on imported food. The structural transformations that have allowed billions of people in richer nations, including China, to leave behind the arduous, high-risk life of manual labor, and shift to more productive and comfortable work in services and manufacturing, have yet to happen in most of Africa.

Professor Huang's message about Africa's potential role in the global food trade and Chinese engagement on the continent was upbeat. "Many African countries have substantial areas of land that are agro-climatically suitable for maize, soybean, and sugar production but are constrained by technology, marketing infrastructure, and farm management. Average yields are generally low, and there has been serious underinvestment in agricultural R&D and advisory services for many years, which China is now helping to strengthen."[18]

A 2013 study by the UK's Overseas Development Institute (ODI) echoed some of this analysis in a briefing entitled, "The End of Cheap Rice: A Cause for Celebration?"[19] The Asian green revolution led to large increases in productivity and the supply of rice, which pushed down the price. Since 2000, however, the price of rice has doubled, reflecting higher costs for fertilizer, fuel, and especially rural wages, in an Asia that is growing increasingly prosperous. In 2011, Africa imported over 10 million tons of rice from Asia, valued at $5.6 billion. While these higher prices could cause hardships for poor and vulnerable groups in Africa, there was a silver lining. In the long run, the ODI argued, this should be seen as Africa's opportunity. If higher prices stimulate Africa "to fulfil its undoubted potential in rice production, that will be no bad thing." And in the very long run, it is possible, even desirable, that Africa will not only feed itself but also send rice to China.

INTO THE BUSH: THE REAL STORY

The question of just what the Chinese are doing in rural Africa has occupied me for a long time. I went to graduate school in the 1980s as a China scholar and studied Chinese agricultural aid in West Africa for my PhD dissertation. I spent nearly a year and a half interviewing Chinese technicians and African farmers and digging through dusty archives in African ministries of agriculture. My first book, *Chinese Aid and African Development*, analyzed the impact of decades of Chinese aid in rural Africa.[20] Over the years, I watched as aid evolved into multiple forms of economic cooperation and investment. In my most recent book, *The Dragon's Gift: The Real Story of China in Africa*, I analyzed China's sharply increased interest in Africa.

In 2011, I was invited to be a senior research fellow at IFPRI, where I began the research for this book. Over the past few years, with the help of a team of colleagues, I have examined each of the alleged Chinese cases of African "land grabbing" collected in online databases, desk studies and inventories, and any other cases we could find (see appendix 1). The portrait drawn in these pages is very different from the headlines, mainly because my colleagues and I actually went to Africa to do our research.

We carried out fieldwork in China and in a number of African countries where major Chinese land grabs were supposed to be happening, including the DRC, Ethiopia, Kenya, Mozambique, Nigeria, Sierra Leone, Tanzania, Uganda, Zambia, and Zimbabwe. We obtained a database of Chinese agricultural investments from the Chinese Ministry of Commerce (MOFCOM), and we interviewed numerous senior Chinese government officials, and employees at many of the major Chinese agribusiness companies in the field and at their headquarters in China. We talked to African government officials in rural areas and in the halls of their ministries. In each country we trekked to the rural areas to visit existing farms or find out why planned investments failed to launch. We also drew on the efforts of IFPRI colleagues stationed across Africa who shed additional light on some cases with their colleagues in ministries of agriculture.

After I began a new position on the faculty of Johns Hopkins' School of Advanced International Studies (SAIS) and became director of the China Africa Research Initiative (CARI), we hosted a major conference, inviting researchers from around the world to share their fieldwork on Chinese agricultural investment in Africa and sponsoring field research by PhD students in Angola, Nigeria, and Uganda. Thus this book reports on my own research but also on that of many other equally curious and intrepid souls who have found themselves driving hundreds of miles into the African bush to find, and interview, the managers of remote Chinese farms and the Africans who work with—or were impacted by—these investments.

Drawing on these multiple methods of research on Chinese agricultural investments (both actual and failed), this book makes five key arguments.

First, although a growing number of Chinese agribusiness companies have pursued investments in Africa, this interest has not, so far, translated into significant land acquisitions. In most cases, the amount of land at stake in these negotiations was far smaller, and the outcomes much more problematic, than reported. Chapters 1 and 5 tell the stories of the investments that *didn't* happen—myths that circulated as facts, ambitious intentions that melted in the face of hard realities. The number of Chinese state-owned firms, individuals, and private companies who see possibilities in Africa is rising, however. Chapters 6 through 8 tell their stories. These suggest that land acquisitions will almost certainly increase from the current very low levels. Indeed, Chinese officials and scholars repeatedly say that they believe Chinese agricultural investment overseas to be "still in its infancy."

Second, these investments often (but not always) display an active role for the Chinese government. We see this especially in the early years, where the guiding hand and pushing palm of the central government is most in evidence. Over the past decade, provincial governments have played an increasingly large role. Some see this as China's "strategic plan" for Africa. In chapter 4, I argue that the government role in these investments should rather be seen as reflecting the framework of China's general "going global" surge of trade and outward foreign investment, increasingly evident in the years since China joined the World Trade Organization (WTO) in 2001. The Chinese government here acts as a "developmental state," following in the footsteps of Japan and South Korea: using a variety of tools and incentives to coax, prod, and nurture its nascent global firms, in agribusiness and other sectors. Yet although the Chinese state is active, we should not make the mistake of seeing every Chinese (or Hong Kong, or Macao) investment as a coordinated action by "China, Inc." This would be a serious misreading of the evidence.

Third, as the case studies throughout the book demonstrate, *all* the actual and planned Chinese agricultural investments we have seen in Africa were either focused on food production for local markets (eggs, poultry, rice, wheat, maize, sugar, mushrooms, etc.) or, like firms from other countries, involved export of traditional agricultural commodities to global markets, including China (sugar, rubber, tobacco, cotton, oil palm). While concern for China's future food security cannot be ruled out as a motive, the evidence is clear that this is by no means the prime incentive.

Fourth, while individual Chinese investors have gone into farming across the continent, we see no evidence of an organized plan to export Chinese settlers to farm in Africa. As researchers Solange Guo Chatelard and Jessica Chu point out in the case of Zambia, many of the new Chinese investors have no prior experience in farming.[21] Like Jack Liu, who founded a company called "Honey King" working with local farmers to export honey from Tanzania, they were entrepreneurs who found a niche that could be exploited by someone with a bit of money and a good idea. These new Chinese investors often chose the agricultural sector after seeing imported vegetables filling African supermarkets or observing the high prices offered locally for wheat, maize, and rice.

Finally, the book emphasizes the key roles played by Africans—as investors, civil society organizations, rural dwellers, and governments. In the dominant storyline, Africa and Africans appear primarily as passive bystanders, even victims. Instead, what we will see is a series of eager and aware African investors who have partnered with the Chinese. We will meet the African governments who have often embraced large projects as desirable due to their promise of rapid modernization.[22] Governments in Ethiopia, Mozambique, Zambia, and elsewhere were impatient with the slower evolution of societal change, confident in the promise of scientific progress, and often disdainful of the claims of farmers and herders who have used parts of "state-owned land" for their modest subsistence. Yet their vision of modern, large-scale agribusiness was not matched by the ability to put in place the roads and power plants, or the humane resettlement schemes, that would make commercial agriculture economically, socially, and politically viable. Local people—farmers, workers, and herders, often backed by local and foreign NGOs and local politicians—pushed back against foreign investors, Chinese and others. For each of the handful of investments that finally succeeded, many more failed because of poor infrastructure, coups, contentious elections, even civil wars.

In *The Dragon's Gift*, I wrote about my efforts, and those of many others, to track down evidence for some of the Chinese agricultural investment stories already circulating through cyberspace. It was already clear then that Chinese companies were interested in overseas agriculture. Indeed, researchers have documented multiple Chinese agricultural investments in nearby countries like Cambodia.[23] In 2007, a Chinese firm signed a memorandum of understanding (MOU) with the government of the Philippines, hoping to lease a million hectares to grow maize, rice, and sorghum (the investment never went forward). I described a conversation I had that year with Wang Yibin in Sierra Leone, which reflected what was then a widespread perception among the Chinese who were coming to Africa. The team leader of a South-South Cooperation project cosponsored with the Food and Agriculture Organization (FAO), Wang had spread his arms wide, saying, "Land plenty in this country, no one use it!" But he had also told me about the failure of his efforts to interest Chinese investors in rural Sierra Leone—mainly due to the poor infrastructure.

The story of China's rise is likely to be the most important story in development for some time to come. China's engagement in Africa has clearly captured the imagination of many who worry about the impact of a newly rising power on a continent that has seen many foreign invasions. Journalists have sometimes stoked a feeding frenzy, circulating rumors as though they were real facts. Getting the details of this engagement right, and avoiding sensationalism, is not easy, but it matters. This is true not only for people in Africa and other parts of the developing world but also for Europeans and Americans who are trying to understand a change that is challenging many of our ideas of development and our place in the world. Although this book draws its conclusions based on my academic research and the evidenced-based assessment of many other scholars, it is meant for thoughtful readers interested in China's rise and what this means for poorer regions, like Africa.

And now let us begin, by diving into the first of our stories and sorting fact from fiction.

CHAPTER 1

China and Mozambique

Fiction and Fact

The year is 2006. Deep in the African bush, drums beat while dancing women lead a delegation of Chinese officials to a set of soft armchairs lined in rows inside a large tent. Outside, a brass band strikes up the national anthem of Mozambique as newly elected President Guebuza steps up to a microphone to make a few brief remarks. Guebuza then turns the podium over to Mapito, the organizer of the meeting. "Listen carefully," a Chinese businessman whispers to his sister. "This is what the future will look like."[1]

After taking a sip of water, Mapito describes a planned helicopter trip along the Zambezi River. "We shall fly over fertile areas that are sparsely populated. According to the calculations we have made, over the next five years we will be able to accommodate four million Chinese peasants who can farm the areas currently lying fallow."

That afternoon, with the thundering clatter of the helicopters drowning out the possibility of conversation, the delegation flies over what appears to be an enormous untouched wilderness. The sea of dark green is broken only by the winding route of a silver river and a scattering of settlements. Later, after dinner, another troupe of local women dance in the firelight. "I take it," the sister says to the Chinese businessman, "that everything's been prepared already."

The scenes described above are fiction. They appear—far more elegantly—in a best-selling thriller published in 2008: *The Man from Beijing,* by the Swedish writer Henning Mankell. The meeting in the jungle never happened. Only in a novel would an elected political leader support a plan to import four million Chinese into his country. Mankell's story reflected exaggerated Western fears about China in Africa, fears that took visual form in the famous March 15, 2008, cover of the *Economist*, with a Photoshopped picture of pith-helmeted Chinese men riding camels across the desert under the banner title: "The New Colonialists."

A slightly less sensational story about the Zambezi valley surfaced in August 2007, when a website hosted by the Swiss Federal Institute of Technology published a short article on China's growing ties with Mozambique.[2] Nearly a year later, the prominent Center for Strategic and International Studies (CSIS) in Washington, DC posted a second short article by the same author with the title "The Zambezi Valley: China's First Agricultural Colony?"[3] The websites appear to have provided no fact-checking, or editorial or peer review. Nevertheless, the two articles created a powerful narrative that would be picked up as fact by NGOs, think tanks, government agencies, and magazines. This story would ultimately become one of the key planks in the foundation of the West's understanding of Chinese intentions in rural Africa. Yet, as we will see, this plank had some very large cracks.

Here is the story as sketched out on these two websites. The Chinese government was "aggressively" seeking large land leases along the Zambezi River valley, trying to "induce" Mozambican officials "to allow them entry into the valley." The Chinese, "crude and rapacious businessmen scavenging for raw materials," were able to "open doors otherwise closed to Western nations." In 2006, the author said, China had given Mozambique a loan of $2.3 billion to build Mpanda Nkua, an enormous dam on the Zambezi River. The two governments, he said, had signed an agreement to allow "as many as 20,000 Chinese settlers" to "move into the valley to run large- to medium-scale farms destined to supply the ever more affluent Chinese market." These farms would be China's "first agricultural investments in Africa." However, the plan to import Chinese settlers "caused great outrage locally" because people in the Zambezi valley feared a return to the dark days of Portuguese colonialism. Indeed, reports of the deal caused "such an uproar" that the Mozambique government was forced "to dismiss the whole story as false."

Nevertheless—the author wrote—the two governments were quietly proceeding with their plans. The government of Mozambique had even decided to make Mandarin a compulsory foreign language for all high school students. The Chinese government had pledged (the author said) to add another $800 million to the earlier loan—a commitment of over $3 billion—all focused on modernizing rice production in Mozambique. Chinese offers of finance for agricultural research and road projects in Mozambique were also "clearly designed to maximize production and facilitate the rapid export of foodstuffs to China." The rice must be meant for China, the author argued, since Mozambicans do not eat much rice.

As further evidence of Chinese intentions, he wrote, China had abolished import tariffs on 400 agricultural products from Mozambique, including rice. "*One thing seems to be certain*," he emphasized, "*China is committed to transforming Mozambique into one of its main food suppliers, particularly for rice.*"[4]

Although it would turn out to be laced with errors, publication on the website of CSIS, one of the world's most respected think tanks, gave the story credibility, while the timing, during the height of the world food crisis, gave it instant visibility. The argument that the Chinese government was leading an aggressive effort to acquire large expanses of land in Mozambique, hoping to settle tens of thousands of Chinese citizens there to grow rice to send home to China, was accepted nearly everywhere, without question. In Washington, DC, IFPRI researchers wrote that "Mozambicans have resisted the settlement of thousands of Chinese agricultural workers on leased lands," citing the CSIS story as their source.[5] The German development agency GIZ included the story in a list of reported foreign investments in land, noting that it was discontinued "due to political opposition."[6] It was cited by newspapers, think tanks, NGOs, and researchers, appearing in reports by GRAIN, the Land Matrix, the Mo Ibrahim Foundation, and South Africa's Standard Bank. Magazines, including the *Atlantic,* repeated the story. In August 2008, the US embassy in Maputo even quoted parts of the CSIS website story in a secret diplomatic cable sent back to Washington.[7]

Only one report commented on the curious lack of evidence. The London-based International Institute for Environment and Development (IIED) had done fieldwork on foreign land grabs in Mozambique and other countries while carrying out a major study for the FAO and the International Fund for Agriculture (IFAD), published in 2009.[8] Citing the CSIS story on China and Mozambique, they noted pointedly that they had been unable to verify its claims. "A common external perception is that China is supporting Chinese enterprises to acquire land abroad as part of a national food security strategy," the IIED researchers noted. "Yet the evidence for this is highly questionable."

When I read these articles, I was intrigued but also puzzled. Many of the statements were simply wrong. For example, rice was *not* of minor importance in Mozambique. According to the International Rice Research Institute (IRRI), "*rice is considered a strategic crop in Mozambique,* where it is expected to contribute to ensuring food security in the country."[9] In 2007, according to FAO statistics, Mozambique—one of the world's poorest countries—had paid over $145 million to import nearly 500,000 metric tons of rice.[10]

It was also not true that Mozambique had made the Chinese language compulsory at any level of schooling. The stories had other errors. For example, in 2006 Beijing had offered to allow duty-free entry for 400 products from Africa's least developed countries (including Mozambique), but fewer than 10 percent of the products were agricultural. The list included knitted bow ties, ballpoint pens, and leather jackets. Rice, a highly protected crop in China, was decidedly *not* on the list.[11] Although the Chinese had expressed strong interest in funding the massive dam at Mpanda Nkua (as long as a Chinese company carried out the work), they had never provided a loan. The author was also clearly not aware that Chinese agribusiness companies had already been investing in agriculture in Mozambique—and other parts of Africa—for over two decades.

These details could be easily checked, and this level of carelessness raised questions about the other claims. There were no references to interviews or fieldwork in Mozambique, or to primary sources that could confirm the more sensational allegations: a massive $800 million Chinese government pledge to modernize Mozambique's rice sector; an agreement to import tens of thousands of Chinese settlers; public protests, expressions of outrage, or government denials of such a plan.[12]

And so I resolved to visit Mozambique. There, a different story began to take shape, one we will return to at various points throughout this book. It is a story of China's emerging global business ambitions and an African government's active concern with food security in a context of weak institutions. It involves not just China but also many other players: Portugal and Brazil, for example. As we will see in chapter 3, the Chinese role in this story begins not in 2006, but decades earlier. This history shaped the present engagement.

"WE CAN'T CONFIRM THIS STORY"

I arrived in Mozambique's faded colonial capital for the first time in June 2009 and was immediately charmed. Maputo was quite unlike the West African cities of Lagos, Freetown, and Monrovia where I had done extensive fieldwork. The warm Indian Ocean washes against the curved beaches that fringe the edges of the city. Acacia, purple jacaranda, and royal palms line its wide avenues, although its crumbling sidewalks covered with a lacework of sand present a hazard to pedestrians. Some prominent buildings are in ruins, cratered with bullet holes, trees branching through arched courtyards.

The bullet holes are a reminder of Mozambique's violent recent history. In 1962, a group of Mozambicans in exile in Tanzania formed the Mozambique Liberation Front, known by its Portuguese acronym Frelimo. Within two years, the Portuguese colonial government found itself fighting armed guerillas that attacked and then melted into the mountains and jungles. For most of the next 30 years, Mozambique would be consumed by war: its own liberation struggle, and then a protracted civil war between Frelimo, and a rival group, the Mozambican National Resistance (Renamo), backed by white-ruled South Africa. The Portuguese would be gone by 1975—the year their own revolution ended decades of dictatorship. But nearly a million Mozambicans would die before South Africa's political transition in the early 1990s brought an end to their conflict.

Under the Portuguese, Mozambicans had acquired a strong taste for rice. Satellite images of Mozambique's major rivers clearly show the ghosts of Portuguese canals marking out rectangular plots of land—drainage and irrigation systems built with *chibalo* (forced labor) starting in the late 1930s. The Portuguese fostered settler agriculture and also disrupted the subsistence practices of local farmers, compelling them to cultivate rice for delivery at low prices to privately owned mills, by threats of beatings and fines. The practice of *chibalo* and the coercive cultivation of rice ended only in the early 1960s. By then, dozens of Portuguese settler farms in areas like the Lower Limpopo had transformed parts of Mozambique into a breadbasket, producing over 10,000 tons of milled rice per year.[13]

As Mozambicans began moving to the cities, the demand for foods like rice accelerated. Local rice yields were extremely low, averaging just over one ton per hectare, compared with over six in China. Yet, as a 2005 study of Mozambique's rice industry funded by the Italian aid agency, Cooperazione Italiana, noted, "*The government of Mozambique sees significant potential to reverse this situation and ultimately produce a surplus of rice to sell both regionally and internationally.*"[14] To become an international rice powerhouse, Mozambique would require new investment on multiple fronts. For example, while paddy rice production costs were comparable to those in Thailand, Mozambique's rice-milling costs were up to six times higher, pushing down farmers' profits. Modern rice mills would be essential to the expansion effort. Weak agricultural research was also a critical constraint.

The Mozambique government identified 20 districts with high potential for rice production and stepped up their efforts to engage international partners.[15] At the government's request, IRRI opened an office in Mozambique. Japan, France, and Ireland provided funding to repair colonial-era irrigation works. In September 2005, President Guebuza met with Chinese President Hu Jintao at the United Nations General Assembly in New York and urged the Chinese to explore agricultural investments.[16] Spurred by this high-level request, the Chinese commercial counselor's office in Maputo translated Mozambique's agricultural investment incentives into Chinese and posted them on the Chinese Ministry of Commerce website.[17]

My first meeting in Maputo that June was with Justiça Ambiental, a local environmental activist group. I asked about the stories I had read. One of the members recalled hearing a rumor from a cooperative in the northern town of Quelimane about Chinese interest in the Zambezi valley, but they knew of no protests about plans to bring in Chinese farmers. "We can't confirm this story," they said.

I met with the staff in charge of agricultural assistance at the World Bank and other international aid agencies, but no one recalled hearing about a Chinese pledge to provide $800 million for rice production or any stories of public outrage or government denials of a plan to bring in Chinese settlers. At the International Monetary Fund's Maputo office, a staff member who had been tracking Chinese investment in Mozambique told me, "Agriculture is a priority area for the Mozambique government. A group of prominent Frelimo people want to find investors for the Zambezi valley. They have offered special tax incentives. There is Chinese interest, but nothing firm." This story was consistent with a March 2006 notice in Chinese on the website of the Chinese economic counselor's office in Maputo: "In recent years, our office has received a number of agricultural cooperation requests. The Zambezi River Basin Development Office has invited Chinese cooperation in growing cotton and rice."[18]

At the Ministry of Agriculture, a group of officials in the office of the permanent secretary, Daniel Clemente, told me: "*We* approached the Chinese to support our agricultural development." The China Export Import Bank was providing a line of credit of $50 million to finance machinery imports and the construction of three Zambezi valley factories for processing cotton, corn, and rice. The Chinese government was also funding an agricultural research demonstration and training center near Maputo with a grant of about $6 million. "This is less than we had expected," the Mozambican officials added. I asked if they had been expecting $800 million. They laughed, shaking their heads, no. "Where does *this* figure come from?"

I worked with several students to search Portuguese-language sources, including archives of the local independent newspapers. We found *no* media reports of an $800 million Chinese investment pledge, *no* stories of any intergovernmental agreement to bring in Chinese settlers, and *no* accounts of protests or outrage leading to the cancellation of any planned Chinese farming project. In dozens of interviews, I failed to find anyone who had even heard of these central pillars of the story. The narrative sketched shimmered like a mirage, until it slowly began to fade away.

In the office of *Savanna*, Mozambique's leading independent weekly newspaper, an alternative story began to take shape. There, I was reminded that Portugal had returned its former colony of Macau to China in 1999, where it had the same kind of autonomy given to Hong Kong. I learned that Stanley Ho, the billionaire Macau gambling magnate, had an interest in Mozambique. In 2005, Stanley Ho's investment company, Geocapital, had joined forces with several wealthy Mozambicans, setting up a local investment company called Zamcorp. "Zamcorp has $500 million worth of plans and projects for the Zambezi valley," an editor told me. "They have been trying to bring in Chinese investors."

"What about Chinese farmers?" I asked. He laughed but then leaned forward and said, "Some Mozambican businessmen connected to Zamcorp have said privately that we should import Chinese workers to transform the Zambezi valley. These are business people. They would like Mozambique to have less restrictive labor laws. For example, they would like to be able to bring in Indian accountants. Local accountants here can get $4,000 to $5,000 a month! But there was no decision to do this."[19]

In 2010, Swedish-Norwegian researcher Sigrid-Marianella Stensrud Ekman, who speaks Chinese and Portuguese, came to Mozambique to dig more deeply into the same story. Her findings paralleled mine (we later wrote an article together for *African Affairs*).[20] In particular, Ekman challenged the idea that "China" had been demanding large land leases in the Zambezi valley. Instead, the government's Zambezi River Basin Development Office "tried hard to get Chinese investment and failed."[21]

Portuguese scholar Ana Cristina Alves elaborated on the strong Portuguese connection missing from the original story.[22] The shareholders in Stanley Ho's Geocapital included Portuguese political and business elites such as Almeida Santos (former president of Portugal's parliament) and Jorge Ferro Ribeiro (former Minister for International Cooperation in Lisbon). By setting up Zamcorp, Alves argued, the private investors hoped to promote the valley's development "through privileged access to Chinese capital." Yet Zamcorp had been unable to develop a single project. Their efforts to pull Chinese investment into the Zambezi valley failed, Alves suggested, because they lacked "formal linkages to the Chinese state."

Clearly, there had been Chinese interest in the Zambezi valley. Yet as the Chinese economic counselor in Maputo would later tell me: "The Mozambique government thinks the Zambezi valley is the best place for agriculture, but it is far from Maputo, from the port, there are problems with transport."[23] His assessment was reflected in a report from Sérgio Chichava, a researcher at the Maputo-based Institute of Social and Economic Studies.[24] Chichava found that in 2010 the Zambezi River Basin Development Office worked with a Chinese group that had asked them to put together a 50,000-hectare concession. However, after conducting a feasibility study, the Chinese investors decided that the lack of infrastructure and problems with water made the Zambezi region too expensive.

As this suggests, had a Chinese company *wanted* to obtain a major concession of land in the Zambezi valley, they would likely have had little problem doing so. Indeed, an Oakland Institute study showed that between 2004 and 2009 Mozambique granted over one million hectares to foreign investors, mainly from Europe and South Africa; Chinese investors were conspicuous only by their absence.[25] Instead of a one-dimensional China aggressively seeking land to settle tens of thousands of Chinese farmers in Mozambique, what I found was an active group of Mozambican and Portuguese elites trying to position themselves to reap what they hoped and expected would be a bonanza of Chinese investment.

Meanwhile, far from the Zambezi valley, a new Chinese project was taking root. In December 2005, China's Hubei Province Department of Commerce led a study tour to Zambia, Kenya, and Mozambique.[26] Since the 1970s, the state farm system in Hubei, one of China's main grain-producing regions, had been sending multiple teams of agriculture experts to Africa under China's aid program. (In 2007, while doing fieldwork in Sierra Leone, I met several of their experts in the small town of Bo, working with Sierra Leone's Ministry of Agriculture on rice cultivation.) When the Hubei delegation reached Mozambique, they visited Gaza province and the former Portuguese irrigation system near the town of Xai-Xai in the Lower Limpopo valley. The Gaza provincial government offered them 300 hectares to start a demonstration farm and transfer technology to local farmers. The delegation brought back samples of the soft, black soil for testing; the quality was excellent. In 2006, Hubei province signed a twinning agreement with Gaza province and asked the provincial bureau in charge of oversight for Hubei's 53 state-owned farms to set up a company.

The bureau brought together a set of 19 investors from some of Hubei's state-owned farms to establish a company called Hubei Lianfeng (United Harvest).[27] The new farm, formally established in May 2007, would be called Gaza-Hubei Friendship Farm. Hubei Lianfeng was also tasked by the Chinese aid program to build a $6 million agro-technology demonstration center (ATDC) for Mozambique, just outside Maputo. "Hubei's project fits very well with Mozambique's national five-year plan," the Mozambican ambassador told a reporter from the *Yangtze Daily News*, in June 2007.[28] The team described plans to produce rice, but also flowers, and perhaps high value-added fruits and vegetables for direct shipment to Europe. Surprisingly, despite all this activity, Hubei province's very real investment project was not mentioned in the articles published on the Swiss and CSIS websites.

MOZAMBIQUE: FICTION AND FACT

This chapter launches us into the book starting with a widely circulated story stemming from a single source. It was premised on assumptions that few questioned: the Chinese government was aggressively trying to implement a grand plan to obtain large swaths of African land to ensure China's food security and planned to move tens of thousands of Chinese farmers to settle in Mozambique. The NGOs, think tanks, and journalists who repeated the Mozambique rumors did not look into the details since the framing of Chinese intentions fit a story that was widely accepted in the West.

This chapter shows how key elements of that story changed when researchers actually went to Mozambique and began to question the details. It illustrates the necessity of relying on evidence, rather than assumptions and rumors, when making an argument. What emerges is still a story—the story of a rising China and its companies beginning to enter global markets. African and European political elites and a Macau billionaire also have roles: hoping to take advantage of China's rise for their own purposes. We see how the Mozambican government asked the Chinese—and many others—to partner with them in helping Mozambique realize its own plans for agricultural modernization.

There is a real story of Chinese agricultural investment in Mozambique, and it has some unusual twists. In chapter 3, for example, we will see that the first major Chinese agricultural investment in Mozambique arrived via Brazil, more than a decade ago. Yet in most other ways, the story of China in Mozambique reflects the history of Chinese engagement in agriculture across Africa. China began providing agricultural aid to most African countries as soon as they became independent. Aid sometimes transitioned into investment. Food security will be a strong theme, but one pushed by African leaders, who were looking to China (and also to Japan, Vietnam, and even Ireland) to help reduce their countries' large and politically risky rice deficits.

Mozambique began to press for Chinese agricultural investment in 1997. It would take almost 15 years, but, eventually, they would succeed in bringing in a private Chinese company whose ambitions matched their hopes. We will meet this company, Wanbao, in chapter 8—not in the Zambezi valley, but more than a thousand kilometers away, on the vast delta along the mouth of the Limpopo River. Though the story of China and Mozambique is not the same story we thought we knew, it still raises deep questions about foreign land acquisitions, commercial agriculture, and food security. In the next chapter, we take a step back to examine some of the differences between China and Africa, and the controversies surrounding these issues. This sets the stage for the rest of the book.

CHAPTER 2

"Begging with a Golden Bowl"

Food Security and Commercial Farms

O n November 17, 2005, Yang Haomin, chairman of Shaanxi province's State Farm Agribusiness Corporation, sat for two hours, pondering a fax that had arrived in his office from the Ministry of Agriculture in Beijing.[1] Would his company be interested in going to Cameroon? Yang described himself as a born optimist. In 1998, he had imported 120 ostriches from Namibia, the nucleus of an experimental farm. People had laughed at the ungainly birds, but his investment grew to become the largest ostrich operation in Asia. Profits from the venture helped build the "Ostrich King" building that now housed Yang's office in Xi'an, home of China's famous 2,200-year-old terracotta army. In the years since China had begun to emphasize outward investment, or "going out," Yang had visited South Africa, Russia, Ukraine, and Brazil, but his explorations had yet to yield a project. He pulled out a map and located Cameroon along the west coast of Africa.

Six weeks later, on Christmas Eve, Yang and a small team of seven experts landed in Douala, the commercial capital of Cameroon. The Cameroon government hosted their visit, paying their expenses and showing them a number of locations where commercial cultivation of rice, cassava, and other crops might be feasible. By mid-January, Yang had decided to invest. Cameroon promised to provide 10,000 hectares of land at no charge, with a 99-year lease. Africa—Yang later said—impressed him with its "enormous development potential."[2] Cameroon seemed to have multiple advantages: warm, with ample water, plenty of sunshine and land, and a ready workforce. Yet every year the country was spending $250 million in scarce foreign exchange to import rice. Drawing on an Asian fable, Yang said: "It's like begging for food with a golden bowl." Yang would later find out that growing rice on a commercial scale in Cameroon was not nearly as simple as he had imagined. But to understand why his investment had such a mixed reception in Cameroon, we need some context.

AGRICULTURE, FOOD SECURITY, AND DEVELOPMENT

Agriculture and food security play critical roles in development. At the most basic level, people need food to survive. The lower a family's income, the larger the share spent on food. In the poorest countries, rural areas experience the deepest poverty: last to gain access to piped water, sanitation, electricity, and roads. Historically, raising the productivity of agriculture has been central to economic development, making poverty reduction possible and financing industrialization. Yet, as we shall see in this chapter, experts engage in passionate debates over the appropriate steps to take to modernize agriculture and ensure food security for all.

Globally, the world's farms still produce plenty of food. Technical change and rising productivity ensured that Paul Erlich's pessimistic predictions of widespread famine by the end of the 20th century did not come to pass. However, standard models used by the less sensational economists at IFPRI suggest that we are indeed at a historic turning point: they predict that prices for the major food grains will nearly double in real terms by 2050.[3]

The underlying pressure for this comes from urban consumer demand generated by Asia's rapid economic growth and from population increases, particularly in Africa, the last major region where families continue to have large numbers of children. As economic development expands, farmers shift from producing mainly subsistence foods to producing marketable commodities. Mechanization releases children from the need to labor manually on their parents' farms. They go to school and eventually move to cities—sometimes by choice, and sometimes because the higher value of land leads powerful people to take control of smallholders' land or to enclose common grazing areas. As poor families urbanize and move up the income scale, their diets change. At first, they put more rice, beans, or chapattis on the table. Soon, animal protein becomes a daily expectation instead of a monthly luxury. To produce a kilo of chicken takes two kilos of grain. For pork, the ratio is four kilos, and for beef, up to seven.[4] Asia's economic rise will mean steady upward pressure on global food supplies. The achievements of the past in raising productivity and output will need to continue.

Yet food security is not simply a matter of production. According to IFPRI's Global Hunger Index, some 870 million people across the globe are chronically undernourished: nearly one out of every eight people.[5] Part of this is explained by short-term shocks—people fleeing conflict; floods and drought—but in other cases, poverty, inequality, and the growing impact of climate change create long-term vulnerabilities. Surprisingly, according to the UN's Hunger Task Force, half of the hungry—and possibly three-quarters of the hungry in Africa—are smallholder farmers, unable to produce enough to feed their families adequately and too poor to buy food in local markets.[6] At a national level, poverty translates into difficulties in purchasing food available in global markets.

Capitalist commercial farming took early shape in England in a long process of scientific advances. But the way these processes played out was never just about science—it was also about power and avarice. As science was making land more valuable, local elites, backed by England's Parliament, enclosed over two million hectares of common lands that had formerly been used by peasants for grazing their animals, hunting, and foraging.[7] Deprived of areas they had relied on for subsistence, villagers became paid agricultural laborers, or they trudged out of villages with their meager belongings and sought work in the new factories of the British Industrial Revolution. Midway through the 19th century, Britain's agricultural workforce had shrunk to only 22 percent of total workers.[8]

The wave of progress, as sociologist Barrington Moore famously put it, rolled over the English peasantry. Yet even today, scholars debate whether the economies of scale created by the English enclosure movement were necessary for the higher productivity that resulted. Were larger farms truly more productive, a necessity for modernization, or did they simply come about through greed? The history of "land grabbing" in today's wealthy countries suggests that agricultural modernization is almost never painless. Commonly, rural-urban income disparities worsen, at least temporarily, and pockets of rural poverty persist: in the United States, the mountains of Appalachia, the small towns of Mississippi, and Arizona's Indian reservations still play this role. China's own modernization reflects these processes.

CHINA: FEED THE PEOPLE

When my mother was a child, parents used to say, "Finish your dinner. There are children starving in China." Famine was sadly common throughout Chinese history. Widespread famine helped invaders from Manchuria sweep to victory over the Ming dynasty in 1644. Famines added to the grievances that sparked the 19th-century Taiping and Boxer Rebellions, leading to the collapse of the final imperial dynasty in 1911. China's last great famine happened more than two generations ago, in the early years of the People's Republic. The disastrous policy failures of the Great Leap Forward (1958–1962), combined with drought and floods, pushed an estimated 30 million Chinese into hunger and then starvation.

There have been no famines in the decades since. The Nobel prize-winning economist Amartya Sen famously argued that democracy and a free press were the easiest ways to prevent famine. Instead, China's authoritarian leaders kept their fingers on the pulse of the rural economy and relied more on internal reporting to adjust their policy framework. Today, China's rural markets overflow with piles of shiny vegetables. Plump chickens squawk in bamboo cages next to baskets heaped with dried corn. With only 9 percent of the world's arable land, China remains the world's largest producer of rice, wheat, and pork.

Food security remains a central concern for China's leadership. Consider this contrast: the United States has a strategic petroleum reserve, with millions of barrels of oil stored in salt caverns along the Texas and Louisiana coast. China has a strategic pork reserve, introduced in 2007 to smooth fluctuations in the price of China's most politically important meat. It also has the world's largest grain reserves.[9] Yet, the nature of food security has changed over time. In Mao's era, facing a US trade embargo that lasted from 1950 to 1971, food security was synonymous with self-sufficiency in grain. Planners set targets, farmers produced according to quotas, and any surpluses were exported to earn foreign exchange. After economic liberalization began in late 1978, farmers were allowed to keep the profits from above-quota production, but the targets remained.

China's agriculture was still quite backward at the start of the reform period. For example, in 1980 nearly 70 percent of the Chinese people were employed in agriculture, but they produced only 30 percent of China's gross domestic product (GDP).[10] China then averaged only 77 tractors per 100 square kilometers of arable land, while Japan averaged 3,019 tractors, and Switzerland had 2,458 for the equivalent area (in Africa levels of mechanization were even lower then, at 33 tractors). Eighty percent of arable land was planted and harvested by hand.

The political importance of food was driven home during the wave of protests that culminated in the 1989 army massacre at Tiananmen Square. Inflation and high food prices had added fuel to the concerns of the protesters. "The ghost of 1989 is still haunting the Party leaders," a Chinese scholar at the National Development and Reform Commission (NDRC) told a team of Belgian scholars in 2008. "Food prices were the main triggers for turmoil in the past."[11]

As we saw in the introduction, the publication of Lester Brown's famous book *Who Will Feed China?* had a powerful effect in Beijing. In 1996, Chinese leaders set the grain self-sufficiency benchmark at 95 percent of China's grain requirements, meaning that China would ensure that it could produce domestically nearly all the staple foods that the country needed. Policymakers decreed that arable land would not be allowed to fall below a "red line" of 120 million hectares to ensure that China could always meet its own grain needs, if necessary. Nevertheless, the Chinese became net importers of food in 2004, a result of increased demand, trade liberalization under the WTO, and sensible policy shifts to promote imports of land-intensive products, like grain, and exports of more labor-intensive and higher value vegetables, fruits, and processed foods. With increased prosperity, the Chinese people are eating less grain but more meat. Today, problems related to obesity are a greater risk than starvation, although poor nutrition and hunger have not been eradicated. As one expert noted, "The cities are full of little fatties, but in the countryside there are children who are malnourished."[12]

By 2012, according to the FAO, China's agricultural exports were worth $63.2 billion and imports worth $112.4 billion. Experts predict that China's overall demand for food imports will continue to grow, stabilizing only in the early 2030s.[13] As with similar shifts in the trade balance of petroleum, iron ore, and other commodities, this reliance on external markets for food evokes a deep unease in many Chinese, making changes in the grain self-sufficiency policy politically quite sensitive, as we will see in chapter 4.

Agricultural modernization remains a work in progress. More than half of China's farmland is irrigated, and nearly half of all plowing, sowing, and harvesting is entirely mechanized. Policymakers test out new policies by experimenting on a local basis, making adjustments, and expanding those that seem to work. Between 1981 and 2010, over 500 million Chinese were lifted out of extreme poverty. While almost 70 percent of Chinese worked in agriculture in 1980, the figure was only 35 percent in 2011. The percentage would be even lower if China lifted restrictions on rural-to-urban migration that keep many Chinese from moving permanently to the cities. The share of agriculture in national income has declined from about 30 percent in 1980 to 10 percent in 2012.

Declines like this are generally healthy developments. The agricultural sector has grown at close to 5 percent a year for three decades, but other sectors have grown even faster, absorbing millions of workers whose labor was not needed in the fields. We can expect these changes to continue as China develops. High-income countries usually do not have many people doing the farming. In the United States, for example, agriculture makes up less than 2 percent of employment, down from 70 to 80 percent in 1870.

Although China is known as the world's workshop rather than the world's farm, agriculture remains central to its political economy. Since 2004, the government has highlighted this by focusing on agricultural modernization in the first policy document published each year. Many Chinese still believe the old adage: "An economy without strong agriculture is fragile; a country without food-grain self-sufficiency is chaotic." Now successful at feeding the people, policymakers' concerns center increasingly on problems of food safety and ecology, conserving scarce water, stemming erosion, cleaning up lands polluted by agricultural and industrial chemicals, and providing insurance and credit to ease farmers' vulnerabilities. Unsurprisingly, given what we know about paths to modernization in wealthy countries, land grabbing has also become an issue. China experiences more than 180,000 protests annually. Researchers believe that over half are sparked by peasants angry at land grabs instigated by local governments in league with unscrupulous property developers.[14]

AFRICA: NOT (YET) THE END OF POVERTY

Fifty years after independence, Africa remains a predominantly rural continent. Despite its vast agricultural potential, the continent's millions of farms produce less, on a per capita basis, than they did at the end of the colonial period.[15] The amount of land under cultivation per person has actually decreased since my first research visit to the continent in 1983. Furthermore, although Asia has more people below the poverty line, Africa boasts the dubious distinction of being the only continent where both poverty and inequality have increased.[16]

Though both experienced foreign imperialism, Africa's history is nothing like China's. In the first great land rush in Africa, European settlers took over 93 percent of South Africa's land and over half the land in what is now Zimbabwe, pushing Africans into the less fertile and more arid areas. Laws barred Africans from owning land in the more productive white settler areas in these colonies.[17] Likewise, Africans were legally excluded from owning land in Kenya's "White Highlands": 3.3 million hectares of the most fertile land in the country.[18]

Liberia was founded in the 19th century by a private group, the American Colonization Society, to house freed slaves from the United States. In 1926, American investor Harvey Firestone obtained a 99-year concession to grow rubber on a million acres (405,000 hectares) in Liberia, 10 percent of the country's arable land. The US government pressured Liberia to accept a $5 million loan (at 7 percent interest) from Firestone to pay for the infrastructure necessary for rubber to be shipped abroad. As early as 1954, the

US government provided cheap American rice to Liberia as food aid, allow-ing Firestone to import this rice to feed its plantation workers. Surpluses were sold locally, depressing Liberian rice prices, which made it more dif-ficult for local rice farmers to make a living. Whether deliberate or not, the end result was an expanded pool of workers for the plantation.[19] Firestone, which produced throughout the Liberian civil war (1989–2003), remains the world's largest rubber plantation today.

These practices were controversial even during the colonial period. A hundred years ago, some colonial administrators resisted foreign interest in large-scale production. In 1907, British soap magnate William Lever, a founder of the firm that later became Unilever, sought land in British West Africa to grow oil palm. He was refused by the UK Colonial Office. As a later analysis put it: "In a region characterized by small, fragmented, and often communally owned farms, it was felt that Lever's scheme would be hard to administer, politically risky, and commercially unsound."[20] Lever developed his plantations in the Belgian Congo instead, planting 47,000 hectares of oil palm on a 100,000 hectare concession, leased for a hundred years. Unilever kept its Congolese plantation until 2009.

In Sudan, British overlords liked the idea of large-scale operations but tried to merge this with their idealized vision of a society based on sturdy yeoman farmers. In 1925, a London-based syndicate launched the mighty Gezira scheme southeast of the capital, Khartoum. More than 130,000 Sudanese tenant farmers began producing cotton for export to British tex-tile mills. Expanded several times, Gezira is now one of the world's largest irrigated areas. A triangle of 880,000 hectares of land between the Blue and White Niles, it is so large that its brown and green checkerboard can easily be seen from space. Cotton is still the major crop at Gezira. Today, critics often disparage the scheme's regimented production and its siltation and infrastructure challenges. I remember reading about Gezira in graduate school as an example of failure. Yet, when a visiting American anthropolo-gist criticized the vast Gezira scheme, a Sudanese acquaintance replied, "Yes, there are some problems with it. But the Gezira Scheme is the best thing we have in the Sudan."[21]

Colonialism had a varied impact on Africa's food supplies. In the British colony of Tanganyika (now Tanzania) colonial policy emphasized food security for local farmers, while in Northern Rhodesia (now Zimbabwe) local farmers went hungry when white settlers were allocated massive amounts of fertile land. During World War II, forced labor and crop requi-sitions by the Belgians in Rwanda led to a famine that killed some 300,000 people.[22] Ethiopia escaped colonial rule but not famine. A prolonged drought and a rinderpest epidemic affecting cattle may have led to the death of a third of the population between 1888 and 1892. Independence did not end famines: the Nigerian civil war (1966–1969) provoked widespread famine in the rebel-held area of Biafra. The Sahelian famine of the early 1970s killed an estimated 100,000 people. People living on the fragile edge of the Sahara Desert and in the Horn of Africa still regularly experience hunger from drought and conflict.

The colonial period set in place a pattern of commodity exports: cotton, rubber, cocoa, tobacco, and coffee. Yet for every dollar the continent earns today in agricultural exports, it spends nearly two dollars on agricultural imports, mainly food.[23] According to the FAO, Africans spent more than $30 billion to import basic grains in 2011. Some of this pattern can be explained by resource-rich countries such as Nigeria, which exports oil and imports food. Indeed, exports of American wheat to Nigeria are an important source of income for US farmers and make up "one of the five largest trade flows of wheat in the world."[24] Nigeria's pattern is not unusual. Ninety percent of African imports of cereals, edible oils, fats, and dairy products come from North America and Europe, while China is an increasingly important supplier of canned and processed foods.[25] Forty percent of the rice consumed in West Africa is imported, mainly from Asia. In Liberia, supermarkets import vegetables from Spain. If current trends continue, food imports will double by 2030.[26]

Why does Africa import so much food when it has some of the world's largest expanses of arable land? The simple answer is technology: Europe's 18th-century agricultural revolution has yet to reach much of rural Africa. Some 65 percent of plowing, cultivating, and harvesting operations rely solely on human muscle—no animal traction or machinery.[27] Up to 20 percent of harvests rot in poor storage or are lost to pests, compared to only 2 percent in the United States.[28] The tall metal grain silos that march across the American Midwest are unknown in much of rural Africa. Few countries have the critical mass of basic engineering and technical skills necessary to support a move up the value chain into even basic milling and food processing. As in Mozambique, the rice mills that do exist are inefficient and costly. Women still spend hours pounding the evening's grain by hand, using heavy wooden mortars and pestles. Consequently, local agro-industries remain underdeveloped. Levels of food consumption per capita and diet have changed little since independence, with cereals, roots, and tubers still making up over 60 percent of calories.[29] Although the picture varies across the continent—South Africa's agriculture is highly developed, and farmers in some other countries have diversified into higher value exports such as flowers and fresh vegetables—FAO statistics show that the bulk of exports appear unchanged. In 1970, Africa's top three agricultural exports were unprocessed coffee, cotton, and cocoa. Four decades later, the same raw materials—cocoa, coffee, and cotton—still head the list.

Agricultural modernization requires investment. Asia's green revolution involved government–research partnerships that produced and disseminated high-yielding seeds, fertilizer, and other inputs. The World Bank's 2008 *World Development Report* noted that government-directed improvements in rural areas explained more than 80 percent of rural poverty reduction in Asia. In Indonesia, for example, policies supportive of smallholders helped spur a reduction of extreme poverty: from 47 percent in 1981 to 14 percent by the mid-1990s. Nigeria failed to support its farmers, and during the same period, poverty in Nigeria increased from 58 to 70 percent.

Government and private spending on research and development is generally meager in Africa, and a shortage of funds can mean that extension agents are unable to bring even these limited research findings to the farmers. As a PhD student in the 1980s, I was able to reach West African farmers' rice fields by hitchhiking on the back of extension agents' motorcycles—after I filled their empty gas tanks. Nebraska's wheat farms and China's rice paddies achieve some 80 percent of the yields in the gold standard of controlled trials, but maize farmers in much of Africa are reaping yields only 20 to 30 percent of those achieved in controlled conditions.

Norman Borlaug, the father of the green revolution, once said that Africa should have three priorities: rural roads, rural roads, and rural roads.[30] India's green revolution was underpinned by a massive road-building campaign. Yet even when roads exist in rural Africa, they are often impassable during the rainy season. I remember waiting for hours with my fellow passengers on an unpaved road at the bottom of a steep, slick Liberian hill. Rainwater streamed down the muddy red ruts, while our "money bus"—a pickup truck modified with seats in the back—lurched and slid in an unsuccessful attempt to climb to the top. In Africa, only 12 percent of roads were paved in 2009. Across the continent, more than half of rural people live in villages that are not reached by an all-season road, and many have no electricity. The Latin American supply of electricity is 50 times higher, per rural worker, than sub-Saharan Africa's.[31] Antiquated and poorly managed ports are a logistical nightmare in some countries. Only 4 percent of Africa's crop area is irrigated, compared with 34 percent in Asia. With all of these constraints, it is remarkable that Africa's farmers have expanded production at all.

African governments have repeatedly promised to increase funding to support agriculture, most significantly in the Comprehensive Africa Agriculture Development Program (CAADP) adopted by the African Union in 2003. Countries participating in CAADP sign a compact pledging to invest 10 percent of their total national budgets in agriculture. Yet poor rural constituencies do not have the clout to push governments to send resources their way. Ten years later, the average for the continent had actually declined to less than 5 percent. Thirty countries had formally signed on to CAADP, but only 13 of them had ever met the 10 percent target.[32]

The policy framework has also impeded progress. For many years, as Robert Bates pointed out in his seminal 1981 study, *Markets and States in Tropical Africa*, African governments taxed their farmers heavily through government-controlled marketing boards without investing much to increase their productivity. As his book was being read in university classrooms and donor agencies, the era of structural adjustment took off. Many marketing boards were dismantled. Export taxes on agricultural products were reduced. Yet, while there are individual cases of success, getting prices right has not had the same kind of response in Africa as the agricultural reforms China undertook in the post-1978 period.

Why is this so? Some point to subsidies in the high-income Organization for Economic Cooperation and Development (OECD) countries that keep global prices low for Africa's exports (sugar, oilseeds, cotton) or the dumping of OECD surplus (and cheap) grain, milk products, and frozen chicken legs in African markets as a factor that discourages African producers, who cannot compete with these cheap imports. Some also blame the very food aid that is ostensibly meant to stem hunger. A study by economists Nathan Nunn and Nancy Qian found that US and EU food aid typically arrives late, responding to a shortfall that happened two years previously and that it arrives whether or not it is still needed.[33] Donated bags of wheat and tins of powdered milk make their way into local markets, depressing prices for local farmers. Yet food aid, which uses our agricultural surpluses, is clearly more popular for donor countries than aid to agriculture. In 2003, the United States spent more on food aid to one country, Ethiopia, than it spent on all foreign aid to agricultural development across the world.[34]

In other ways, foreign aid has not played the role in Africa that it played in Asia's agricultural modernization. At the end of the 1970s, the OECD countries were giving 18 percent of their official aid to agriculture. By 2004, direct funding for agriculture had sunk to a low of 3.5 percent. World Bank funding for agriculture made up 32 percent of all loans to sub-Saharan Africa in the late 1970s and only 12 percent at the end of the millennium. The drop was even sharper for aid from the United States. Agriculture used to command 25 percent of our aid in the 1980s, but it dwindled to 1 percent in 2008. Aid for agriculture has ticked up again in the past decade, but it is still a far cry from earlier levels.

Why did agricultural aid fall so sharply? In part, the drop is a legacy of the end of the Cold War. During the 1960s and 1970s, concerns about communism and rural revolution helped keep rural poverty and agricultural development on the West's agenda. These concerns died down when

Mao died, and China's great reformist leader Deng Xiaoping shifted China toward the free market. However, as economist Carl Eicher has noted, donors also turned away from the long-term building of agricultural research, extension, and higher education, to short-term funding for NGOs and community-development approaches.[35] At the World Bank, an internal review reported complaints by staff that debates about strategy made agricultural projects more contentious than other kinds of projects.[36] As we will see, these debates about agriculture and development have only intensified since the 2007–2008 food crisis. Three are particularly relevant for us: the role of smallholders versus large commercial farms; export-oriented farming versus local food sovereignty; and the issue of land tenure.

AWAKENING AFRICA'S SLEEPING GIANT?

A controversial 2009 World Bank study on the prospects for commercial agriculture, *Awakening Africa's Sleeping Giant*, estimated that the continent had 60 percent of the world's useable but currently uncultivated land—some 400 million hectares—and some 33 million smallholder farmers, who, as noted earlier, often cannot produce enough food to feed themselves and their families. Sixty-nine percent of African farms are less than two hectares, similar to the average for Asia. In the United States, only 4 percent of farms are that small.[37]

African governments appear to like the idea of large, mechanized farms with their shimmering promise of modernity and progress. To urban elites, Africa's rural areas are not romantic; they appear backward: low-yield subsistence farms scratched into the hillsides; blackened trunks of trees standing among the thinly seeded fields; women wiping sweat from their brows as they harvest together, their machetes cutting across the stalks of maize or sorghum, or warily watching barefoot Fulani pastoralists driving cattle that threaten to bolt into their meager fields. Modernize all this? How much easier it seems to offer a 99-year lease and tax credits to a promising investor or issue a tender for a foreign company to build, operate, and transfer a state-owned farm, as Angola is doing.

Yet for many Africans and Africanists, large-scale, foreign investment in commercial agriculture is deeply controversial. These controversies go beyond the widespread, shared concerns about powerful agribusiness companies pushing small farmers off of their traditional lands—concerns reflected in a *Guardian* headline from 2008: "A New Wave of Food Colonialism Is Snatching Food from the Mouths of the Poor." Development experts simply do not agree on whether large commercial farms should ever play a role in the rural development of poor countries and, more particularly, in strategies for food security and poverty reduction. And for some governments, commercial farms are not the issue but rather foreign ownership—or even, as in Zimbabwe, ownership by local minorities of a particular (European) ancestry.

Many experts see modernizing smallholder agriculture as the only possible solution for poverty alleviation and rural development in Africa. After an extensive review of large-scale farming, World Bank land-tenure experts Klaus Deininger and Derek Byerlee stated flatly that the global experience with large farms is "largely negative" regarding efficiency, productivity, employment, or poverty reduction.[38] Flexibility, local knowledge, and the hard and often unpaid work of family members can provide advantages for small-scale farming when management is costly and product quality or standardization are not at issue.

Yet given that African governments have largely been unable or unwilling to support millions of smallholders to modernize their farms, others argue that large-scale commercial farms may offer the best hope for putting more land under cultivation, rapidly modernizing African agriculture, and expanding food supplies. Economist Paul Collier took this position when he famously skewered what he called a "giant of romantic populism . . . the [Western] middle- and upper-class love affair with peasant agriculture."[39] Smallholder farming is unlikely to be the main route for African prosperity and poverty reduction, he argued. Large companies are able to finance the lumpy investments in irrigation systems and roads, transfer the capacity to manage research and development, and implement the increasingly stringent standards for imported foods in large export markets such as the European Union.

Large farms that specialize in one crop tend to emerge for crops like sugarcane, which ferments quickly and requires speedy processing, or oil palm, which also deteriorates rapidly. Both enjoy scale advantages in "vertically integrated" operations that encompass the entire supply chain, from farm to fork.[40] Some sugarcane operations in Brazil are over 300,000 hectares. When rural workers can maintain their own family or communal farms, or when plantations allocate plots to their workers for growing food, opportunities for wage work can sometimes provide a useful source of income for rural families.[41] Yet, as stereotyped in films of the antebellum South, low-wage plantations with dispossessed workers can be one step up from slavery: archetypes of exploitation and misery.

Plantations can also coexist with smallholders in contract farming, sometimes called outgrower farming. Companies with processing operations often combine a centrally run plantation with contracted purchases from independent farmers, with the central farms helping ensure a reliable level of supply for scale economies. In Southeast Asia, where some oil palm plantations are over 200,000 hectares, large nucleus plantations with their own factories often work with small outgrowers. Smallholders grow a third of Indonesia's oil palm, and many others find part-time employment in the sector. Higher incomes from oil palm—compared with subsistence farming or other cash crops—have apparently contributed to Indonesia's impressive poverty reduction.[42] Eighty percent of the world's rubber is actually produced profitably on labor-intensive small farms of two to three hectares, many linked to processing operations owned by larger farms. In Mauritius, where rural poverty rates are the lowest in Africa, half the sugarcane land is owned and planted by smallholders who sell their cane to factories owned by large sugar plantations. In the 1990s, smallholders in Kenya supplied three-quarters of all exported vegetables and two-thirds of all fruits. Other studies suggest that it has sometimes proven difficult to integrate smallholders into global supply chains with stringent standards. Contract farming arrangements can fail when smallholders divert their output to local markets and do not repay the credit and inputs provided by the buyer. The Chinese call this mode of production "company + farmer mode." As we will see, despite its risks for investors, the Chinese government is now promoting contract farming as one of the most promising areas for Chinese agricultural investment in Africa.

EXPORT AGRICULTURE AND FOOD SECURITY

A second issue for some critics, particularly those in the "food sovereignty" movement, is a perceived trade-off between local food security and commercial agriculture exports.[43] For example, a European organization concerned with environmental justice wrote in a 2015 report that "export orientation is often associated with negative impacts on food self-sufficiency."[44] On the other hand, Ousmane Badiane, director for Africa at IFPRI, has stated flatly: "There is no evidence whatsoever that export agriculture is bad for food security [and there is] plenty of evidence to the contrary."[45] In his view, African food security will be strengthened when African farmers move up the value chain, increasing the use of more productive technology for cultivation, harvesting, and postharvest—whether for export or local consumption. A World Bank report, *Growing Africa: Unlocking the Potential of Agribusiness*, points out that one prosperous Asian country, Thailand, has more agricultural exports than all of sub-Saharan Africa.[46] Ironically, rice-consuming countries in Africa are likely destinations for some of Thailand's rice. Nigeria is expected to import 3.5 million tons of rice in 2015, for example.[47]

RIGHTS TO LAND

The last thorny issue involves justice: Who has rights to the land? In the industrialized world, land has long been alienated from its original use as the means of subsistence for man and beast, becoming a "factor of production," a commodity to be bought and sold. That is not the case for much of rural Africa, where different forms of land tenure have existed uneasily together for several centuries. The large plantations and settler farms of the colonial period were built alongside varied systems of customary land tenure.

Some efforts were made to shift to a more capitalist system as colonialism was ending. Britain's East Africa Royal Commission (1953–1955) recommended the establishment of a land-titling system in Kenya to allow "energetic and rich Africans to acquire more land and bad ones less land thus creating landed and landless classes . . . *a normal step in the evolution of a country*."[48] Yet this rarely happened. At Senegal's independence, for example, only 2 percent of land was held with registered title.[49] After independence, most African countries continued to sidestep the onerous and expensive "cadastral" surveys necessary to establish titles, and the struggles that would inevitably ensue. They simply declared that land not already held with a registered title was owned by the government. Today, only seven countries in Africa give legal protections to customary landholding, and, even there, enforcement of these protections is uneven.[50] Across the continent, millions of African farmers are—in the eyes of the law and their own governments—squatting on state-owned farmland, stealing firewood from state-owned forests, and allowing their cattle to forage on state-owned pastures. Their uncertain status would come to haunt investors like Yang Haomin. And now let us return to Cameroon, where the Ostrich King was preparing a major investment.

"QUIETLY ROOTED IN THE AFRICAN CONTINENT"

Yang returned to Cameroon in March 2006 with a team of 13 experts, just three months after his original visit. Shaanxi Agriculture Group set up a subsidiary, China-Cameroon Yingkao Agricultural Development Co. Ltd. (also known locally as Sino-Cam IKO), and agreed to begin by rehabilitating around 100 hectares of rice fields at Nanga-Eboko, a Taiwanese aid project near the northern banks of the Sanaga River, abandoned in 1971 after Cameroon officially broke diplomatic ties with Taipei (the Republic of China) in favor of Beijing. The team planned to test varieties of rice, maize, soybeans, and cassava. The Cameroon government promised to arrange for another 2,000 hectares of land close to Nanga-Eboko to grow rice and 4,000 hectares in the nearby Ndjoré District for cassava. Another 4,000 hectares would be in Santchou, in western Cameroon, on the site of a state-owned rice company liquidated during the era of structural adjustment after failing to turn a profit.[51]

The team moved quickly into the decaying buildings left by the Taiwanese. As an admiring Chinese reporter described it later, the land they were to work appeared completely barren: no people, electricity, or roads; thick with shrubbery and tall grasses that completely hid the old irrigation system. They struggled through six kilometers of thorny forests to find the source of the irrigation water, encountering snakes and wild animals. Within two months, they had planted a vegetable patch, found a way to conquer weeds unlike any they had seen before, cleaned nearly five kilometers of irrigation channels, and rebuilt the access road. Local Cameroonians joined the Chinese, learning to drive tractors, working from seven in the morning until nearly nightfall, and forging, it was said, a "profound friendship." Living without electricity, suffering from malaria, without a day off, the team triumphantly harvested their first crop of rice that December. They were well on their way, a Chinese reporter explained, to being "quietly rooted in the African continent."

Local people described the arrival of the Chinese somewhat differently. Villagers employed on the rehabilitation of the station did welcome the employment, but the Chinese refused to give them formal contracts or to pay above the local rate for farm labor, between two and three dollars a day. "We earn a pittance," Keman Essam, a bulldozer operator, complained to a reporter. Jean Assamba, a 46-year-old father of six, quit after six months. "They work hard, never get tired, and it is impossible for a Cameroonian to keep up with them. Me, I was forced to resign because I couldn't take it. And they pay so poorly. If you complain, they say that we are getting more than Chinese workers would get in China." Although he grudgingly admired the Chinese work ethic, he was left feeling bitter: "The Chinese are wicked!" The project was plagued by minor thefts, and the Chinese team acquired a German shepherd guard dog. "Touching an abandoned papaya is forbidden," a former worker reported. "If they catch you with some rice in your pocket, you are directly sent to the police, accused of theft."

Struggles over land tied the project in knots, and the government of Cameroon was not able to roll over the protests of all the farmers asked to cede land to the Chinese investors. Villagers were accustomed to use these spaces for hunting, grazing animals, and gathering firewood and other products from the forest. Tucked in among the trees were patches of land cleared for small subsistence farms. A local man, Joseph Embolo Fa'a, claimed customary rights to 1,015 hectares of land in Nanga-Eboko. In May 2011, he and others were arrested for protesting the government's decision to allocate part of their land to the Chinese investors. When Fa'a and a local forester cut down three trees to block the government surveyor's access, he was slapped with a four-month jail sentence. "We still don't know if we will be compensated for the land loss and, if so, how much money we will receive," he said later. "This land is very important to us. Our ancestors are buried here, and the forest feeds us with termites, worms, and other produce."

European journalists and television crews visited the project. Some warned that the Chinese might try to control the entire chain of rice production in Cameroon. A French article with the title "When Cameroon Feeds China" led with the sentence: "The Cameroonian government has ceded land to an Asian enterprise that exploits local peasants to cultivate rice destined for China." Other reporters interviewed the project's manager, who told them that their signed agreement specified that all the rice produced on the project would be milled and sold in Cameroon. Few had actually seen this agreement, however. The reporters decided to believe local activists who showed them bags of rice covered with Chinese characters for sale in the village market. Although the bags were likely imported from China (hence the Chinese characters), the activists argued that this was proof that the rice was meant for the Chinese market: "When they can fill a boat, the rice will leave to China!" Rice, they predicted, will "follow the trail of bananas and cotton." Yet the price of rice in Cameroon's markets was nearly double the price in China.[52] Would a businessman come to Cameroon to produce rice and pay to ship it off to China at a huge loss? Or perhaps Yang Haomin had a long-term plan to sit quietly in Africa and wait for prices to rise in China?

Furthermore, in both the Western and the Chinese press, the Chinese farm was always described as a "10,000 hectare investment." Yet Cameroon's farmers and activists had been able to pressure their government to stall on land allocation. After working for four years at the old Taiwanese station, the Chinese company still had not been able to obtain any additional land. "We only have 100 hectares," the Chinese manager growled at a visitor who had asked about conditions for local workers. "We have also been exploited!" The project contract was still sitting in the office of the prime minister, under study by an interministerial committee: "They are making us wait years just for a piece of paper!" the manager complained. "It is time for the people of Cameroon to understand that the future is in agriculture," he said. "It can no longer continue in these times cultivating with a hoe and a pickax. That will get you nowhere." In 2011, Cameroon's imports of rice rose to over 552,000 metric tons; yet, as one study pointed out, 90 percent of the land fit for growing rice was still not being used by anyone.[53]

We started and finished this chapter with the story of a troubled Chinese agricultural investment in Cameroon. Yang Haomin's company was warmly welcomed by the Cameroon minister of agriculture, who had visited China. The minister believed that Chinese expertise could contribute to his task of modernizing agriculture and that he would reap some of the credit when visitors observed vast, modern fields brimming with waving stalks of rice, an increase in local food supply, and perhaps even self-sufficiency. To him, land was owned by the government and could be reallocated to other uses, if the government so chose. On the other hand, local people quite naturally resented the proposal that some of their ancestral land be given to a foreign investor. They were concerned that they would not be compensated. They feared permanently losing access to common lands where they and their animals had traditionally foraged for food.

Cameroon was no stranger to commercial agriculture. Vast rubber plantations built during the early years of independence stretch across the south of the country, and an American company, Heracles, has drawn fire more recently for its plans to develop a 73,000-hectare oil palm farm.[54] In 2008, as we will see in chapter 8, a Chinese company would become a majority shareholder in GMG Global, a firm that would win the rights to over 100,000 hectares of Cameroon's rain forest. We will return to Yang Haomin's story in chapter 5. Cameroon—like most of Africa—stands now at a critical juncture. The decisions they make about commercial agriculture and foreign investment are likely to shape the future prospects and even stability of their rural areas.

In the next chapter, we will see how China, at a similar juncture, used foreign interest in its own agribusiness sector to drive innovation, transfer technology, and boost productivity. When Chinese firms began exploring investment in Africa, they would come with expectations and visions shaped by their own history of foreign investment and the way their government interacted with investors. It is often said that China's development experience may provide lessons for other countries. For Africans, perhaps, some of the most useful lessons might be learned by studying how China dealt with its own foreign agribusiness investors.

CHAPTER 3

Seeds of Change

Foreign Agribusiness Comes to China (and Chinese Agribusiness Goes to Africa)

In West Africa's winter months, the *harmattan* winds blow cooler air across the soils of the Sahel, dry after the short rainy season. On some days, the sun rises and sets in a ghostly haze. A fine red dust settles in the towns and villages, finding its way into cupboards while coating each blade of grass. Local people pull on wool caps and sweaters against the chill.

During the height of the 1962 *harmattan*, seven Chinese agricultural experts landed at the airport in Bamako, the capital of the West African country of Mali.[1] They had come at the request of the young Malian government, newly independent, and headed by a friendly socialist president. Could China assist them in adding value to Mali's agriculture—perhaps by constructing the country's first sugar complex, a cotton-textile mill, and a tea factory and plantation? Both countries were then very poor: annual income per person in China was about $117 and in Mali, $275, although China was relatively more industrialized: manufacturing made up nearly 30 percent of Chinese production, compared with only 6 percent in Mali.

The Chinese experts would probably have journeyed first to the Office du Niger, northeast of Bamako, where the Mali government had inherited a massive irrigation scheme on the Niger River, constructed by forced labor during the French colonial period. Before independence in 1960, the French sponsored the cultivation of cotton for French industries on 100,000 hectares of the Niger River's *delta mort,* an alluvial plain that stretches for nearly one million hectares. At the time of the Chinese team's visit, less than half of the irrigated area was being cultivated.[2] Mali grew no sugarcane or tea and had little in the way of agro-industries.

The Chinese experts also traveled southeast to Sikasso, crossing a network of rivers and stopping at the picturesque waterfalls on the Farako River—the "river of stone" named for the wide, flat rocks below the rushing water. Here, they decided, near the point where Mali's dry savannah transitioned into rain-fed forests, conditions would be good to grow tea. The projects would be financed out of a 1961 Chinese aid commitment of approximately $16 million.[3]

By 1968, the Chinese had built the Dougabougou sugar plantation and factory and a cotton-textile mill in nearby Ségou, where the Office du Niger has its headquarters. The Farako tea plantation and a factory for processing tea opened near Sikasso in 1973. When Mali requested a second sugar project, the Chinese agreed. The Sribala sugar complex was completed in 1974.

Over the next two decades, the Chinese aid program would construct similar state farms in other parts of Africa (see table 3.1). In Tanzania, for instance, China agreed in 1965 to finance the construction and meet the initial operating costs of the Ruvu State Farm, a large mixed farm and cattle ranch located 50 miles west of Dar es Salaam. Six years later, Chinese teams developed the Mbarali rice farm, which featured poultry, dairy, and its own hydropower plant.[4] The island of Zanzibar received finance and Chinese assistance for a mixed farm and a sugar cane plantation. Chinese teams built other state farms for governments in Mauritania, Guinea, and Zaire (now the Democratic Republic of the Congo, or DRC). Most of the farms grew rice, where Chinese technologies were clearly superior, or were mixed farms with grain, vegetables, fruit trees, poultry, and orchards. Several focused solely on sugarcane—in Mali, as we have seen, but also in Zanzibar, Togo, Sierra Leone, and the DRC.

During the 1970s and 1980s, the Chinese aid program shifted to emphasize much smaller demonstration farms, working with local farmers to teach rice farming and vegetable cultivation. The last large state farm to be built under the aid program was the Doho rice farm in Uganda, completed in 1990.[5] Two decades later, a Ugandan newspaper noted that Doho was still providing benefits for local people. Although the old rice mills crush the rice "into small pieces that cannot be sold on the market . . . children in Butaleja are not like other Ugandan children for whom rice is a delicacy, reserved for only big days like on Christmas or Idd."[6]

Until the 1980s, all the Chinese aid projects were built, operated for two years by local staff with oversight by the Chinese teams, and then handed over to be run by the African hosts while the Chinese teams returned to China. However, as we shall shortly see, this system was about to change. China's great market transformation was about to begin, and the Chinese

Table 3.1. MAJOR CHINESE AGRICULTURAL AID PROJECTS
IN AFRICA (1961–1999)

Year Started	Year Completed	Country	Project Name	Crop(s)	Size (ha)
1975	1980	Benin	Malanville	irrigated rice	516
1975	1976	Benin	Dévé (Mono)	irrigated rice	150
—	1981	Burkina Faso	Banzon	irrigated rice	454
1973	1983	DRC/Zaire	Kingabwa	irrigated rice	400
1973	1976	DRC/Zaire	N'djili	irrigated rice	100
1975	1986	DRC/Zaire	Lotokila	sugarcane and mill	3,000
1979	1983	Ghana	Afife	irrigated rice	880
1990	1991	Ghana	Nobewam	irrigated rice	124
1979	1982	Guinea	Koba Farm	sugarcane, mill, rice	1,800
1981	1987	Liberia	Kpatawee	upland seed rice	323
1962	1964	Mali	Dougabougou	sugarcane and mill	1,654
1962	1964	Mali	Farako	tea	402
1970	1974	Mali	Siribala	sugarcane and mill	3,520
1968	1972	Mauritania	M'pourié	irrigated rice	1,000
—	1980	Niger	Sébéri	irrigated rice	360
1976	1982	Nigeria	Itoikin	irrigated rice	170
1972	1977	Sierra Leone	Rolako Farm	irrigated/upland rice	316
1977	1981	Sierra Leone	Magbass	sugarcane and mill	1,280
1978	1985	Somalia	Fanole	irrigated rice	440
—	1971	Somalia	Bala Weyne	irrigated rice	300
1965	1969	Tanzania (Zanzibar)	Upenja	rice, mixed farming	526
1965	—	Tanzania	Ruvu	rice, mixed farming	2,834
1971	1977	Tanzania	Mbarali	rice, mixed farming	3,530
1974	—	Tanzania (Zanzibar)	Mahonda	sugarcane and mill	1,216
1978	1985	Togo	Anie	sugarcane and mill	1,200
1973	1982	Uganda	Kibimba	rice, mixed farming	697
1987	1990	Uganda	Doho	irrigated rice	800
				Total	27,992

Note: Partial list; includes only projects of at least 100 hectares and does not include projects originally developed by Taiwan. Sources and more details available at SAIS-CARI.org.

role in Africa would be profoundly affected. Chinese teams would start to return to manage their old aid projects in rural Africa. But China would also begin to open up its own rural areas to foreign investment. Much later, the assumptions of people like Shaanxi businessman Yang Haomin about the role of foreign cooperation, foreign investment in agribusiness, and aid to agriculture would be shaped by the events that were about to happen.

CHINA OPENS UP

In the summer of 1980, after a year of intensive Mandarin classes in Taiwan, I took a train across what was then a sleepy border between the British colony of Hong Kong and mainland China. Traveling slowly from coastal Guangdong province to Beijing, taking a riverboat that passed through the Three Gorges of the Yangtze, I visited communes and brigades that were on the verge of enormous change. The five-year plan still loomed large, but agriculture was at the foundation of the great transition period that started in the late 1970s when Deng Xiaoping released market forces in rural China. Little was yet visible to outsiders, but the communes and production brigades I saw as I explored the provinces of Anhui, Shandong, and Wuhan were being dissolved. Farm households responded with sharp increases in production. Yet the Chinese understood that while market incentives were necessary, market liberalization alone would not modernize Chinese agriculture. International cooperation—through investment, trade, aid, and loans—would be critical. In China, given political hesitations, changes like these would be gradual. Foreign loans were introduced experimentally in the late 1970s, mainly via Japan, and expanded when China joined the World Bank in 1980. Heilongjiang province provided a testing ground for China's tentative embrace of global finance, technology, and aid.

BEIDAHUANG: THE "GREAT NORTHERN WILDERNESS"

Located in the far northeast of China, Heilongjiang province was carved from an area known historically as Manchuria. The Chinese have long called the region Beidahuang, the "Great Northern Wilderness." In 1949, there was almost no one living on the alluvial Sanjiang plain, where the silt of three rivers produced a rich black soil. Only 3 percent of the area had been cultivated.[7] Its miles of lonely wetlands echoed with the calls of red-crowned and hooded cranes. Manchurian tigers still prowled in forests of white birch and dragon spruce.

The Chinese determined to turn what they saw as wastelands into farms. During World War II, General Wang Zhen—one of the "Eight Immortals" who founded modern China—led the 359th army brigade to counter a Japanese blockade, establishing the famously self-sufficient Nanniwan Farm in an arid wasteland in Shaanxi province.[8] Wang's farm fed the troops of Mao's rebel army and established a pattern of soldier-farmers struggling against climate and geography to be self-sufficient in grain. After China became independent in 1949, Wang later carried out similar land reclamation work in the autonomous region of Xinjiang, and became minister of State Farms and Land Reclamation under Mao.

Inspired by the Shaanxi and Xinjiang experiences, over a hundred thousand active and demobilized soldiers went to tame the wild lands of Beidahuang, building *junken* (army farms) that allowed the military to grow its own food and not be a burden on the local peasantry. Chinese magazines profiled some of the Chinese settlers who, "in the spirit of revolution and hard work," fought to build these farms.[9] Before relations soured in the late 1950s, advisers from the Soviet Union helped out, building Youyi (Friendship) State Farm in Heilongjiang. At over 120,000 hectares, Youyi is today still China's largest state farm. The early settlers' children were born in "wilderness huts," while their parents dug drainage systems and irrigation channels—sometimes by hand, sometimes with inefficient Soviet machinery—turning the vast swamps into fertile farms. Particularly after the break with the Soviet Union in 1960, the farms took on a military mindset. "We prepared for invasion," recalled Zhao Yufu, an agricultural specialist. "We trained in a boot camp. We learned to use a bayonet. We ran a lot."

In the 1960s, some urban Chinese youth were sent to the *junken* farms, in the "up to the mountains, down to the villages" movement. Many never returned to the cities. Over three decades, some two million hectares of the Great Northern Wilderness was opened for cultivation and mechanized production. This process was repeated in other provinces of China. In the late 1950s, there were only 107 state farms; by 1977, China had more than 2,000. Later, when China became a more significant outward investor, the *nongken* or state farm system would be in the lead.

Japan became one of China's most important partners in the early reform period. In 1979, as China began to open up, the food division of one of Japan's major *zaibatsu*—business conglomerate groups—Nichimen, arrived to explore agribusiness opportunities.[10] Nichimen was not a stranger to Manchuria. In the boom years after World War I, the firm sold Japanese cotton cloth and bought Manchurian soybeans for export to Japan. Japan's defeat in World War II and the communist takeover in China ended Nichimen's involvement in Manchuria, but Deng Xiaoping's reforms rekindled the relationship. Within a year, Nichimen had a preliminary agreement for a joint venture to help carve out the new 20,000-hectare Honghe Farm from the wetlands of Heilongjiang's Sanjiang plain.

The original plan had been for Nichimen to supply modern Japanese agricultural and engineering machinery, while the then leading US hybrid-corn seed company, DeKalb AgResearch, would supply the technology to raise high-quality poultry and hogs.[11] DeKalb backed out of the arrangement, but Nichimen stayed in. They arranged a $13 million Japanese loan that allowed Heilongjiang to pay for high-performance machinery to develop the wetlands. Honghe Farm grew corn and soy-beans. The soybeans were exported to Japan over a period of four years by Nichimen and sold to repay the loan—a kind of countertrade. During the 1980s, Nichimen arranged at least two additional countertrade loans, both again repaid through the export of soybeans to Japan. The World Bank also became involved in land reclamation in Heilongjiang in 1983, providing an $80 million loan to finance the development of an additional 200,000 hectares of virgin land.

With finance and technology from abroad, the deep, fertile black soils of Heilongjiang became the breadbasket of China. By 2009, the province had nearly 10 million hectares under cultivation, producing 4.4 million metric tons of soybeans, wheat, and other grains.[12] The *junken* farms created by the People's Liberation Army to tame the wilderness would become part of the commercially oriented Beidahuang Group. And, as we will see in chapter 8, Heilongjiang's *junken* farms and the spirit of the Great Northern Wilderness would later surface in a most unexpected place: Mozambique.

BRINGING IN FOREIGN INVESTMENT

In 1980, foreign investment—inconceivable under Chairman Mao—became possible in China. By the mid-1980s, markets for fruits and vegetables had been liberalized. In 1984, China's Ministry of Agriculture combed through its assets and announced that China would invite foreigners—including overseas Chinese from Hong Kong, Macao, and elsewhere—to invest in joint ventures involving 303 state-owned farms, dairies, rubber plantations, and agro-processing factories.[13] Vegetable growing, sugar, coffee, spices, and flowers were all slowly opened to foreign capital.

The array of institutions and actors changed profoundly in this period as China moved from the state-guided plan to the market guidance of a developmental state. Under the state-planning system, the Ministry of Agriculture had presided over a series of provincial and local farming bureaus, while land reclamation (*nongken*) came under a separate ministry. In 1980, some provinces and municipalities were allowed to begin sepa-rating their government and enterprise functions. Thus was born a series of agribusiness corporations that would be responsible for managing and operating the state's farming assets.[14] For example, in 1980 the Ministry of State Farms and Land Reclamation created China State Farm Agribusiness Corporation (CSFAC), while the Beijing Animal Husbandry Bureau, in charge of building the municipality's swine and poultry farms, established the Beijing Huadu Group. Over time, these corporations and others like them were separated from their ministries and became China's pioneer agribusinesses. As we will see in chapters 4 and 6, they would also be the first to seek business in Africa, some as early as 1982. As Han Xiangshan, vice president of CSFAC would later put it: "Decades ago we were at the forefront of China's campaign to reclaim wasteland. Now we apply our skills in African countries."[15]

China's eagerness to earn hard currency also led to a revival of the country's earlier role as a supplier of labor for overseas projects. In the 19th century, Chinese indentured workers fanned out around the world to build railways, dig for gold, and work on plantations. These labor exports resumed in the late 1970s, with Beijing's blessing. For example, as the *New York Times* reported in 1987, a Manhattan-based company set up by K. K. Soo, a Chinese-American entrepreneur, arranged with CSFAC to supply Chinese farm workers on temporary work visas to American farmers during an acute shortage of farmworkers in some southern and western states.[16]

Another early policy decision would profoundly shape China's engagement with the outside world and its stance toward foreign investment. In 1986, Beijing formally applied to resume its membership in the GATT (General Agreement on Tariffs and Trade), the forerunner of the World Trade Organization (WTO). Concerns about China's agricultural productivity and its relationship with global markets intensified during 15 years of tough negotiations. Many feared that Chinese farmers would suffer from trade liberalization and stiffer competition and that this could be politically destabilizing.[17] The Chinese government decided to take a longer-term view: Chinese farmers needed the tools to compete. China's closest neighbors in Asia, including Japan and Thailand, could bring in the new technologies and show Chinese farmers how allowing foreign competition could be a stimulus for modernization.

AN EMPIRE BUILT ON CHICKENFEED

The Bangkok-based CP Group may be the most successful foreign investor in China today, but their story begins nearly a century ago in the 1920s.[18] After the collapse of the last imperial dynasty in 1911, China descended into chaos. Warlords carved up the different regions and fought for control of the state. Many Chinese fled abroad. In 1921, two young Chinese brothers from the Guangdong area arrived in Thailand with a small cache of Chinese vegetable seeds. They set up a family-run seed and agrochemical store, Chia Tai, on a crowded street in Bangkok's Chinatown. Over the years, the younger brother ran the company in Thailand, while the older brother, Chia Ek Chor, expanded their trading firm across Southeast Asia.

As their company grew, Chia relocated their headquarters to a coastal Chinese city, Shantou: one of the six treaty ports forced open by the British during the 19th century Opium Wars.

Chia Ek Chor's youngest son, Dhanin, was born in Thailand in 1938. When the increasingly nationalist Thai government closed the Chinese language schools in Bangkok, Chia brought his son to Shantou. The fluency Dhanin gained in Mandarin Chinese would later stand him in good stead. When the Communists nationalized the Shantou headquarters in 1949, Chia moved the company back to Thailand, and the family adopted the Thai name Chearavanont. The young Dhanin Chearavanont became head of the family firm at the age of 25 and proved to be a visionary leader. By the early 1970s, the little seed shop had evolved into the massive, vertically integrated Charoen Pokphand (CP) Group. Contract farmers grew corn for its feed mills; its hatcheries supplied day-old chicks to other farmers; and the company operated its own poultry, hog, and shrimp farms across Southeast Asia. High-quality feed remained the core of the company, while the rest of the business across the value chain acted to stimulate demand for CP Group's feed.

In 1979, as China was opening its doors, Dhanin began to travel to Beijing. He dined with Deng Xiaoping and laid out his vision of a mutually beneficial future. The CP Group set up the first foreign company incorporated in China; they still hold the Chinese company registration number 001. Two years later, in 1981, CP Group partnered with the American firm Continental Grain to build a $4 million modern feed mill in the newly created special economic zone of Shenzhen, just outside British-controlled Hong Kong.

The decision to leap into a risky investment paid off handsomely. Chinese feed was low quality and cheap. CP Group introduced higher quality feed, hired sales agents, sponsored feed demonstrations, and worked with local government agencies on a commission basis. Soon they were selling chicken feed and their specially bred day-old chicks in more than 80 Chinese cities. Within 10 years, CP Group was operating feed mills, chicken and hog farms, meatpacking plants, and fish and shrimp aquaculture in 23 Chinese provinces. CP Group became a supplier to Kentucky Fried Chicken (KFC) in 1987 when KFC became the first US fast food company to enter the Chinese market. Five years later, CP Group controlled 33 percent of the Chinese chicken-feed market, sold 42 percent of China's chickens, and accounted for 30 percent of China's poultry exports. Before the CP Group arrived in China, customers purchased chickens much as I did when I was a student in Taiwan. For my first dinner party, I decided to make the famous Shaoxing "drunken chicken," marinated in traditional wine. At the market, I selected a live chicken that rolled its eyes at me and flapped wildly as the stall owner took it around back. I heard the thump of the ax, the head came off, and then the whole chicken was placed in a tub with rubber fingers that rotated to pull off the feathers. Minutes later, the stall owner set the still warm chicken in my basket, and I headed home on my bicycle, feeling slightly queasy. Chinese customers can still buy their chickens the old-fashioned way, but busy families have embraced the convenience of plastic-wrapped chicken, and, concerned with food safety, they appreciate the CP Group's famous obsession with hygiene. In 2011, Forbes magazine chose Dhanin Chearavanont—now the wealthiest man in Thailand—as Asian businessman of the year. CP Group had also become China's largest foreign landlord, producing poultry, livestock feed, and other crops on over 200,000 hectares of Chinese land.[19]

CHINA: HUNGRY FOR INVESTMENT

Foreign direct investment (FDI) in agriculture rarely exceeded 2 percent of total FDI in the decades following China's initial opening, but it was not insignificant. Between 1979 and 1998, for example, foreigners sank more than $9 billion into China's agricultural sector.[20] CP Group's strategy for success in China's agribusiness sector involved meeting Chinese leaders' expectations. "It's not enough just to be [ethnically] Chinese," Dhinan noted. "You have to offer them something they want or need."[21]

The Chinese needed to modernize agriculture and bring in high-technology. They saw that a leading foreign firm could offer this, while also providing a model and serving as a training ground for Chinese managers. For example, corn is a staple of chicken feed, but, as in much of Africa today, Chinese corn yields were low, and the crop took four months to mature. CP Group's proprietary hybrid corn, developed with the American firm DeKalb AgResearch, combined high yields and short duration, maturing in 90 days. Chinese leaders also wanted to maximize export earnings. CP Group provided distribution channels overseas and a Chinese brand with economies of scale, quality, and reliability. Its products sold in European and Japanese supermarkets but also in small Chinese shops across Asia.

At the same time, CP's agribusiness approach accommodated Chinese realities. As a CP official told an *Asian Business* reporter in 1994, "At first the Chinese authorities refused to believe that a Thai company could teach them anything. So they went to look at feed meal and poultry operations in America. But in America, everything is automated and employs few people. They came back to Thailand, because we still use a lot of labour." Another CP official added: "We are able to take Western technology, modify it and adapt it to a developing country's environment."

Finally, as historian Rajeswary Ampalavanar-Brown noted in her study of the Thai conglomerate, CP Group had a critical advantage in its "stable and enduring relations" with the Chinese state. In its first dozen years of heady expansion in China, most of CP Group's joint ventures were with mainland partners: provincial grain bureaus and city or county governments. In Shenzhen, CP Group's subsidiary told a reporter for the *Far Eastern Economic Review* that they paid the state-owned company in charge of the zone, Shenzhen Development, 15 percent of earnings "to act as a godfather to us." These close ties with (and financial gains to) Chinese agents provided enormous advantages, helping overcome bureaucratic barriers, providing inside information and access. They allowed CP Group to use the government's distribution channels, lowered their risks, and provided critical market information.

Over the years, the Japanese company Nichimen also formed other joint ventures in China, including one with US agribusiness giant Archer Daniels Midland (ADM) and COFCO (China National Cereals, Oils and Foodstuffs Corporation), China's largest agricultural commodities trader.[22] Together with two Chinese state farms, Nichimen set up a company to process polished white rice in Heilongjiang province.[23] Then, Nichimen used its distribution expertise to build an export market for the province's specialized *japonica* rice, shipping it to Japan, Russia, Singapore, and France.

Contract farming became the preferred model for foreign investment in commercial agriculture in China because it added to the skills and capacity of China's rural farmers. For example, in the late 1980s, when McDonald's decided to open its first Chinese restaurants, local Chinese potatoes were deemed too short and round for the company's famously long french fries. An Idaho company, Simplot, began testing longer American varieties north of Beijing in a joint venture with a state-owned firm. Their contract farming model mixed 5,000 individual Chinese growers on 2,000 hectares of land with centralized input supply and marketing, lowering risks and improving productivity. A decade later, *China Daily* noted approvingly that Simplot's innovations were "expected to help Chinese farmers meet the challenges brought by [China's] WTO entry."[24]

Like African governments today, China's provinces competed to entice foreign investment in agriculture.[25] Liaoning province, a major grain and soybean producer, announced that joint investments could count on five to 10 years of lower taxes if they developed farms in wastelands or hilly areas. In 1997, Xinjiang became the first province to offer 50-year land leases for wholly foreign-owned enterprises. Coastal provinces like Jiangsu and Guangdong set up special, export-oriented agricultural zones where companies could receive tax breaks and transferable land rights at concessional rates for up to 70 years.

The coastal province of Shandong, with its peninsula jutting into the Yellow Sea, was particularly successful in attracting Japanese investment—as direct producers and through contract farming schemes.[26] By 2001, the province was exporting so many shiitaki mushrooms and scallions to Japan that Japanese farmers cried out for protections. Shandong province made investment attractive and easy. For example, when Shandong invited Asahi Breweries to set up a model organic dairy farm—which would also supply fertilizer for an organic sweet corn and strawberry venture—the province provided 526 hectares of land, rent-free for three years, built a road to the site, and installed electricity lines. As this was happening, novice Chinese investors were beginning to explore Africa. They expected this kind of encouragement; aside from the rent-free provision of land in exceptionally long leases, they rarely found it.

AID, INVESTMENT, AND TRADE: BUILDING BUSINESS IN CHINA

Foreign investors employed a mix of aid, trade, and investment to succeed in China. In 1983, for example, California-based, multinational food producer Del Monte would help Shanghai to build a three-hectare experimental farm on Zhong Ming Island in the Yangtze River delta, planting Del Monte varieties of sweet pea pods, sweet corn, asparagus, and tomatoes.[27] PepsiCo, maker of Lays potato chips, operated eight potato demonstration farms in partnership with China's Ministry of Agriculture to show Chinese farmers how more scientific crop-management systems could raise yields and incomes.[28]

In other cases, foreign governments stepped in to construct demonstration centers that would boost commercial opportunities for their country's firms. For example, Israel built demonstration farms to showcase commercial methods of growing and processing fruit, vegetables, and flowers in Shandong province, as well as a demonstration dairy farm on the outskirts of Beijing.[29] "Israeli cows are the most productive in the world, yielding more than 10,000 litres a year," an Israeli embassy official told a journalist. "We will bring our equipment and know-how to the farm. Investors can come and learn and buy them."[30]

With its own expertise in agriculture to promote, the Netherlands actively involved Dutch horticultural firms in its Chinese training and demonstration centers.[31] A Dutch expert who learned the flower business from his father and grandfather explained how this cooperation worked: "I've been coming to China [since 1997] as part of a joint Sino-Dutch project to assist bulb and flower producers here while also assisting Dutch producers looking to do business in China. It's been a win-win situation for both parties."[32] In Fujian province, the Netherlands supported the Sino-Dutch Horticultural Training and Demonstration Center. The center covered 100 hectares, with greenhouses, classrooms, conference rooms, and training equipment—a model quite similar to the agro-technology demonstration centers China would later develop in Africa. Dutch companies provided seeds, young plants, and horticultural equipment, and taught courses to demonstrate (and create demand for) their technologies.[33] As we will see in chapter 4, this blending of assistance, training and investment would characterize some of China's agricultural ventures in Africa.

FROM "BRINGING IN" TO "GOING OUT"

By the time China joined the WTO in 2001, its agricultural sector had been transformed. McDonald's was serving french fries in Chinese cities, using potatoes grown by Chinese farmers. Chinese poultry farms competed with CP Group to sell their broilers to KFC. In Japan, housewives bought traditional Japanese vegetables grown in China and air-freighted across the Yellow Sea. Even more astoundingly, China's soybean sector was dominated by foreign firms. An assortment of 64 foreign firms controlled 60 percent of soybean-crushing capacity, while four giant multinational commodity traders—Archer Daniels Midland, Bunge, Cargill, and Louis Dreyfus, known collectively as "ABCD"—supplied 80 percent of China's soybean imports."[34] Fears that liberalization would destroy China's agriculture proved unfounded. Liberalizing on its own terms, forging relationships with the world's most prominent sources of agribusiness knowledge and experience, China was well on its way to becoming a global player in agriculture.

As they moved out of China, Chinese investors would be shaped by these experiences. With their roots in the frontier farms established at the founding of the People's Republic, CSFAC and the Beidahuang Group specialized in opening new areas of previously uncultivated land for large-scale mechanized cultivation. China Complete Plant Import and Export Corporation (Complant) had experience in developing large plantations, factories, and other turnkey projects under China's foreign aid; they would manage sugar factories in Africa. China's state policy banks would draw on their early experience with Nichimen to establish commodity countertrade as a model for securing loans in risky environments. In 2006, the Chinese government would experiment with helping its new agribusiness firms set up demonstration farms abroad, mixing aid and investment in the hope of future business and a more sustainable technology transfer. Role models, like CP Group, would likely have been in the minds of Chinese entrepreneurs like Li Li, who arrived in Zambia in 1993 when her husband was sent by CSFAC to set up a mixed farm. At one point, they would supply at least 10 percent of the eggs sold across Zambia. Yet, as we will see in chapter 6, CSFAC could not out-compete other commercial farmers—often Europeans that had settled earlier in the country—or serve as a role model for Zambian investors. They never developed the vision or the ability to control the value chain the way CP Group had done in China.

Many other Chinese agribusiness investors in Africa would follow CP Group's model of seeking joint ventures with local governments or their officials. They hoped that this would help them navigate different systems with different expectations, but their African "godfathers" were not used to smoothing investor risks. When African governments promised to deliver land concessions, Chinese companies would expect land to be delivered unencumbered, as in China—and would not expect to be involved in the process of consulting stakeholders or arranging compensation. They would expect local governments to supply roads and electricity lines. Their very different experiences of governance did not prepare them for countries where governments were not developmental states or cases where the peasantry—as in Cameroon—was able to push back against the "wave of progress" about to roll over them.

SEEDS OF CHANGE IN AFRICA

While China was moving from the planned to the free market, change was also underway across the world, in Africa. During the first decades after independence, many African governments operated state-owned farms. African cash crops were sold abroad by marketing boards that, in theory, invested some of their proceeds back into the growing of the crops, while levying taxes to transfer agricultural surpluses into other uses.

All this changed as the full impact of two oil price shocks in the 1970s helped precipitate a sharp shift toward the free market. African governments found themselves in debt as commodity prices plunged and interest rates on their foreign loans soared. Under pressure from the World Bank and the International Monetary Fund (IMF), they tried to auction off their state-owned farms and dismantle their marketing boards. Through the 1980s and 1990s, austerity programs meant that there was little in the budget for support to extension services or to build rural roads. As we saw in chapter 2, donors failed to make up the difference. This is the context in which the Chinese found themselves when their own economic reforms after 1978 pushed them to put their African engagement on a more financially sustainable footing. Let us return to see how these changes played out in Mali and in Mozambique.

MISSIONARIES TO MALI

In late 1982, Chinese Premier Zhao Ziyang traveled to 11 African countries to explain how China's reforms at home would affect its foreign aid and economic cooperation on the continent. China wanted to emphasize the mutual benefits that should result from its engagement in Africa as opposed to simply giving aid. Chinese companies would welcome joint ventures. Countries could swap some of the debt they owed to China for equity shares in these ventures. Teams could be invited to manage—for a fee—the Chinese-built state farms and factories that had declined under host-country management. If countries did not have the foreign exchange they needed to buy spare parts for their Chinese machinery and factories, they could pay through countertrade, exporting products to China, as Nichimen had arranged to do with soybeans in Heilongjiang province.

Like rural households in China, Chinese state-owned companies operating overseas under China's aid program were given a "responsibility system": allowed to keep up to $1 million in any foreign exchange they earned after delivering their planned quota.[35] Chinese embassies began helping the companies find opportunities. And this is how Chinese teams returned to the two sugar plantations, the textile factory, and the tea plantation in Mali, two decades after that initial trip.

Malians had been running the factories for 10 years and more, but they had found it difficult to manage them efficiently or to import spare parts for the Chinese machinery. In 1984, they invited the Chinese to return. Chinese experts from China Light Industrial Corporation for Foreign and Technical Cooperation (CLETC) were appointed as the general manager and heads of all departments at the two sugar complexes, their salaries paid from the profits of the factory. According to a Chinese source, output increased by nearly 100 percent.[36] Mali was under IMF pressure to privatize its loss-making state-owned companies. Despite the renewed production, the sugar complexes, with 2,100 employees, were still operating at a loss. They needed new varieties of sugarcane and greater production efficiency. And although the Chinese were not pressing hard for repayment, Mali was also in debt to China.

It took four years to negotiate the privatization of the sugar complex and arrange a debt-equity swap, but in 1996 the two sugar plantations were combined in a joint venture, known as Sukala. China Light Industrial Corporation for Foreign and Technical Cooperation held 60 percent of

the shares, and the government of Mali, which contributed the land, 40 percent. The Chinese government provided additional loans so that CLETC
could upgrade the factory equipment. As we will see in chapter 7, Sukala
made headlines when the company decided to greatly expand the area
under sugarcane cultivation and build a new refinery, in competition with
an American firm.

The Chinese also sent a team to run the textile mill at Ségou: COVEC
(China Overseas Engineering Corporation), the company that had originally built the complex.[37] COVEC was entrepreneurial. In the late 1990s,
the World Bank sponsored several rural development projects in Mali.
One tried to boost commercial opportunities in Mali's agricultural sector.
"Donors can no longer be expected to fund the bulk of land development
now that they have helped make it profitable," the Bank reasoned. "Private
investment will be needed." Foreign investors would be given 30-year
renewable leases. A second project involved the extension of the irrigation
perimeters of the Office du Niger in several villages about 80 kilometers
from the textile factory in Ségou. Part of COVEC's purpose in returning
to Mali to manage the textile factory was to use it as a base for expanding
their construction business. They won the World Bank's irrigation project
construction contract to develop several thousand hectares of irrigated
perimeters.

While the construction was going on, Mali went on a "charm offensive"
to attract foreign investment, sponsoring an advertising campaign and setting up a new investment promotion agency. In 1998, COVEC decided to
invite rice experts from Jiangxi province to join them in a commercial rice
venture. The company invested over $3 million, receiving a 30-year lease on
1,000 hectares near M'Béwani. COVEC uprooted shrubs, leveled the land,
and constructed canals. But the first two years of mechanized rice cultivation on an initial 200 hectares were deeply disappointing. The machinery
did not work as well in Mali as in China, and the irrigated area did not have
the hard bottom layer necessary to support the machines. Perhaps most
frustratingly, thieves stole most of the rice.

COVEC decided to rent out the irrigated plots to more than 300 local
farmers, keeping 10 hectares as a demonstration plot. Tenants—mostly
local government officials and elites who could afford the rent—paid 60,000
Mali francs (about $120) per hectare, per six-month season. A Xinhua
reporter who visited in 2007 described standing under a tall breadfruit
tree, viewing the "endless green paddy fields." Some of the Malian farmers
were bent over, working in the fields. Others were fishing for African carp
in the clear green waters of the canal. From time to time a large flock of
egrets would startle upward, a white cloud with flapping wings. COVEC
had become a landlord, earning hundreds of thousands of dollars each year.

And the tea factory at Farako? The Chinese returned, but there the story took a different twist.[38] The Chinese technicians left in 1976 after several years training their Malian counterparts. The tea bushes continued to produce glossy dark green leaves, sheltered by rows of mango trees, but Malian management was "not satisfactory" as a Malian newspaper put it. In the early 1990s, a team of experts returned to Farako from Shimen State Farm, in Zhejiang province, home of the famous gunpowder tea. As Wang Guohua, one of the team members, later recalled, they drove from Bamako in a very old yellow van. Red dust poured in from the dirt road. Twenty-five kilometers from the factory, the landscape changed. They felt they had entered a movie set, with beautiful scenery and a landscape thick with trees. However, their arrival at the Chinese experts' compound filled them with dismay. A fence surrounded a few dilapidated red mud huts, shaded by mango and palm oil trees. Small striped squirrels dashed from tree to tree, bees nested in the walls, four-foot-long snakes crawled across the yard, and, at night, bats flew out of the eaves of the huts.

The experts, described in a Chinese blog as "tea missionaries to Mali," saw much that reminded them of pre-reform China. The state-owned factory was now deeply in debt. Pickers plucked large, tough leaves, and the factory let the dry leaves pile up in a warehouse. The Chinese taught Malians how to apply fertilizer more scientifically, plow deep to encourage better root formation, and pick tender leaves. "The tea was being sold fresh," Wang Guohua said. "To make the tea sell well, we roasted it first."

In 1993, the Chinese team agreed to a 10-year lease-management contract but was unwilling to invest in the project. When they left in 2004, the plantation and its machinery were both 40 years old. Some bushes had died; the plantation had shrunk by 12 hectares. There were still no electricity lines to the factory, which relied on ancient generators for its power. Jérémie Togo, secretary general of the tea workers' trade union, was hired in 1975, just as the original Chinese team was leaving. "I've lived through the different epochs of this factory," he told a visiting journalist. "You know, when the Chinese built this factory, their goal was not to promote the cultivation of tea, but get us Malians accustomed to consuming tea."

History shows that Malians had actually been accustomed consumers of Chinese tea since the colonial period. Europeans brought the strong, green, gunpowder tea favored in Mali from China to northern Africa in the 18th century. It moved south with the Tuareg and Arab nomads to northern Mali and then spread across the Sahel. A local company took over the lease. Today, the factory struggles to compete against imports; its costs per kilogram are nearly three times greater than those in China. The new manager, Souleymane Koné, worried that rehabilitating the factory would cost at least $4.3 million. "We are in discussions with some donors," he confided to a journalist. But probably not the Chinese.

CHINA ENTERS MOZAMBIQUE

Mozambique became independent only in 1975, and its Marxist government began almost immediately to consolidate many of the Portuguese plantations and surrounding subsistence areas into large state farms. By the early 1980s, the country had 69 state farms covering some 131,400 hectares.[39] During this time, China's aid program sent at least 120 agricultural experts to help develop Mozambique's state farms.[40]

In the early 1990s, as Mozambique's civil war was drawing to a close, the Frelimo government began a rapid transition toward a free market economy. The state farms were privatized, and Frelimo began to actively court foreign investment. Chinese Premier Li Peng visited Mozambique in 1997 on a seven nation Africa tour. The Chinese news agency Xinhua reported that the two governments would promote joint ventures in agriculture.[41] Several months later, Mozambican leaders met with Chinese ambassador Shao Guanfu in Maputo to push for Chinese investment in agriculture. Groups of Chinese experts conducted preliminary studies of mixed farming, shrimp cultivation, and sugar cane. In early 1999, a delegation from the city of Chongqing toured Mozambique's main rice-growing areas. Mozambique's minister of Agriculture and Forestry told them that Mozambique was dependent on imported rice but had a lot of land. "*China should play its role in helping Mozambique improve its rice production,*" he urged.

Yet, despite all this urging, Chinese firms were reluctant to take the plunge. Between 1990 and 2000, Mozambique received only one Chinese agricultural investment: the 20-hectare Zhong-An vegetable farm near Maputo, which did not go well. In 2002, China's Ministry of Commerce reported that the small farm was "in a state of paralysis."[42] Two years later, however, a major Chinese agribusiness company finally came to Mozambique: China Grains and Oils Group (CGOC). Although their joint venture with Mozambican businessman Zaide Aly would end abruptly, its history shines a light on the key role played by Mozambicans in persuading Chinese agribusiness firms to invest in their country.

Zaide Aly lives in the northern city of Beira where he is president of the Chamber of Commerce. I was lucky that he happened to be visiting Maputo on my second trip to Mozambique, in November 2014. We met for lunch at the Hotel Cardoso with its striking view of Maputo's bay. Zaide Aly's great-grandfather had come to the Portuguese colony from India during the colonial period; his family has been in the country for generations. Aly had served in the Portuguese army before independence and eventually entered the business world with a small restaurant, a hotel, and ambitious goals. In 2003, he decided to buy the lease on a property of some 15,000 hectares, about 100 kilometers from Beira. The farm was originally a Portuguese plantation and had later been operated by the British company Lonrho in a joint venture with the Mozambican state. It boasted a school, a hospital, offices, and housing for 150 workers.

Aly knew something about farming. "My first job after independence was running my father's 47-hectare farm," he told me. But he didn't know much about soybeans, so he traveled to another Portuguese-speaking country, Brazil. There, he ran across a delegation from CGOC conducting a study tour of Brazil's soybean sector.

Aly went back to Mozambique with a soybean expert from Brazil, but the Chinese he had met stayed on his mind. "I checked them out," he said, and then he decided to visit them in Beijing. Aly proposed that CGOC join him in Mozambique: growing and processing soybeans and maize, and running a modern poultry farm. CGOC sent a team, and, after seeing the potential of the area, they decided to invest. "We planned to do something very big," Aly told me. They secured approval for a $6 million investment, brought in a dozen Chinese experts, 20 tractors, and all the equipment for producing eggs and poultry. Aly would be a minority partner. The stage could have been set for another CP Group.

Yet by 2006 the project had been abandoned. South African researcher Philippe Asanzi reported that the venture had problems because of soil conditions and difficulties securing work permits for some of the technicians they wanted to bring in from China.[43] The Chinese economic counselor in Maputo added that the core of the problem was that Mozambique had no institutional support for soybeans; no research institutes or private companies to turn to for continuous variety testing or recommendations on fertilizer use and disease control.[44] Aly said that the main problem was water. "The farm needed an irrigation system," he explained. In 2005, after the seeds had been planted, the rains failed to arrive. A major drought affected more than 1.4 million people across the region. The China Grains and Oil Group began lobbying Beijing for a loan to build a dam on the nearby Zangue River. "If we had built this, the project would have worked," Aly recalled. "The soil was perfect for soybeans. In our first year we were getting five tons to the hectare, almost double what they get in Brazil."

Unhappily for the project, halfway across the globe, China's giant state-owned companies were going through another round of restructuring, in the hopes that they would be better suited to become national champions. In 2006, CGOC was taken over by COFCO, becoming a subsidiary of China's largest commodity trader.[45] "COFCO decided to close our company," Zaide said. "They thought Mozambique was too risky." Years later, the chairman of COFCO, Ning Gaoning, would reflect on this Africa experience, advising Chinese investors not to acquire land in Africa but to buy the products of African farmers.[46]

When I told him about Ning Gaoning's comments, Aly shook his head at the memory. "I had taken out a mortgage on my hotel," he told me. "I nearly lost it. We both lost something." But as we walked across the lawn at the Cardoso after our lunch, he concluded that the experience was a net gain: "the Chinese were wonderful; I learned so much from them."

This chapter puts China's current engagement in Africa in historical and comparative context. We can see how Chinese interest in agricultural investment in Africa was less dramatic and more gradual and experimental than is often believed. We can also see how in China, the governments of more advanced countries, and their companies mixed aid with business, building demonstration centers that could showcase their technology. The discipline of an impending WTO accession added urgency to the necessity of agricultural modernization in China, making the government supportive of involving foreign companies. In later chapters, we will see many echoes of these patterns as Chinese engagement in Africa expanded. Experiences at home set expectations for Chinese government planners, advisers, and companies as they experimented with ways to move economic cooperation forward in Africa.

How did this translate into policies? In the next chapter, we take a close look at that question, drilling down to widespread rumors about Chinese plans to send millions of farmers to Africa and examining stories about central government policies to acquire land overseas to secure China's food supply.

CHAPTER 4

Going Global in Agriculture

Incentives, Institutions, and Policies

B etween 2006 and 2009, Chinese reporters broke stories that sent
shock waves through the international media. One cluster of stories
suggested that Beijing would send Chinese peasants to settle as farmers in
Africa. The other hinted that China was considering a policy of acquiring
large expanses of land in Africa (and elsewhere) to grow its own food.

Let us begin with the Chinese farmers.[1] In late 2006, rumors emerged
that tens of thousands of farmers from Hebei province had settled in
"Baoding villages" across Africa. The following year, Li Ruogu, the president of the China Export-Import Bank (China Eximbank), made a speech
at his bank's newly opened Chongqing branch. Millions of Chongqing
farmers would be moving off the land in the coming years, Li remarked.
If the Chongqing government would organize groups of these farmers to
open farms in Africa, China Eximbank could provide funds and technical
assistance. In some versions of this speech, Li Ruogu apparently added that
Chongqing's labor exports would really "take off" if the government could
convince Chinese farmers "to become landlords overseas." African blogs
and newspapers reacted with alarm: "China to Dump Its Unemployed
Rural Laborers on Africa," represents a typical headline. Finally, in 2009,
reports emerged that China's National People's Congress had apparently
debated a proposal to send a million peasants to farm in Africa. As noted in
the introduction, this later became—for at least one American journalist—
a debate over sending "100 million" Chinese to Africa.

The slightly separate—but related—land acquisition story began to take
shape in the spring of 2008. In the short span of two months, global prices
for rice soared by nearly 75 percent; the cost of a kilo of maize doubled.

Fearful and angry, residents in Haiti's slums rioted for a week; their government fell. In Cairo, fights broke out as lines for subsidized bread stretched
for blocks. With food prices skyrocketing, Chinese reporters broke another
story that was picked up by the *Financial Times* with a dramatic May 8
headline: "China Eyes Overseas Land in Food Push." The story alleged that
China's Ministry of Agriculture had drafted a proposal to boost Chinese
food security by securing large overseas farms.[2] Although China had policies to boost offshore investment in banking, manufacturing, and oil, the
article said, there were none for agriculture. Consequently, Chinese overseas landholdings were "limited to a few small projects." It would be "particularly problematic," the article warned, if Chinese companies used Chinese
labor in their overseas farming investments. Thus, the *FT* linked the land
acquisition issue neatly to the controversies on Chinese migration.

How accurate were these reports? All were widely circulated and discussed in and outside of China. They are the foundation of the idea that
China is acquiring large amounts of land in Africa to grow food to send back
to China and sending Chinese farmers to do this. As of 2015, there is no
evidence that anything like this is happening. Yet to understand what *was*
happening at this critical juncture, we first need to see how Chinese policy
in this area started out—and how it evolved. This chapter draws heavily on
Chinese language media discussions and documents to probe these stories
and highlight the incentives, institutions, and policies that shape China's
outward investment in agriculture. Bear with me while I walk you through
this in a bit of detail.

FROM AID TO BUSINESS

First, we have seen that Chinese agribusiness companies already had several
decades of experience overseas at this juncture. Chinese companies were
legally allowed to invest abroad as early as 1979.[3] During his 1982 visit to
Africa, Chinese Premier Zhao Ziyang signaled that China wanted to pursue
joint ventures on the continent. However, overseas investment proposals
faced an arduous system of approvals. Ironically, given China's huge foreign reserves today, policymakers worried that China did not have enough
foreign exchange to risk in large-scale, outward investments. The focus on
control also reflected unease about markets, and realism about the inexpe-
rience of Chinese firms. These controls would be relaxed very gradually.

Despite these difficulties, investments *did* happen. In fact the first
Chinese investments in Africa were not in the mineral or petroleum sectors,
but in agriculture, along with manufacturing and offshore fishing. As we
saw in Mali (chapter 3), most of the early companies had originally come

to Africa as part of China's aid program. In the mid-1980s, when I was a PhD student stepping gingerly along the edges of West African rice paddies, I met some of these Chinese agribusiness investors.[4] In Sierra Leone, a company called China Agricon arrived in 1984 to offer consulting services, lending Chinese expertise to other agribusiness investors. The Chinese firm Complant was managing Sierra Leone's Magbass sugar complex. China State Farm Agribusiness Corporation already leased at least seven farms in more than half a dozen African countries *before* the first Chinese oil investment occurred in Sudan (1995) and the first mining investment in Zambia (1997). In chapters 6 and 7, we will meet some of these pioneering companies.

Still, China's overseas agribusiness investments were slow to expand. By 2008, China had become deeply integrated in global agricultural trade: "The world's fourth-largest importer of agricultural products and the fifth-largest exporter of agricultural products."[5] Yet although China had received more than $30 billion in foreign investment in its own agricultural sector since 1978, the country's stock of outward investment in agriculture only amounted to $900 million that year.

SETTING UP TO GO OUT

The term *zuo chuqu* (variously translated as "going out," "walking out," or "going global") began to be widely used at the turn of the millennium as China was about to join the WTO. China's top policymaking body is the State Council. Three government ministries, two policy banks, and the system of state-owned land reclamation and state farm agribusiness companies that we met in chapter 3, known collectively as "China *Nongken*," are at the heart of the Chinese developmental state's framework of support for going global in agriculture.

Ministry of Commerce

Stretched out imposingly in the center of Beijing a little north of Tiananmen Square, the Ministry of Commerce (MOFCOM) dominates several blocks of Chang'An Avenue in a new building with a stylized pagoda roof. MOFCOM oversees the Chinese Economic and Commercial Counselor's office in Chinese embassies overseas. Chinese companies looking for support for outbound business can find it in MOFCOM's Department of Outward Investment and Cooperation. In the developmental state tradition, the department creates incentives for firms—carrots that induce them to risk investments abroad—using money allocated by the Ministry of Finance.

Ministry of Agriculture

The Ministry of Agriculture (MOA) is also centrally located but in an older building on a less fashionable street. Although we focus only on agriculture in this book, the MOA is also in charge of forestry, animal husbandry, and fishery activities. Most of their tasks are domestic: boosting output, ensuring food security, and helping with structural transformation and upgrading. However, MOA also has two units to support going global: the Department of International Cooperation and the Foreign Economic Cooperation Center. Their tasks are similar to MOFCOM's Department of Outward Investment and Cooperation: planning, appraising, and helping implement overseas (agricultural) cooperation projects. They also work with other parts of the government to develop strategic plans for going global.

Ministry of Foreign Affairs

Diplomats at China's Ministry of Foreign Affairs (MOFA) also play a role in China's overseas economic engagement. The Ministry gives advice, helps negotiate agreements, and coordinates with other parts of the government on major diplomatic initiatives with an economic thrust. Their Department of International Economic Affairs works most closely on supporting the going global strategy. The Ministry of Foreign Affairs and the Ministry of Commerce work together on economic diplomacy, for example, jointly launching catalogs to guide outward investment, country by country.

China Development Bank

China Development Bank's gleaming curved facade occupies a commanding position near Beijing's main financial district. The CDB is at the heart of China's developmental state. Tasked with using finance strategically to break through bottlenecks in China's own development, CDB was set up in 1994 as a government-owned policy bank. Although CDB is primarily domestic, its role in China's global business is growing. CDB provides commercial-rate finance; its loans are not directly subsidized. CDB has forged strategic partnerships with some of China's flagship corporations and announced lines of credit to support going global in areas as diverse as cultural industries (e.g., film, television), petroleum exploration, and tele-communications. In 2007, CDB established the China Africa Development Fund (CAD-Fund), an investment fund that began with $1 billion and is expected to reach $5 billion.

China Export-Import Bank

China Export-Import Bank (China Eximbank) was also established in 1994 as a policy bank and serves as China's official export credit agency. Two-thirds of the bank's loan portfolio consists of export seller's credits. These can support Chinese firms' exports, but also their offshore invest-ments. China Eximbank is supposed to operate on a break-even basis—not making a profit, but not requiring regular subsidies. It can use profits from its commercial-rate loans to subsidize its policy loans, including its prefer-ential export buyers' credits for borrowing governments. It also receives transfers from the Ministry of Finance to subsidize its concessional for-eign aid loans (about 3 percent of its portfolio). Like CDB, it is implicitly guaranteed by the Chinese state and enjoys the same strong credit rating as the central government. China Eximbank has offices in South Africa and Morocco and a regional office in Paris that also supports their work in Africa.

The *Nongken* System

We met the forerunners of China's *nongken* (land reclamation and state farm) companies in the Great Northern Wilderness in chapter 3. As China reformed, the *nongken* companies were separated from their parent minis-tries and commercialized, becoming responsible for their own profits and losses. Some went out of business and others were merged to help create giant agribusiness corporations. In 2004, for example, China State Farms Agribusiness Corporation and a number of other state-owned companies became subsidiaries of China National Agricultural Development Group Corporation (CNADC).[6]

Provincial-level *nongken* companies are accountable to their provincial governments, not directly to Beijing. Most have become corporate enter-prises, like Xinjiang Production and Construction Corps (now active in Angola) and Heilongjiang Beidahuang Nongken Corporation (active in Mozambique, as we will see in chapter 8). Some provinces have merged the state farm functions into their local departments of agriculture, while

others are transforming their *nongken* systems into policymaking and planning bureaus.

By the mid-1990s, the institutions that would support China's globalization
were in place, yet the first State Council document offering guidance on how to
encourage Chinese outward investment was only issued in 1999 (see box 4.1).
All of this is to say that for Chinese companies and the government, figuring out
how to do outward foreign investment is relatively—but not entirely—new.

OVERSEAS FARMING IN THE GOING GLOBAL
FRAMEWORK (2000–2008)

From the beginning, policymakers assumed that going global would naturally include overseas farming. These were not secret plans. For example, in
January 2001, the State Council and the Communist Party of China (CPC)
announced that officials "correctly" implementing the going global strategy
in agriculture would encourage Chinese companies to set up agro-processing factories abroad and boost efforts to *develop foreign land resources*.[7] This
guidance came from the highest levels, including former Chinese President
Hu Jintao, who in 2003 called for Chinese firms "to go abroad *to develop
land*, forestry, fisheries and other resources."
    Furthermore, Africa was clearly an early focus. In September 2002,
MOFA and MOFCOM teamed up to hold a seminar on African agricultural cooperation.[8] Representatives from 21 ministries attended, along with
more than 60 Chinese companies. Wei Jianguo, China's vice-minister in
charge of foreign aid, gave a speech to the delegates. Food self-sufficiency
is a strategic priority for African states, he explained, and they are keen to
cooperate with China. China had provided a lot of aid to African agriculture,
but in the future, Wei said, foreign aid will play a smaller role: "China-Africa
agricultural co-operation in the new century must be conducted by enterprises and should be market-oriented. *We encourage Chinese companies to
invest in the farming sector in Africa*."
    As this quotation suggests, Chinese investment was positioned, at least
publicly, as a way to help *African* countries achieve food security. Some
Chinese officials also assumed that going out would help *China's* food security, yet there was no clear message on this. For example, on May 24, 2004,
Xinhua noted that the government was trying to help solve China's food
problems by "encouraging enterprises to produce grain overseas by leasing
foreign farmland."[9] Xinhua quoted prominent Peking University economist
Justin Yifu Lin (who later became chief economist at the World Bank).
China's shortages of farm land and water, he said, made overseas farming an

obvious option. Just four days earlier, however, Niu Dun, the director general of the Ministry of Agriculture's Department of International Cooperation, had emphasized to *China Daily* that China would feed its own people.

In June 2004, MOFCOM held its first international forum on the going global strategy. An official told assembled guests (including representatives from the EU and Africa) that China would be experimenting with "multiple approaches" to build agricultural bases overseas.[10] Finally, in 2006, MOFCOM, the Ministry of Agriculture, and the Ministry of Finance formed a 14-department interministerial working group to "accelerate" the going global strategy in agriculture. Their work would include modernizing China's own agribusinesses and commodity traders, moving Chinese agricultural exports up the value chain, and developing new incentives for overseas investment.

Thus, as the 2008 global food crisis was looming on the horizon, the Chinese government was gradually refining its existing incentive structure for going global in agriculture. Below, I provide a few details on this incentive structure, which included catalogs to guide outward investment, special funds managed by MOFCOM, economic diplomacy headed by MOFA, and strategic cooperation agreements with China's policy banks. We will also see that Chinese companies did not see those policies as effective and pushed for *more*.

Catalogs Guiding Outward Investment

For decades, China has published catalogs that guide foreign investors seeking business *inside* China. In July 2004, MOFCOM and MOFA published the first of three catalogs offering guidance on *outward* investment.[11] The catalogs, still available only in Chinese, covered five broad sectors (including agriculture) and dozens of countries. For each country, the catalogs highlighted specific areas where foreign countries were eager to receive investment and also those of particular interest to China. These could be very specific—potato farming in Thailand or jute in Bangladesh—but most were fairly general. Firms that were certified to invest abroad were more likely to be given priority access to Chinese benefits, including financing, foreign exchange, tax exemptions, customs, and immigration assistance—if they followed the catalogs' suggestions.

What signals can we see here about Chinese farming goals in Africa? In 2004, Africa played a very minor role. Only 13 of the 67 countries listed were African. The 2005 catalog added 10 new African countries, while the third, published in 2007, added an additional 10 from Africa. Together, the catalogs mentioned farming or the cultivation of crops as a recommended investment in only 12 of the 33 African countries. Most noted one specific crop: tobacco (Zimbabwe), sisal (Tanzania), or cotton (Egypt). Several mentioned clusters of crops: fruit and vegetables (Gabon), fruit and nuts (Nigeria). In six African countries—Cameroon, Ethiopia, Zambia, Guinea, DRC, and Benin—the catalog encouraged the broad category of "farming crops" (*nongzuowu zhongzhi*). Whereas rice was suggested in the Philippines and "grains" in Laos and Cambodia, none of the catalogs listed rice or grain as a sector for encouragement in Africa. We have to conclude that investment in African agriculture was on the radar but in a modest way, at least through 2007, and that the government was not encouraging Chinese firms to grow grain in Africa to feed the Chinese people.

Special Funds

In December 2005, MOFCOM and MOF established the first special fund for foreign economic and technical cooperation (FETC), offering general support for going global.[12] Since then, Chinese companies investing in agriculture and a range of other priority sectors have been able to apply for interest rate subsidies and rebates of some preinvestment expenses, up to RMB 30 million (about $4.6 million). Although MOFCOM has no funds *specifically* targeting agriculture, it has been listed from the beginning as a sector covered by the FETC special funds. Provincial governments also have special funds to support their firms to go global; some are said to offer a higher level of support than MOFCOM does at the national level.

Economic Diplomacy: FOCAC and Foreign Aid Programs

In the new century, China's Ministry of Foreign Affairs has become an active player in economic diplomacy, particularly through the establishment of "cooperation forums" in regions with many small countries (the Caribbean, South Pacific, and Africa). The Forum on China Africa Cooperation (FOCAC) was founded in 2000.[13] These forums allow economies of scale in building economic ties, offering loans, hosting investment fairs, and cementing political relationships through pledges of foreign aid.

For example, as part of the goal of making cooperation less about foreign aid and more about business, FOCAC commissioned a well-known management consultant, Shi Yongxiang, and 40 experts to develop an Africa Investment Roadmap for the November 2006 Beijing FOCAC summit. The Investment Roadmap recommended that Beijing follow the path carved out by the Dutch, Israelis, and others in China: use foreign aid funds to construct agro-technology demonstration centers (ATDCs) with state of the art research labs and student dormitories. Beijing would provide three years of foreign aid funding for the companies to run the centers, offer courses, and train local counterparts, before handing them over to the host governments. These were duly announced at the 2006 FOCAC summit. The Chinese firms were encouraged to use the centers as platforms for other investments and to seek ways for the centers to earn income and become self-financing. Not only would this alleviate problems of sustainability that had plagued China's earlier agricultural aid efforts, it would also "create a lot of opportunities for China's agricultural enterprises," as Shi told a journalist.[14]

Over time, more than two dozen ATDCs would be built in Africa (see appendix 3). African governments could point to the shiny new buildings as visible proof of their desire to promote agriculture. And as we have already seen, they were attractive to some Chinese agribusiness companies: Hubei Lianfeng in Mozambique, for example. Yang Haomin's Shaanxi State Farm Agribusiness Corporation in Cameroon would take charge of building the ATDC for Cameroon.

MOA and China Development Bank: Strategic Cooperation Agreement

Finally, we see that in 2006, the Ministry of Agriculture and China Development Bank signed a five-year agreement to work together to help modernize China's agriculture.[15] China Development Bank had signed strategic agreements before in a number of sectors, including natural resources, shipbuilding, and overseas construction, but this was their first with the Ministry of Agriculture. Proposals to acquire more advanced technology, improve trade logistics, or develop "land and water overseas" were eligible for loans. By 2010, CDB had disbursed some $2.5 billion under the agreement. Most of the funded projects had focused on China's domestic agriculture, but about $420 million was devoted to going out projects.

"WALKING WITH DIFFICULTY"

Despite these measures, Chinese companies remained reluctant to invest in agriculture overseas, even those from the famously entrepreneurial province of Zhejiang. "We've been encouraging companies to go out," a Zhejiang province official told a reporter in 2008, "but so far not many have gone. There is interest, but there are a lot of problems."[16] A study commissioned by the MOA reported that more than 20 firms from Guangxi province had invested in agriculture abroad, but the average investment was only two million yuan (about $300,000). A company from Guangdong province was trying to establish a rubber plantation overseas, but it couldn't afford to tie up large amounts of capital for years while the rubber trees matured.

In 2006, Xia Zesheng, the director of overseas development at CSFAC, argued that risks were particularly high for agricultural investment in Africa: some firms with investments in Africa were "walking with difficulty."[17] (In chapter 6, we will see what he meant.) Xia used his soapbox to push for more government attention to Africa's agribusiness potential. At least 44 African countries need to use their scarce foreign exchange to import food, he said. They have preferential policies to achieve local self-sufficiency. *This provides an opportunity for Chinese companies.* Xia suggested that the government set up a special fund just for China-Africa agricultural cooperation. China should build a "national team" of government ministries and major companies to develop strategies for going out in Africa.

In response to all this, MOFCOM and the Ministry of Agriculture held a meeting in 2007 with representatives of China's more prominent agricultural provinces and their agribusiness firms.[18] Hubei Lianfeng showcased their efforts to establish the Gaza-Hubei Friendship Farm in Mozambique. The Ostrich King from Shaanxi described his company's efforts to invest in Cameroon. Both explained that they had plunged into their investments before getting support from MOFCOM and were now having some difficulty. Private firms complained that it was nearly impossible to access MOFCOM's special funds. After the meeting, the MOA set to work to develop recommendations for new incentives for agribusiness to go global. Around the same time, China's National Development and Reform Commission (NDRC), the main planning body under the State Council, created a task force with 14 ministries and bureaus to develop a medium- and long-term national food security plan.[19] MOFCOM and the China Council for the Promotion of International Trade were already planning to hold a major conference on outward investment in April 2008. They decided to add several panels that focused on agriculture. And now we arrive at a windy spring day in Beijing, the moment that would lead to the disquieting headline: "China Eyes Overseas Land in Food Push."[20]

APRIL AND MAY 2008

On April 22, 2008, over 600 people gathered in Beijing for the start of the second annual Chinese Enterprises Outbound Investment Conference.[21]

A cold front swept in from the northern steppes. Officials and investors hurried through the doors as strong gusts of wind blew sheets of rain across the Beijing sidewalks. Inside, plenary sessions outlined general policies and opportunities, while in the afternoon, a series of concurrent seminars focused on special topics. Officials from foreign governments made presentations: Invest in Quebec: Your Smart Choice; An Offshore Gateway to Europe—the Advantages of the Isle of Man; and Join the Winning Team: Why Düsseldorf has the Fastest Growing Chinese Business Community in Germany.

Two seminars highlighted investment policies and opportunities in agriculture. An official from the Ministry of Agriculture spoke in the first seminar. The Chinese government was developing new incentives to encourage Chinese companies to expand their overseas agricultural investments, he said. After a tea break, officials from Brazil, Burma, Egypt, Kazakhstan, and Canada gave presentations on agricultural opportunities in their countries.

On the second day, Zhang Xichen, an executive from the Suntime (Xintian) Group, a Xinjiang provincial conglomerate, gave a speech. In the late 1990s, Zhang's company had established Cuba's largest agricultural joint venture, growing 5,000 hectares of irrigated rice for local sale. In 1998, Suntime bought 1,255 hectares in Campeche, Mexico, to grow rice, watermelon, and kidney beans. The initial years of the Mexico investment were a disaster, but Suntime persevered, and by 2005 they were making a tidy profit. Zhang told the guests that China should give more support for companies to "rent land to grow grain" or even "buy land to grow grain."[22] If they could sell this grain back to China, this would help safeguard China's food security, he said.

Liu Yinghua from the *Beijing Morning Post* seems to have been the only reporter to write about the conference. His article noted "sources close to the Ministry of Agriculture said recently that Chinese companies going overseas to develop agricultural resources will help close gaps in China's domestic supply." The Chinese headline for the article spun this a bit differently, saying: "Ministry of Agriculture recommends that companies overseas 'rent land to grow grain.' "[23] The wording was nearly identical with the comment in 2004 that China was "encouraging enterprises to produce grain overseas by leasing foreign farmland." Yet the timing was completely different. As we saw at the start of this chapter, high food prices had created panic in a number of countries and concern was already growing about land grabbing in poor countries.

The foreign press latched onto the story. On May 4, the Associated Press wrote: "As Beijing scrambles to feed its galloping economy, it has already scoured the world for mining and logging concessions. Now it is turning to crops to feed its people and industries. Chinese enterprises are snapping up vast tracts of land abroad and forging contract farming deals."[24] Four days later, on May 8, a Chinese newspaper repeated the *Beijing Morning Post* story but added that the Ministry of Agriculture was busy trying to clarify its position, telling reporters that the MOA had no special incentives for companies to buy or lease land to grow grain overseas.[25] The *Financial Times* article was published later that day, with the hugely influential statements that we have already seen:

> Chinese companies will be encouraged to buy farmland abroad, particularly in Africa and South America, to help guarantee food security under a plan being considered by Beijing. A proposal drafted by the Ministry of Agriculture would make supporting offshore land acquisition by domestic agricultural companies a central government policy.[26]

With a readership of several million people, the *Financial Times* article commanded attention. The Chinese government reacted. The Ministry of Agriculture assigned Xie Guoli, an English-speaking official who had been at the April conference, to meet with reporters. Rowan Callick in the *Australian* quoted Xie: "China is encouraging its companies to co-operate more internationally. But we are not providing financial support, and we are not at this stage studying or recommending any specific country as an investment target."[27]

In Britain, the *Guardian* carried another explicit denial from a Chinese MOA official. "It is not realistic to grow grains overseas, particularly in Africa or South America. There are so many people starving in Africa, can you ship the grain back to China? The cost will be very high as well as the risk. It is the government's policy to encourage all companies to go abroad, including agricultural firms, just like the mining and oil companies," the official continued. "As far as I know, the government is not working on any detailed plan to support such investment." Then implying that such a plan might unfold down the road, he added: "It's too early, we need to wait and see how the investments mature."[28]

Let us pause for a moment. Looking back over nearly a decade and a half of evolution in the going out policies (see box 4.1), we can see that the idea of Chinese companies farming overseas was not a sharp break from the past. Rather than a sector that was ignored until global food prices rose, agriculture was always included in the general framework of support for Chinese companies moving outward. Learning how to support different sectors like agribusiness was gradual, involving much experimentation. But as we have seen, Chinese agribusiness companies and analysts were impatiently pushing for targeted policies to encourage Chinese firms to invest in agriculture overseas. They wanted the developmental state to get more involved.

Box 4.1

GOING GLOBAL IN AGRICULTURE: CHRONOLOGY
OF POLICY LANDMARKS

1979   Chinese companies first allowed to invest overseas.

1989   CSFAC first overseas agricultural investment (Australia).

1994   CDB and China Eximbank established.

1996   Information Office of State Council, "Grain Issue in China," white paper.

1999   State Council: Opinion on encouraging companies to carry out overseas processing and assembly investment.

2000   FOCAC launched in Beijing (November).

2001   Tenth five-year plan (2001–2005) launches going global.

2002   MOFCOM/MOFA seminar on African agricultural cooperation.

2004   Chinese media reports Beijing "encouraging enterprises to produce grain overseas by leasing foreign farmland."

2004   First Catalog for Guidance of Outward Investment.

2005   Second Catalog for Guidance of Outward Investment.

2005   Guidelines for Foreign Economic and Technical Cooperation (FETC) Special Fund: *Cai Qi* [Finance Regulation] [2005] 255 (December).

2006   Eleventh five-year plan (2006–2010).

2006   MOA/MOFCOM/MOF: Opinions on accelerating implementation of agricultural going out strategy.

2006   MOA/MOFCOM: Three-year plan for China-Africa agricultural cooperation.

2006   MOA and CDB sign strategic agreement to work together on agricultural modernization.

2006   Interministerial working group formed to accelerate going out strategy in agriculture.

2007   No. 1 Policy Document: Speed up implementation of going global strategy in agriculture.

2007   Third Catalog for Guidance of Outward Investment.

2007   MOA: Agriculture going out development plan formulated (January).

2007   CAD-Fund established (March).

2007   China Eximbank president Li Ruogu speech in Chongqing (September).

2008   Second annual Chinese enterprises outbound investment conference (April).

2008   State Council: Long-term plan for food security published (November).

2008   MOA and China Eximbank create Foreign Agricultural Cooperation Loan Program (December).

2010   No. 1 Policy Document: Speed up international cooperation in agriculture technology and agriculture development.

2010   CAAIC established with RMB 1 billion ($116 million).

2010   MOA Minister Han Changfu: "time is ripe for the country's agricultural companies to go out."

2011   Twelfth five-year plan (2011–2015): MOA portion includes going global plan for agriculture.

2011   FETC Special Fund: key sectors include overseas agriculture. *Cai Qi* [2011] 76.

2012   FETC Special Fund: key sectors include overseas agriculture. *Cai Qi* [2012] 141.

2012   MOA/CDB: Joint agreement of financial support for Chinese international agricultural cooperation.

2013   Third Plenary Session of the 18th CPC Central Committee: accelerate agricultural going out pace.

2014   No. 1 Policy Document: emphasis on accelerating pace of agricultural going out (January).

2014   CPC Central Rural Work Conference: China *nongken* companies should go abroad to develop resources (December).

Did these stories give an accurate account of what was happening behind the scenes in the halls of power? The *Financial Times* was correct that new policies were being drafted, but, from what we have seen, it is hard to find evidence for some of the key assumptions and conclusions of the article: that the interest in overseas farming was new, stemming from high food prices; that policymakers had paid no attention to agriculture in the going out policies so far; or that Beijing was developing a major new policy of offshore land acquisition in Africa and Latin America.

AFTER THE HEADLINES

As of this writing, seven years have passed since that stormy spring when high food prices, combined with ongoing Chinese efforts to evolve their going global policies in agriculture, created a public relations nightmare for the Ministry of Agriculture. Chinese policymakers clearly did not expect the international backlash that erupted because of the perception that China wanted to acquire large amounts of land overseas to grow food to ship back to China. One of the reporters who covered the story for the

Chinese press in 2008 told me: "In China we talk about this issue openly. No one thinks the government would be wrong to encourage offshore land acquisition, rather, they think the government has been slow. The Ministry of Agriculture criticized me after I wrote my article. They said my work promoted the 'China threat' theory—I really did not expect this."

As we will see, there is still no clear evidence that the Chinese government was considering a major new policy of securing land overseas, in Africa and elsewhere, as a plank in China's food security plan. At the December 2013 CPC Central Rural Work Conference—which provides an important annual political signal on agricultural policies—Chinese President Xi Jinping repeated a stock phrase: "Our bowls should be filled mainly with Chinese grain."[29] Jiao Jian, author of a major report on China's food security published in China's leading finance and economics magazine *Caijing*, in late 2013, commented that the role of overseas agriculture in China's food security strategy remains "pretty unclear."[30] At the same time, we can put together some of the pieces.

Long-term Food Security: "Fill Our Bowls with Chinese Grain"

The working group that developed the long-term framework for Chinese food security for the National Development and Reform Commission (NDRC), China's apex strategic planning body, included none of the institutions one might have expected if foreign farming was being considered as a major policy. MOFCOM was not at the table, nor the Ministry of Foreign Affairs, nor the policy banks.[31] The national framework for food security 2008–2020 was published in November 2008 and unsurprisingly, did not mention anything about relying on overseas land.[32] The going out section of the framework emphasized trade: China would build long-term, stable partnerships with the world's top grain- and soybean-producing countries—such as Brazil and the United States.

The NDRC held a press conference to present the framework. A reporter from the Voice of America asked whether the plan's encouragement of Chinese firms to go out referred to the rumored plan to set up large-scale overseas farms to boost China's food security. The plan is not to set up large overseas farms, spokesman Zhang Xiaoqiang answered. "We want to have a stable and reliable system to be able to import a broad range of foods, including soybeans and edible oils."[33] This reply would have reminded many in the room that when China opened its soybean sector after joining the WTO, its domestic soy-processing firms tumbled badly in the face of far more efficient foreign competition. Archer Daniels Midland, Bunge,

Cargill, Louis Dreyfus, Wilmar, and other foreign firms soon controlled almost 60 percent of China's total soybean-processing industry.[34] Zhang finished by saying: "International cooperation, logistics, and so on particularly for soybean procurement—*this* is what we are very concerned about."

The Governor's "Rice Bag"

Food security is not only a central government responsibility in China, but something that each provincial government must ensure. This is colloquially known as the "governor's 'rice bag' (*mi daizi*, which can also be translated as grain supply) responsibility." Security is not the same as self-sufficiency. Provincial officials can make sure their populations have access to supplies of food through local production quotas, imports from other provinces, or even securing land in other parts of China. This helps explain several instances in which provincial companies and analysts have promoted overseas land acquisitions in Africa for *provincial* food security.

In 2010, two Hubei-based analysts, one of whom worked for a branch office of China Development Bank, recommended that Hubei establish "overseas granaries" for the province.[35] Several years later, as we will see in chapter 8, Wanbao, a private company from Hubei province, would describe their Mozambique-based Friendship Farm in similar fashion. The farm would first help solve food supply problems in Africa, but, in the long term, it could become an "overseas production base" for China. The idea that southern Africa might provide an "overseas granary" for China's food security also animated a strategic cooperation agreement signed in 2014 between the Food Industry Association of the large coastal city of Xiamen in Fujian province and the Common Market for Eastern and Southern Africa (COMESA) to address "Xiamen's food security problem."

Provinces in China are known for conducting their own foreign economic relations, and, as noted above, many have set up their own special funds to support going global. Some—Anhui for example—even have provincial funds focused on overseas agriculture. While overseas granaries might not be a central government policy, some provinces may see foreign farms as a way to help keep the governor's rice bag full.

Follow the Money

Significant shifts in funding should provide the most important clues to policy about overseas land acquisition as a strategy for Chinese food security. And here we have another important piece of the puzzle. In December 2008,

China Eximbank quietly signed its own strategic cooperation agreement with the Ministry of Agriculture to establish a Foreign Agricultural Cooperation Loan Program with up to $8 billion available to finance Chinese agribusiness firms going global.[36] The MOA-China Eximbank program created a substantial new source of funding to help Chinese agribusiness firms globalize. As with the CDB program, loans were available for a wide range of projects, including working capital or construction costs for overseas farming (but not land purchases). This program was almost certainly what Li Ruogu was referring to in Chongqing in September 2007. As Li had said, the loans came with the promise of project assistance from the Eximbank and from the Ministry of Agriculture. This may also have been the program that MOA officials were thinking about when they spoke at the April 2008 conference about an evolving plan to help Chinese agribusinesses.

Yet so far, the Foreign Agricultural Cooperation Loan Program has not fostered major overseas investments: the first 80 loans averaged only $10 million each.[37] One successful applicant was a joint venture between Anhui State Farm Agribusiness Corporation and the Zimbabwe Ministry of Defense (see chapter 8). "We came to Zimbabwe in December 2010," the manager said when I visited in June 2013. "China Eximbank helped us. They gave us RMB 50 million [$8 million] in a preferential loan to put this farm back into production." As collateral, Eximbank requires either a property mortgage or a share of stock (for listed companies), limiting the attractiveness of these loans.

In June 2010, China National Agricultural Development Company joined with the China-Africa Development Fund to set up the China-Africa Agriculture Investment Company (CAAIC). Funded at RMB 1 billion (US$161 million), CAAIC provided a modest platform to promote China's farming, fishing, animal husbandry, livestock, and agro-processing and marketing investments in Africa.[38] By April 2012, the CAD-Fund had itself only invested a total of $57 million in agriculture-related projects.

As it happens, both China Development Bank and China Eximbank are offering far more financial support to *African* governments to invest in their own agricultural sectors. In 2009, China Development Bank provided a $1.5 billion line of credit for the Angolan government to invest in agriculture projects. As we will see in the next chapter, three Chinese firms are developing seven of 13 large state farms commissioned by the Angolan government. China Eximbank reportedly advanced the Ethiopian government $123 million to enable the construction of a sugar factory in the northeast, while in 2013, CDB pledged over $500 million to Ethiopia to build two sugar factories in South Omo.[39]

In March 2013, China Development Bank made what appears to be its largest single agricultural loan in Africa so far: $500 million.[40] This finance will allow Indonesia's largest oil palm producer, the controversial but very experienced Sinar Mas Group, to develop a $1.6 billion oil palm project in Liberia. Rather than securing land for China's food security, this transaction showcases CDB's growing role as an international commercial bank.

In thinking about the global agribusiness priorities held by Chinese leaders, we can compare China Eximbank's $8 billion Foreign Agricultural Cooperation Loan Program with over $9 billion in funding provided by Chinese policy banks between 2011 and 2013 to just one agricultural commodity trading company: COFCO.[41] China's leaders do want to modernize agriculture at home and promote overseas agribusiness investment, but following the money suggests that they *deeply* want to develop at least one national champion to compete with the Cargills of this world.

FOREIGN FARMERS

What of the fears that China was planning to offload its displaced farmers to Africa? I have never found any hint of an official policy of promoting large-scale *resettlement* but rather a continuation of the familiar policy of promoting labor exports on temporary contracts, something China has been doing since 1978, as described in chapter 3. China Eximbank president Li Ruogu's 2007 speech was less a clarion call for migration than an advertisement for services his bank would be providing through the Foreign Agricultural Cooperation Loan Program. The relatively small loans they were planning might be feasible for a group of investors assembled from the provinces—the kind of group that Hubei province assembled to create Hubei Lianfeng's venture in Mozambique (chapter 1). Chinese peasants would be unlikely to flood into Africa under this program. The dozens of Chinese overseas farming investments that already existed in Africa by this time were using very few Chinese workers. This was unlikely to change in any significant way.

And the "Baoding village" legend? This story was traceable to one person: Liu Jianjun, an entrepreneur and former government official from the Hebei province city of Baoding. Liu enjoyed considerable media attention because of his claims to have settled at least 15,800 people from Baoding in dozens of "Baoding villages" in 17 countries across Africa. However, field researchers—Barry Sautman, Yan Hairong, Josh Maiyo, Solange Guo Chatelard, myself, and others—have been unable to find even one example of a Chinese farming village anywhere on the continent.[42] "This is a fairy tale," Imataa Akayombokwa, a director in Zambia's Ministry of Agriculture, said when I asked him in 2008 about Liu Jianjun's claim to have established a wealthy "Baoding village" with 380 Chinese farmers in his country.

A team of anthropologists from the Netherlands and Australia reported that Chinese netizens had mounted their own "Baoding Villages: Where Are You?" investigative campaign in 15 African countries alleged to have these settlements. They also failed to find any. Yet like a zombie, the story refused to lie down and die.

Finally, what about the so-called National People's Congress "debate" about sending a million Chinese farmers to Africa? This has been described as though the legislative branch debated a serious, official proposal of some kind. There *was* a proposal—from NPC delegate Zhao Zhihai, a renowned agricultural scientist and "model worker" known as the "father of hybrid millet." Zhao's institute at the Hebei province Academy of Agricultural Sciences had been conducting commercial hybrid-millet trials together with the Ethiopian Institute of Agricultural Research, about 130 kilometers outside Ethiopia's capital Addis Ababa. Zhao had visited Ethiopia to oversee the tests.[43] As he told a Chinese reporter, this experience led him to suggest that China adopt an official strategy to solve its unemployment problem and Africa's food shortages by sending up to a million unemployed Chinese to work in Africa. When I asked a colleague at the Chinese Agricultural University about Zhao's proposal, she winced and asked: Surely your Congress gets some strange proposals from delegates, too? It is unlikely that his proposal was seriously discussed at the NPC, but, as we will see later, it *was* debated on the Internet.

IS THE TIME RIPE?

In December 2010, Agricultural Minister Han Changfu met with China's top agribusiness companies and told them that conditions had matured: "The time is ripe for China's large agricultural enterprises to seize the historic opportunity of globalization, and make Chinese agriculture 'going out' a major force in international markets."[44] Five years later, China's large companies had not (yet) seized this opportunity, and many remained decidedly unenthusiastic about going out. In his December 9, 2013, *Caijing* cover story on China's food security, analyst Jiao Jian noted that China was a latecomer in overseas agribusiness. If we disregard the pressure of international public opinion and carry out foreign land acquisitions, he said, we face the same efficiency-raising challenges that we have in China but in an unfamiliar environment with greater risks. Furthermore, which companies should take the lead? State-owned firms have more resources, but they are easily demonized. Private firms lack financing and have problems scaling up. There are no easy answers.

We leave this discussion of China's agricultural going out policies with an appreciation for its slow evolution and the profound challenges faced by planners responsible for the food security of a fifth of the world's population. Outside China, people remained deeply concerned about any hint of a large-scale Chinese appetite for land overseas. Chinese leaders need no reminders that foreign land remains a hot-button issue. In 2014, although China had begun to relax its approvals process for overseas foreign investments, the government decreed that any proposal for large-scale land development was "sensitive" and would have to be approved by the State Council.[45] At the same time, a number of vocal critics inside China complained that overseas agricultural investment needs a far higher position in China's strategic planning. These tensions made it politically difficult for clear policy guidelines to emerge.

I came to another conclusion during the months our China Africa Research Initiative (CARI) team spent exploring Chinese-language media discussions about Chinese policies toward outward investment in agriculture. This investment may be about to sharply increase, although it is not clear that Africa will be the target. The first clue was a small notice posted in December 2014 describing the outcome of the CCP's Central Rural Work Conference. "Next year," the notice said, "the central government will step up the reform of China's centrally managed *nongken* companies, urging some of the giant *nongken* corporations to go abroad to develop resources."[46]

The second clue was larger. Chinese analysts repeatedly say that Chinese offshore investments in agriculture are "still in their infancy."[47] As an indicator of this, we need look no further than an opinion piece published in June 2014 by Ding Xuedong, chairman of China's $650 billion sovereign wealth fund, China Investment Corporation (CIC). Writing in the *Financial Times,* Ding announced that his fund planned to increase its investments in agriculture across the value chain, with a focus on increasing global food supply. "Crops will not plant themselves," he said. "Meeting the world's need for food will require long-term investment."[48]

However, if the future emerges from the past, China's policies toward outward agribusiness investment will continue to evolve gradually, not dramatically, as Chinese planners experiment and learn from experience. China will likely continue to produce rice and wheat in quantities to ensure basic food security at home, protecting these crops from outside imports, much as Japan does today with its 800 percent tariff on rice. We will continue to see a Chinese policy focus on meeting Africa's food needs. We may even see MOFCOM and the MOF set up a special fund devoted just to agriculture. What we are unlikely to see is the Chinese government pushing its firms to acquire land in Africa to grow food to send home to China.

CHAPTER 5

Feeding Frenzy

"The Dangerous Allure of Google"

In 2011, the Voice of America (VOA) published a critical story on China's overseas investments.[1] An Africa expert at the Atlantic Council in Washington, DC, was quoted as saying that a Chinese company had leased "over a quarter of a million acres of land in southern Zimbabwe for the raising of maize, which it exports back to China." VOA also interviewed an American business school professor, coauthor of a book called *Death by China*, who seemed to confirm this story: "There are a lot of Chinese farmers there now tilling Zimbabwean soil, growing crops that are sent back to China while the people of Zimbabwe starve." Had this been true, it might have confirmed many of the fears about Chinese investment in Africa, yet both experts were simply recirculating what we might call a "rural legend"— a 10-year-old rumor about a nonexistent Chinese farm.

Another of the most widely circulated myths about Chinese "land grabs" was an alleged three-million-hectare oil palm investment in the Democratic Republic of the Congo. This story burst into the international media in May 2008 under the title "China Farms the World to Feed a Ravenous Economy."[2] "A Chinese telecommunications giant, ZTE International, has bought more than 7 million acres of forest to plant oil palms," the article claimed. The story was repeated in the *Economist* a year later and has since been widely cited—by the International Food Policy Research Institute, the United Nations' Human Rights Council, numerous NGOs, activists, and even a number of scholars.[3] As we will see, ZTE did go to the Congo, and they had did have big plans, but they only obtained 200 hectares for their project.

The Western news media is not alone in circulating tales of large-scale Chinese land acquisitions that never happened. Xinhua, the Chinese official news agency, reported in 2008 that that Ouyang Riping, a private Chinese entrepreneur, was "bankrolling the production of 150,000 tons of sesame on a sprawling 60,000 hectare farm" in Senegal.[4] Although Ouyang Riping did have an investment, he did not have a farm.

In chapter 1, we saw how the chief economist of the African Development Bank wrote that China was Africa's "biggest 'land grabber.'"[5] His source appeared impeccable: an April 2012 World Bank conference. In reality, the World Bank had no data on Chinese land acquisitions. Instead, their conference provided a platform for the first release of the Land Matrix, a database of media reports of land grabs—including those mentioned above.[6] The Land Matrix was a project of the International Land Coalition, a consortium of more than a hundred academic and nongovernmental groups with a worthy goal: raising awareness of the substantial risks that the wave of investor interest posed to subsistence farmers and traditional landholding communities. Unfortunately, although supposedly cleaned in-house before it was released that April, the *beta* version of the Land Matrix database was riddled with errors.

An expert on African land investments who combed through the *beta* version reported being "struck by a horrendous sense of dismay . . . we were promised verified data, [yet] no thorough verification appears to have taken place."[7] More than a quarter of the Africa entries were "duplicates, unverifiable, or simply incorrect." Thirty-two deals—involving 6.6 million hectares—were included as "investments" by countries, even though they were so vague that they lacked even the name of a company. Flawed as they were, these databases would become authoritative sources for people like the AfDB's chief economist, who would reference their "data" on Chinese land acquisitions.

This chapter provides a link between chapter 4, focused on fears about Chinese policies, and the rest of the book. It introduces the 20 largest cases of alleged Chinese land grabs in Africa, published in various databases, through December 2014 (table 5.1). A handful of these *were* real: large, new investments. We will read about them in the next few chapters. Yet we will concentrate in this chapter on the startling fact that more than half of the alleged Chinese land acquisitions in these databases, *including the five largest,* never took place, while many of the others were far older, or far smaller, than heralded in the feeding frenzy of media stories.

The Internet is a wonderful tool, but it creates a challenge for those seeking to know the real dimensions of phenomena like Chinese land acquisitions in faraway places. As we saw in the case of Mozambique, myths can appear as facts in books and articles by writers who assume, because it featured in the *Economist,* the *Guardian,* or the website of a famous think tank, it must be true. University of London professor Carlos Oya warned

Table 5.1. TOP-20 REPORTED "CHINESE" FARMLAND ACQUISITIONS IN AFRICA, 2000–2014

	Country	Farm Name/Location	Reported Investors	Year of Report	Largest (Reported) Land Leased (Ha)	Actual Size of Lease in 2014 (Ha)	Source of Report
1	Angola	Pedras Negras; Sanza Pombo; Cuito Cuanavale	CITIC/CAMC	2010	20,000	0	1, 2
2	Cameroon	Nanga-Eboko	Shaanxi SFAC (Sino-Cam IKO)	2006	14,000	100	1, 2, 3, 4,
3	DRC/Congo	Equateur Province	ZTE Agribusiness (Zonergy)	2007	3,000,000	200	1, 2, 3, 4,
4	Ethiopia	Gambela Region	Hunan Dafengyuan	2010	25,000	0	1, 2
5	Madagascar	Ambilobe, Namakia and Morondava	Compliant	2008	22,000	29,470	1, 2, 3, 5
6	Mali	Malibya/Office du Niger	Mali govt./ Libya/China	2008	100,000	0	1, 3
7	Mali	N'Sukala/Office du Niger	CLETC; Mali govt.	2009	20,000	20,000	1, 2, 3, 4
8	Mozambique	Gaza-Hubei Friendship/Xai-Xai district	Hubei Lianfeng/Wanbao	2007/2010	20,000	20,000	1, 3, 4
9	Mozambique	Malanga	Luambala Jatropha	2008	8,789	(not Chinese)	1
10	Nigeria	Akotogbo	Wems Agro	2014	25,000	(not Chinese)	1
11	Nigeria	Patigi, Ebba	ZJS International	2011	5,000	(not Chinese)	1
12	Senegal	n/a	Datong	2008	60,000	0	2, 3, 4
13	Sierra Leone	Tonkolili district	Shanghai Construction	2012	30,000	0 (still under discussion)	2, 3, 5
14	Sierra Leone	Magbass/Tonkolili district	Compliant	2005	8,100	1,845	1, 2, 3, 4
15	Sudan	Merowe "North"	ZTE Agribusiness (Zonergy)	2010	10,000	60	1, 3
16	Tanzania	Rudewa & Kisangata/Morogoro	CSFAC/CAAIC	2000	6,900	6,900	3, 4,
17	Uganda	Hebei Hanhe/Luweero	Hanhe Int'l Ag. Inv. Co/Qiu Lijun	2009	41,000	162	1, 3
18	Zambia	Northern Province	Wuhan Kaidi	2009	2,000,000	0 (abandoned)	1, 3, 4,
19	Zimbabwe	Nuantesi Ranch	CIWEC	2003	101,171	Construction contract only	1, 3, 4
20	Zimbabwe	Chinhoyi	Zim-China Wanjin Ag. Dev. Co.	2010	50,000	10,000	3, 5
				Total, As Reported	5,566,960		
				Actual Total		88,837	

Sources: (1) Landmatrix.org; (2) GRAIN, "Land Grab Deals," February 23, 2012, http://www.grain.org/article/entries/4479-grain-releases-data-set-with-over-400-global-land-grabs; (3) Carin Smaller, Qiu Wen, and Liu Yalan, "Farmland and Water: China Invests Abroad," International Institute for Sustainable Development, Manitoba, Canada, August 2012 (table 5.1 includes only projects listed in Smaller, Qiu, and Liu as "in operation" or "contract signed"); (4) Irna Hofman and Peter Ho, "China's 'Developmental Outsourcing': A Critical Examination of Chinese Global 'Land Grabs' Discourse," *Journal of Peasant Studies*, 39, no. 1 (2012): 31–37 (from Appendix: Table of Investments); (5) Author's research. Sources detailed in this book and also available at SAIS-CARI.org.

of the risks of this approach. Media reports are not hard evidence but "a mix of actual facts, perceptions, intentions, rumours, guesstimates (when the event is confirmed but its scale cannot be verified) and outright lies ... In other words, we face a complex mix of facts and 'factoids.' "[8] A group of colleagues alarmed about the poor scholarship on this issue put it especially well: "*The rapidity of easy access to 'data' and the dangerous allure of Google have facilitated the recycling of facts long after their sell-by date.*"[9]

In the case of Chinese agricultural investments in Africa, the gulf between field researchers and the compilers of databases was surprisingly vast. For example, as we saw earlier, researchers from the London-based International Institute for Environment and Development (IIED) did fieldwork for the FAO and IFAD in China, Ethiopia, Ghana, Madagascar, Mali, Mozambique, Tanzania, and Zambia, investigating land grabs. Their study, published in 2009, cautioned that although there was clearly Chinese interest in agricultural investment, the conventional wisdom appeared to be incorrect: "As yet, there are no known examples of Chinese land acquisitions in Africa in excess of 50,000 hectares where deals have been concluded and projects implemented."[10]

The Center for International Forestry Research (CIFOR) also sent researchers to investigate two of the most sensational and widely circulated stories—an alleged request by "China" for two million hectares of land in Zambia (discussed in chapter 8) and the alleged three million hectare Chinese "land acquisition" in the DRC.[11] CIFOR reported in 2011 that the concessions actually under negotiation between the two companies and the host governments were just *4 percent* of the amount circulating in the media. "China," a CIFOR researcher said, "is not a dominant investor in plantation agriculture in Africa, in contrast to how it is often portrayed."[12]

Unfortunately, once a database is populated, it will be used. In 2013, for example, the National Academy of Sciences published a peer-reviewed paper on global land grabbing. The authors created a combined database of 416 cases culled from a number of other lists of land grabs.[13] Their "meta-database" included 16 alleged Chinese land grabs in Africa, totaling 3.4 million hectares. This paper is a jaw-dropping example of the kind of "false precision" Carlos Oya warned against. The authors, who were not themselves experts on the topic, assured their readers that "most of the contracts underlying the land acquisitions . . . have been verified." Their primary source turned out to be a list published in 2012 by the Spanish non-governmental organization GRAIN. Yet GRAIN had specifically warned that their list had "*not been verified against realities on the ground.*"[14]

The nature of knowledge circulation is such that first impressions are very hard to erase. For example, when some of the more egregious errors in the Chinese cases were corrected by the Land Matrix in a 2013 relaunch, the amount of land reportedly acquired by Chinese companies in Africa fell far below that linked to other investors. The United States rose to the top as the largest (alleged) investor in African land, followed by the United Arab Emirates, Saudi Arabia, the UK, and India. One of the Land Matrix organizers then remarked: "In the press you see China everywhere, but in the database there is not as much China as we think there is."[15] This "nonstory" received little media coverage.

Table 5.1 draws on the Land Matrix, GRAIN, and other databases to list their 20-largest reports of "Chinese farmland acquisitions" in Africa between 2000 and 2014. The table only lists reported deals with at least a smidgen of evidence: the name of a company, for example. Vague reports about "China" wanting land or "a group of Chinese businessmen" exploring an investment are not included. "Intended size" provides the largest figure reported by a media source. If Chinese companies had actually acquired the maximum amount of land reported for these 20 projects, they would have been farming 5,566,960 hectares in Africa. In reality, these 20 cases add up to 88,837 hectares of land, less than 2 percent of that claimed.

This is not the total area acquired by Chinese agribusiness firms in Africa. For example, GMG Global (discussed in chapter 8) is the largest Chinese farming investment so far in Africa. Its two major rubber concessions in Cameroon were never recorded as Chinese land acquisitions by any of the land grab databases. (Appendix 1 provides further details on GMG Global and all known cases of Chinese farming investment in Africa larger than 500 hectares, between 1987 and 2014.) Keep in mind that modest as our figure is, chapter 4 suggests that it is very likely to increase substantially in the future. Several large projects remain under discussion in Sierra Leone and Madagascar, among other places. Yet a more accurate analysis of what has (and what has not) happened so far in Africa should provide a better foundation for understanding this evolution, if it does in fact occur. Now, let us turn to the details.

ZTE IN THE CONGO

What really happened in the Democratic Republic of the Congo, where a Chinese company was alleged to have acquired three million hectares of land to grow oil palms? The glossy red fruits of the oil palm produce the most heavily consumed edible oil in the world. The trees are highly productive: a hectare of oil palm produces five times more oil than a hectare of peanuts, and nine times as much as soybeans. Native to West Africa, the bushy oil palms grow only in a narrow climate band along the rainforests of the equator. Africa used to be the world's top exporter, yet decades ago, planters in Indonesia and Malaysia took over the global market for oil palm. Palm oil remains an important food in countries like Liberia, but palm oil is also a potential biofuel.

In 2006, Hou Weigui, the president of telecommunications giant ZTE, one of China's largest listed firms, decided his company ought to diversify into renewable energy. ZTE's board was probably surprised by Hou's announcement at the April 2007 board meeting: ZTE would be the major shareholder in a new, $171 million energy company.[16] Just a few weeks after the board meeting, Hou led a delegation from ZTE's headquarters to Kinshasa, the capital of the Democratic Republic of the Congo, which I will refer to as "the Congo" or "DRC."

ZTE began doing business in the Congo during the brutal civil war that lasted from 1995 to 2002 and was operating a joint venture with the Congolese state-owned telecoms company. In the capital, Kinshasa, Hou Weigui met the man who was then Congo's 37-year-old Minister of Agriculture, Nzanga Mobutu. "Put him in a pair of black, horn-rimmed glasses and a leopard-skin hat, and he would look a lot like the late dictator Mobutu Sese Seko," a *Washington Post* reporter had written when Nzanga Mobutu ran unsuccessfully for president in the 2006 elections.[17] This was not unexpected: Nzanga Mobutu was Mobutu Sese Seko's son.

On May 29, 2007, Mobutu held a press conference; Hou stood silently by his side. Mobutu announced that the Chinese wanted to invest "a billion dollars" to grow oil palm on three million hectares in the DRC.[18] They would set up a processing plant for biofuels and provide jobs for 100,000 people. The Congolese press was ecstatic: the Congo would become the Saudi Arabia of the tropics! Critics warned that some of the targeted districts were home to the Congo's remaining Pygmy groups, already threatened by European and Malaysian timber activities.

Hou flew back to China. On November 1, 2007, Mobutu and ZTE's regional sales manager, Wang Kewen, held another press conference in the Lubumbashi Salon of the Grand Hotel. There, they signed a three-page agreement.[19] The Ministry pledged to supply at least 100,000 hectares to the venture. ZTE would invest an estimated $600 million. The agreement was good for three years, during which time feasibility studies would be carried out. The investment would go forward only if the studies indicated a promising outcome.

ZTE's global plans for biofuels were ambitious—but also unclear and sometimes inconsistent. No one at ZTE ever spoke publicly of the plan announced by Mobutu in the Congo—to grow three million hectares of oil palm in the Congo. Their website listed only the agreed figure of 100,000 hectares.[20] In early 2008, the Chinese ambassador in the DRC told a Congolese reporter that ZTE's project was expected to be 300,000 hectares, not three million. Yet later that year, Xinhua reported that ZTE's planned project in the DRC could ultimately be one million hectares.

In Beijing, in December 2013, I learned from a Chinese consultant that as feasibility studies were underway in 2008, ZTE's long-term business plan for the Congo had included a target of two million hectares. Then, in the summer of 2008, oil prices began a sharp decline. A year later, in July 2009, an official from ZTE Agribusiness Company noted that the firm still hoped to acquire a million hectares of agricultural land "overseas" within 10 years, with a focus on Indonesia and Malaysia. But there was no longer any mention of the Congo.

All this is to say that ZTE's ambitions were indeed very large (and Chinese news agencies could also circulate those ambitions as though they would move smoothly from a gleam in an investor's eye to the actual acquisition of land). Yet, despite all the hype, three years after the partnership agreement was signed, ZTE's oil palm project had melted away like so much palm butter under the hot tropical sun. By early 2010, a Congolese official told *Africa-Asia Confidential* that the project was moribund: "nobody talks about it anymore."[21] Ironically, on the Internet, it was rapidly becoming a prime example of Chinese "land grabbing" in Africa, with reports usually citing the figure of three million hectares as though it had already occurred.

What happened?

In December 2013, on a bleak wintery day, I met with three ZTE staffers in a glass-walled building in the Beijing office of ZTE's energy subsidiary, now called Zonergy. "We are still interested in oil palm," a smartly dressed young woman told me, "but there is a general misunderstanding about the scale of our business." The young man sitting to her right gave a short, rueful laugh: "We do very large-scale research," he said, "but not large-scale investment. Since 2007, we've invited a lot of experts to do feasibility studies in the Congo, Indonesia, even here in China on Hainan Island, but so far we are only growing thirty thousand hectares of oil palm—in Indonesia, not in the Congo."

ZTE had no experience in oil palm, so in 2008, they signed a short-term agreement with the Indonesian oil palm conglomerate Sinar Mas Group to explore opportunities together in Indonesia, Malaysia—and the Congo.[22] A small team of Malaysian experts carried out ZTE's feasibility study in the Congo. In 2015, I interviewed ZTE's former regional manager, Wang Kewen, who is now based at ZTE headquarters in Shenzhen. An IT specialist with a master's degree from the UK, Wang told me how the experts hired a plane and flew above the jungles of Equateur province in western Congo, taking photographs of the land below. They also traveled to the remote Bikoro region in Equateur, taking soil samples; studying the transport situation; and holding meetings with local leaders, community members, and the provincial governor.

Technically, Equateur province seemed to be an excellent location. The Congolese agreed to allocate ZTE 200 hectares of government land for an oil palm nursery near Mbandaka. Clearing land would allow income from tropical timber to support the larger project, but the experts warned that the infrastructure was terrible, logistical costs would be high, and the threat of conflict was never far away. "The business proposal was very positive," Wang told me. "But it was also very, very risky." With no working roads in the area, ZTE would need to float the timber and, later, the palm oil, down the Congo River.

Wang Kewen hired a boat, put together a team of Chinese river transport experts, and set off up the Congo River. "We initially planned to go seventeen hundred kilometers," Wang told me. "But it took seven days just to get to Mbandaka," normally a three-day trip. "The Congo is a natural river," Wang explained. "Everywhere, you meet sandbars. Our boat broke down several times. You can break down anytime, anywhere." It would be a nightmare to transport bulldozers and tractors. A refinery would have to be built on site; they would need to bring all the construction materials and machinery in by river. The Chinese experts told ZTE that it would take "more than a hundred years" to develop the river for transport. "The Congo River was very beautiful," Wang told me. "I still remember everything from that trip. But this was a very big reason why we stopped the project."

ZTE tried other projects.[23] In March 2010, they signed a five-year renewable agreement to manage 600 hectares held by the Congolese Ministry of Agriculture at N'Sele, the former private farm of ex-president Mobutu, on the outskirts of Kinshasa. "I don't want to see any weeds growing here!" the new minister of agriculture told reporters when the agreement was signed. Wang Kewen had arranged for funding from MOFCOM and the Ministry of Agriculture in Beijing to set up one of the agro-technology demonstration centers (ATDC) promised under the FOCAC. Sixty hectares of the N'Sele Farm would be allocated to the ATDC. ZTE planned to develop and operate the remaining 540 hectares for the commercial production of soybeans, maize, and peanuts. "But although this is government land, many, many villagers live there," Wang told me. "They are the offspring of the military. It is very tough to send them away." There were further challenges. On the day ZTE surveyed the land for the ATDC, they counted 20 villagers living on the 60 hectares. "Once they heard we were going to develop this land for the center, the next day there were 200 villagers." And they were all demanding compensation.

"For our company, this was a big loss," Wang said. "We were supposed to finish the construction in 13 months, but because of delays like this, it took 21 months." Once, his team planted 10 hectares of maize, only to find the ripe cobs harvested by thieves overnight. (It is also possible the maize was stolen by local people who used to live on that land and were not compensated by the weak Congolese government.) "So many challenges in the Congo, every day I had a headache," Wang told me.

ZTE IN SUDAN

In June 2009, a team from ZTE's new energy company arrived in Sudan to explore agribusiness investments.[24] Three months later, ZTE signed an MOU to set up a pilot project in the Merowe region of Sudan's northern state, about 200 miles north of the capital. Within two months, experts from China were in place in the Sudanese desert. In the first winter season, they irrigated 60 hectares, planting trial rows of wheat, corn, sorghum, sesame, white kidney beans, and vegetables. In May 2010, the first crops were harvested, as the Sudanese minister of defense looked on. A reporter from *Xinhua* covered the event: "The wind rolls through the golden grains of wheat," he wrote. "Harvesters rumble through the fields."[25]

In 2010, the Sudanese Ministry of Agriculture gave ZTE a concession of 10,000 hectares to take the trials into commercial production. ZTE submitted a proposal for funding from China Eximbank's agribusiness line of credit.[26] But in Beijing, I found that China Eximbank had refused to fund the project, citing high risks. The staff at ZTE told me they had given back the concession, although the project remained on their website, which suggested that the company still held some hope of a return.

CIWEC IN ZIMBABWE

We started this chapter with an introduction to the legend of the 100,000-hectare Chinese maize farm at Zimbabwe's Nuanetsi Ranch, a three-hour drive south of the monumental ruins of the 15th-century city known as Great Zimbabwe. Nuanetsi is vast, more than 400,000 hectares of dry, scrubby, mopani forest, dotted with acacias and rock outcroppings. Limpopo bushbuck and blue wildebeest mingle with wild buffalo, elephants, and zebras. In 2002, amid food shortages and the chaotic "fast track" land reform, the government of Robert Mugabe held a tender for bids to develop a portion of Nuanetsi for irrigated maize. China International Water and Electricity Corporation (CIWEC), a large, state-owned construction company already active in Zimbabwe, won the tender.

In February 2003, Zimbabwe's state-owned newspaper, the *Herald*, crowed that the project would transform 100,000 hectares into farmland, grow three crops of corn per year, and make Zimbabwe once again the breadbasket of the region.[27] The land being cleared by the Chinese firm would be managed by Zimbabwe's state-owned Agricultural and Rural Development Authority (ARDA) and allocated to local farmers. The Nuanetsi Ranch was virgin bush; it had not been seized from white farmers. Yet several days later, a British paper, the *Guardian*, published a story on the contract, with the headline "Mugabe Hires China to Farm Seized Land."

In Beijing, MOFCOM announced further details of the project.[28] CIWEC had only won a contract to develop the first phase: 10,000 hectares, for which they would be paid about $11 million. CIWEC immediately ran into problems. Zimbabwe's inflation was then running at nearly 600 percent; shops and gas stations had long lines. CIWEC appealed to the Zimbabwe government for fuel and funds. They couldn't even begin work until Zimbabwe's parliament passed a special supplementary budget allocation of five billion Zimbabwe dollars for the project. In a hyperinflationary economy, these billions did not last long. A year later, CIWEC had only managed to clear about 800 hectares of land. In April 2005, after multiple requests for funds to carry out the work, CIWEC abandoned the project, which was by then $7 million in arrears, according to the Chinese. A senior official from Zimbabwe commented: "It now appears our government negotiated in bad faith."

When I visited in 2009, CIWEC was still registered as a construction company, but no one answered the phone. Yet it wasn't necessary to visit Zimbabwe to track down the fate of this project. All the information was available on the Internet—if anyone had looked. As of mid-2015, the project was still mistakenly listed as a "Chinese investment" on the Land Matrix website. We have seen how a Voice of America article perpetuated this myth in 2011, including the accusations that Chinese were growing maize to export to China, while Zimbabweans starved. As recently as March 2014, a Harvard professor wrote in the *Christian Science Monitor* that China "grows cassava, maize, and sorghum in such places as Zimbabwe . . . and ships the produce home."[29]

Zimbabwe does export tobacco to China (and to the United States), but as we will see in chapter 8, tobacco is grown by Zimbabwean farmers. During droughts in 2002 and 2005, *China* sent maize to Zimbabwe, partly as food aid. According to the FAO's database of agricultural trade statistics, there has been no other trade in staple foods between China and Zimbabwe since 1990. In 2012, the latest year for which FAO data is available, Zimbabwe spent $270 million importing maize from abroad. All this supports the explanation provided previously: the Nuanetsi project was the brainchild of the government of Zimbabwe, which believed it could use Chinese technology and expertise to cover gaps in its own food supply.

Chinese companies were not trying to grow maize in landlocked Zimbabwe for export to China.

MALIBYA: LIBYA, MALI, AND CHINA?

Another of the largest Chinese "investments" was an alleged 100,000-hectare joint venture in Mali. In May 2008, while Colonel Gaddafi was still ruling Libya, his government signed a six-page agreement with the government of landlocked Mali to allow the $66 billion Libyan sovereign wealth fund to set up an investment company (Malibya) to develop 100,000 hectares to produce rice.[30] China Geo-Engineering Corporation (CGC) had an office in Mali, having arrived in the 1980s to construct wells for a Chinese foreign aid project. The CGC managers, as they put it, "seized the opportunity to actively seek in-depth contact" with local officials as soon as they learned of the proposed project.[31] Thus in the summer of 2007, CGC invited Amadou "Bany" Kanté, the Malian head of the West Africa office of the Libyan sovereign wealth investment fund and a special adviser to the president of Mali, to bring a delegation to Beijing.

China Geo-Engineering Corporation arranged a stop in Hunan so that Kanté and his group could talk to rice experts at the China National Hybrid Rice Research and Development Center in Changsha. The Center showcased their expertise in variety testing and hybrid seeds. Kanté was very interested. This would solve a big headache: neither Mali nor Libya had the technical expertise for the project. The Chinese did.

As I learned when I visited Hunan in December 2013, it took several rounds of negotiations for Malibya and the Chinese companies to decide what form their cooperation would take. Ultimately, CGC, Malibya, and the Center set up a joint-stock company to provide Chinese seeds and rice-growing expertise to Malibya over a three-year period. The Libyan side held 70 percent of the shares of this company and would supply all the funds, while the Chinese side would supply rice seed, carry out variety trials, and provide several experts to help plan and coordinate the project.[32] As we will see later in this chapter, similar arrangements would be negotiated among Chinese agricultural companies, Chinese construction companies, and the government of Angola.

The Center brought in two tons of rice seed and began variety testing on 28 hectares. With a separate contract, CGC began to dig a 40-kilometer canal and build a paved road between the project area in the Office du Niger and the Niger River. Under the agreement, the Malian government was supposed to resettle villages and provide unencumbered land to the project. As in so many of these cases, although the land was technically owned by the state, thousands of Malians had built their small farms across the area blocked out for the canals. Without waiting for disputes over compensation to be resolved, CGC began construction, bulldozing everything in its path. As a visiting NGO reported:

> The construction of the irrigation canal and adjacent road has caused massive disruption in Kolongo and communities in their path. Houses have been razed, market gardens and orchards bulldozed, and the broad canal now divides single villages that find themselves cut in two by the broad expanse of the canal. A cemetery was unceremoniously unearthed in the village Goulan-Coura. Local people there were shocked to find human remains scattered about the construction site before the contractors then plowed them into the ground.[33]

A *New York Times* reporter visited the site in late 2010 and interviewed Kassoum Denon, the regional head for the Office du Niger. Denon accused the Malian organizations protesting the project on behalf of local villagers of being "paid by Western groups that are ideologically opposed to large-scale farming."[34]

"We are responsible for developing Mali," he said. "If the civil society does not agree with the way we are doing it, they can go jump in a lake." We will sometimes see this attitude repeated by other African government officials, although never quite as vehemently as in this case.

The Libyan civil war started in February 2011. With the triumph of the coalition forces a few months later, the Malibya project stopped in its tracks. Its construction task finished, CGC walked away with the $55 million it had been paid for construction, while the stunned villagers began to adjust to the new canal cutting through their lands. In 2012, the Mali government was overthrown by a coup, while armed Tuareg nomads and Islamist rebels threatened to sweep down from the country's northern deserts.

Given the official attitude toward rural villages expressed by Kassoum Denon, it should not be surprising how easy it was for Islamists to ignite simmering resentments. It should also be a warning to Chinese companies to consider their partners more carefully. In Hunan, no one appeared to have done a political analysis of the risks. Even in 2013, the Chinese I spoke with during my visit to Changsha saw the project quite differently from its critics, who believed that this was a North African land grab and that the rice would all be sent to Libya. "Gaddafi wanted to help Mali," a Chinese agricultural scientist earnestly told me. "We hope this project will restart. It was supported by the former president of Mali. It will be useful for the country." In truth, it was never clear exactly where the Malibya rice would have been sold. In 2007, according to the FAO, Libya imported just under

174,000 metric tons of milled rice. However, in recent years, Mali's dependence on imported rice has been even higher than this. The project could have substituted for those imports.

HUNAN DAFENGYUAN IN ETHIOPIA: BAD LANDS

So far we have seen a proposed investment that failed a feasibility test (ZTE in the Congo), two construction projects that were not Chinese investments (Zimbabwe and Mali), and one 10,000-hectare concession that was abandoned by ZTE in Sudan. In Ethiopia, we have another case where a Chinese company, Hunan Dafengyuan, intended to invest but ultimately decided against it. The 25,000-hectare concession they were awarded reverted back to the Ethiopian state.

Hunan Dafengyuan Agricultural Company was established by two Hunan firms: Yuan Longping High-Tech and Ershisanye Construction Group, a Hunan subsidiary of the national conglomerate China Minmetals.[35] In November 2010, Ethiopia's Ministry of Agriculture agreed to give Hunan Dafengyuan a 40-year lease for 25,000 hectares of land in the southern state of Gambela. The project had moved relatively quickly. In March 2010, MOFCOM's Hunan province branch held a large workshop in a local hotel, bringing a number of Chinese stakeholders, including a local representative of China Eximbank, to discuss the project. Hunan Dafengyuan received investment approval from MOFCOM on September 22, 2010, and signed the Ethiopia lease two months later.[36] The lease required Hunan Dafengyuan to make a down payment within 30 days, conduct an environmental-impact assessment within three months, and begin to develop the land within six months. Failure to follow these rules would invalidate the lease. The Ethiopian government committed to deliver the land "vacant" and "free of impediments" 30 days after receiving the down payment.

The Gambela region is sparsely populated, although photographs of the area on the company's website showed some scattered dwellings. The Ethiopian government had implemented a villagization program to move people into villages where, according to the government, services could be delivered more easily. In 2012, Human Rights Watch published a report based on interviews in the region, charging that people were being violently expelled from land expected to be allocated to commercial farming in Gambela.[37] Gambela also contained a national park; fortunately, the location of the proposed farm would be far from the boundary of the park. However, there were no roads to the remote concession area.

In November 2011, I visited Ethiopia with a small team of IFPRI researchers to do a scoping study of Chinese agricultural engagement.

"Hunan Dafengyuan has returned to China," a member of the Chinese business association told us. "Things looked good at the beginning, but the land they were given is not good. They were not happy." The Chinese economic counselor in Addis Ababa insisted that the company had not abandoned the project. "They have already paid four million birr [$200,000] for the down payment," he explained. "The problem is the road. How can they access the land to develop it if there isn't any road? The Ethiopians plan to build a road," he added, optimistically, "but they are not sure when this will happen."

Yet in March 2012, the *Hunan Daily* published a notice that Hunan Dafengyuan was being disbanded, its assets liquidated.[38] That July, I was again in Ethiopia on another IFPRI mission. By this time, Hunan Dafengyuan's website was inactive. "We have not seen them in over a year," Esayas Kebede, the head of the Agricultural Investment Support Directorate told us. "After they signed the agreement, they visited the area. Once they saw Gambela, they saw the challenges of the road, and they gave up. They are not interested in hardship."

SESAME AND SNAKE OIL SALESMEN

Two of the largest alleged investments in table 5.1 are associated with private Chinese companies: Hebei Hanhe Farm in Uganda, listed as a "confirmed" 40,500 hectares in the Land Matrix *beta* database, and the alleged 60,000-hectare sesame investment in Senegal. Dutch student Josh Maiyo had hoped to do his PhD thesis on Chinese agricultural investments in Uganda, including Hebei Hanhe Farm. He found that the farm existed, but it had only 160 hectares.[39] Back in China, I was told that founder Qiu Lijun's investment company was under investigation for fraud. Allegedly, Qiu sold shares in his firm by claiming to have access to far more land than was in fact the case and suggesting that he had official funding from the China-Africa Development Fund (he did not).

A 60,000-hectare "Chinese investment" in Senegal appeared to be more solid, with Xinhua as a source. The investor, Ouyang Riping, majored in French at a Changsha university in Hunan province, graduating in 1977. He began working as a translator just as Deng Xiaoping's reforms were creating an open door for business. Sent to West Africa, he left his Chinese government job in 1991 to establish Datong Trading Enterprises in Côte d'Ivoire, importing and assembling agricultural machinery from China. Over the years Datong expanded to Mali and Burkina Faso and began purchasing sesame seed.

In 2008, sesame was on the list of products enjoying duty-free import to China from the least-developed parts of Africa, while strong markets also existed in Latin America and Europe. Senegal looked promising for an expansion of Datong's business. Ouyang decided to invest over $5 million to set up a processing operation in Dakar. They arranged to provide sesame farmer associations with credit for seeds and fertilizers, which would be repaid from their harvests. No land was transferred.

The problems hit six months later when Datong's contracted farmer associations began selling their sesame to competing buyers, who did not need to recoup the cost of inputs and could thus offer higher prices. This "side-selling" would ultimately sink the Senegal venture. "We've warned the Senegalese government and called them to help us recover credit and supervise associations," Ouyang told a Reuters reporter in 2009.[40] "If there are no guarantees, who will want to invest in this game?"

In 2014, PhD student Nama Ouattara looked further into the denouement of this story. "It was a complete fiasco," she told me. "Datong was very disappointed." Although Datong thought they had good relations with officials, the Senegalese government declined to intervene. Datong was left to try to settle the matter by bringing the farmers' association to court.

LUAMBALA JATROPHA, ZJS INTERNATIONAL, AND WEMS AGRO: NOT CHINESE

Three of the largest Africa projects listed as "Chinese" in the Land Matrix database did not actually involve any Chinese investors. The largest of these was a planned 25,000-hectare rice project in Nigeria, labeled as Chinese even though the website and investment proposal of the investor, Wems Agro, state that the company is proudly Nigerian—they planned to draw on Chinese technical expertise to grow the rice.[41] Another Nigerian project mistakenly listed as "Chinese" was ZJS International's 5,000-hectare project to produce corn, rice, and soybeans in Kwara state. The two sources provided by Land Matrix did not identify the company as Chinese. Searching for clues on the Internet, I tracked down the website of a Korean company, Juyong-Tech.[42] Juyong-Tech established ZJS International Ltd. in Kwara state in 2008 to seek out industrial and construction projects in the Nigerian market. An Asian investment (if it actually occurred), but not Chinese.

The investors in the 8,789-hectare Luambala Jatropha project were recorded in the Mozambique investment promotion center's list of approved investments as Chinese. This seemed to be a good source, and so I included it in a 2012 article that listed Chinese investments approved in Mozambique.[43] It also appeared in the Land Matrix database as Chinese. In 2014, tracking down Luambala Jatropha on the Internet to check the status was not hard, but the results were confusing. One source said that the project was Finnish, while a second claimed that the investors were jointly Italian and Mozambican. What was going on?

I shot an e-mail to my colleague and coauthor Sigrid Ekman, who had just finished a detailed field study of emerging economies' agricultural investments in Mozambique for CIFOR.[44] I could practically hear her exasperated sigh as she typed out her reply: Luambala Jatropha was mislabeled. It was a subsidiary of Chikweti Forests, a "sustainable forestry" project owned by a group of socially conscious Dutch, Swedish, and Norwegian investors. A series of articles on Chikweti Forests confirmed this and also showed a troubling pattern of protests with accusations that local communities had been inadequately consulted and compensated.[45] These problems have also plagued Chinese firms. But Luambala Jatropha was clearly not Chinese.

CITIC: NOT LEASING LAND IN ANGOLA

In 2014, a flurry of articles appeared claiming that CITIC, formerly known as China International Trust and Investment Corporation, had a lease on 20,000 hectares of land in Angola and was preparing to invest $5 billion to develop an additional 500,000 hectares.[46] "Angola needs 4.5 million tons of grain a year to feed its 20 million people, but at the moment it can produce only 1.5 million tons," a spokesman said. "Even with the 2 million tons that our project will be able to contribute, there will still be a shortage."

CITIC is a state-owned investment company, set up in 1979. CITIC's subsidiary, CITIC Construction, is one of the world's top-50 engineering firms. CITIC (and its subsidiaries) did not actually have *any* land under lease in Angola. Like CIWEC in Zimbabwe, and China Geo-Engineering Corporation in Mali, CITIC Construction had been eager to secure contracts to carry out the development of a new wave of state-owned farms in Africa. While Robert Mugabe's government lacked the funding or the credit worthiness to pursue that particular dream and Libya's government fell in a civil war, governments in some oil-rich countries have partnered or plan to partner with Chinese companies to develop state-run farms and irrigation systems. Chinese banks have supported some of this construction.

In Angola, 27 years of war left a country with a decimated agricultural sector. Much of the countryside was laced with landmines. Angola used to feed itself, but according to the FAO, Angola spent over $2 billion to import food in 2011, including $467 million worth of frozen chicken. In 2010, China Development Bank provided a line of credit for $1.5 billion to Angola's government to be used for agricultural projects. Some of this was used to finance the construction of seven (out of 13) new state-owned farms managed by Gesterra, a land management company owned by the Angolan Ministry of Agriculture, Rural Development, and Fisheries.

CITIC Construction won two of Gesterra's state farm tenders: for Pedras Negras and Sanza Pombo, each around 10,000 hectares (see appendix 1). In 2014, a Chinese PhD student, Zhou Jinyan, visited CITIC in Angola with funding from our China Africa Research Initiative.[47] CITIC and the other construction firms had five-year contracts: two years to build the massive farms and three years to operate them and train the Angolan staff. CITIC arranged for 11 Angolan graduates to do master's degrees in agricultural management at Xinjiang Shihezi University.

However, CITIC Construction is best known in Angola for building the massive $4.2 billion satellite city of Kilamba Kiaxi, now housing over 70,000 people outside the capital, Luanda. The Kilamba Kiaxi project was financed by Chinese banks, not CITIC. The $5 billion project under discussion? It bears watching. Zhou Jinyan told me that CITIC *was* interested in the project as a real estate investment, but they would be unlikely to invest more than $500 million. The major investor would be the Angolan government, carrying out its goal of building new multipurpose satellite towns in the provinces. These represent both Angola's modernist dreams and a Chinese construction firm's savvy marketing of combined residential and production zones modeled on similar developments in China.

MIRAGE IN THE DESERT

The differences I have sketched out here between realities on the ground, grand plans, and (sometimes) even grander exaggerations in the media are not unique to reporting on China in Africa. Consider the case of Gulf States' investment in African agriculture, as recounted by German scholar Eckart Woertz.[48] Arab states of the Persian Gulf were deeply dependent on cereal imports, and they had the cash and incentive to fund large, export-oriented agribusiness ventures in Africa. Gulf countries had a real interest in land acquisitions, Woertz concluded, yet he also found little implementation: "The widespread media perception of large-scale cultivation by Gulf countries abroad and export of agricultural produce to the Gulf countries is inaccurate."[49]

In an op-ed for CNN, "Mirage in the Desert: The Myth of Africa's Land Grab," Woertz and Harry Verhoeven, a PhD student at Oxford, took a close look at the case of Sudan. Just a fifth of the agricultural investments approved in Sudan had actually moved to any degree of implementation. "The land grab phenomenon in Sudan and in many (though not all) African countries," they wrote, "resembles a *fata morgana*, a mirage in the desert."[50]

Woertz later deconstructed an article, "The Man Who Stole the Nile," by journalist Frederick Kaufman, published in the July 2014 issue of *Harper's* magazine.[51] Kaufman purported to tell the story of Saudi-Ethiopian billionaire Mohammed Hussein Al Amoudi's Saudi Star project in Ethiopia's Gambela region, the same area originally targeted by Hunan Dafengyuan. Food now outranks gold and oil as the most valuable of assets, Kaufman wrote, and "Al Amoudi is getting his hands on as much of it as possible, flying it over the heads of his starving countrymen, and selling the treasure to Saudi Arabia. Last year Al Amoudi, whom most Ethiopians call the Sheikh, exported a million tons of rice, about seventy pounds for every Saudi citizen."

A sensational story—yet as Woertz pointed out, also totally bogus. It was true that Saudi Star had a lease for 10,000 hectares in the wetlands of Gambela. But in the 2013–2014 season, the Saudi project was still in a pilot phase, with only 250 hectares under cultivation. It was facing deep production and financial challenges, violent protests from villagers in Gambela, and had yet to address the same poor infrastructure that made the Chinese investors of Hunan Dafengyuan give up. As for the sensational claim that, in 2013, Al Amoudi exported a million tons of rice from Ethiopia to feed Saudi Arabia? According to the US Department of Agriculture, Saudi Arabia imported 1.2 million tons of rice in 2013. India supplied about 70 percent, while the United States, Pakistan, and Thailand supplied nearly all the rest.[52] Not a grain came from Ethiopia.

GREEN DREAMS

In this chapter, we have worked our way through more than half of the 20 projects in table 5.1. We have seen the reflection of a lot of interest by Chinese investors in the green lands of Africa. But by now, two central points should be fairly clear. First, there have been far fewer Chinese farming investments in Africa than the media headlines would lead one to believe. Some of the early efforts to collect data on Chinese investments have been flawed by the inclusion of cases that were not Chinese, not investments, or that failed to move much beyond a press conference or an expression of interest. We have seen little so far that would qualify as an actual land grab: a recent Chinese land acquisition where African smallholders and villagers lost land they relied on for planting, grazing, or forage.

However, the second point is that like other companies, Chinese firms have been exploring a wide range of potentially commercial crops in Africa, from biofuels to rubber, from sugar to sesame, and some have been primarily interested in construction or project-management opportunities.

In the next three chapters we will meet the Chinese agribusiness firms that went to Africa and stayed to invest. We will also meet some of the African officials, civil societies, and scholars who facilitated, resisted, or studied this growing trend. There is much to learn from the stories of the Chinese firms that *have* invested in African agriculture, and even from some whose efforts failed. But before we go, let us return to the Ostrich King's dream of a 10,000-hectare rice plantation in Cameroon.

We left the Shaanxi province team of Chinese at the end of chapter 2, managing the demonstration farm at the old Taiwanese foreign aid project at Nanga-Eboko, frustrated that their land-lease approval was still "being studied" by a committee in the prime minister's office. Cameroonians were angry and frustrated as well—particularly those whose land was staked out on maps for allocation to Yang Haomin's company.

Shaanxi State Farm Agribusiness Corporation had an MOU with Cameroon to obtain 10,000 hectares for their Sino-Cam IKO investment, but they never had a lease. They were able to secure a pledge of loan support from CDB for the project, but, when appraising the project, CDB decided against disbursing the loan.[53] In March 2015, we spoke with Yang Haomin by telephone at his home in Shaanxi province, nearly 10 years after his first trip to Cameroon.[54] "It got really complicated," Yang said. Their company was never able to expand beyond the 100 hectares of the ATDC. Securing land was part of their difficulties, but "money was the biggest problem," Yang told us. "Shaanxi SFAC used some of its assets as collateral for the China Development Bank loan, but then CDB decided that the project was too risky. There were some operational risks. One of our staff died of disease just one day before he was due to depart for China. But CDB also thought the political risks were too high."

Shaanxi SFAC handed over the 100-hectare ATDC to a new company in 2012: Shaanxi Overseas Investment and Development Co., Ltd., estab-lished by the Shaanxi provincial government to manage all the overseas investments by its provincial state-owned firms. Yang Haomin retired. In 2013, the Philippines-based International Rice Research Institute wrote that Cameroon had the potential to be the rice granary of Central Africa.[55] Yet later that year, the country's rice imports hit a new record, breaking 600,000 tons.

CHAPTER 6

Taking Root in Africa

China State Farm Agribusiness Corporation

It is late May 2013, the start of the dry season in Zambia. Our taxi crawls through Lusaka, the capital, on the way to the China-Zambia Friendship Farm, an hour away. A thin layer of red dust coats the trees, dulling the rich green I remember from my first visit, five years earlier. We pass an enormous advertisement, a statue of a white chicken, perched firmly atop a pedestal in the middle of a traffic circle: *Hybrid: Zambia's finest chicks for over 50 years.* Traffic is heavy as we enter the industrial area on the outskirts of the city. In the shadow of another advertisement for Hybrid Poultry (*My country. My chicken),* a feed mill posts a smaller sign: "Wanted: Soya Beans." Zambia does not have many tofu eaters, but soybeans are an important input for its rapidly expanding poultry feed and vegetable oil industries. We turn off the paved road when we see the sign for the farm. The truck stops short at a tall fence; the gate is locked. The taxi waits. In the distance, a pick-up truck moves toward us on the farm road, kicking up a cloud of dust. In a few minutes, we are inside.

China-Zambia Friendship Farm is one of the earliest Chinese commercial investments in Africa. China State Farm Agribusiness Corporation (CSFAC) and a provincial firm, Jiangsu State Farm Agribusiness Corporation (JSFAC), bought an existing farm in December 1990, taking it over from a Chinese state-owned import-export company that did not have the experience or the finances necessary to run the farm.[1] When we arrive at the farm's small office, Song Guoqiang, the middle-aged farm manager, tells me that he came to Zambia in 2006. "I wanted some adventure," he said. His wife accompanied him as the farm's accountant. Three other Chinese help manage the 40 Zambian employees. Now he stays because their teenaged daughter is happily enrolled in the expensive American school in Lusaka. "It's our family's dream, for her to study in America."

The 630-hectare farm lies in Zambia's water-rich agricultural belt, with abundant groundwater. The Chinese company purchased it for $317,500, along with a renewable 99-year lease. During the dry season, the farm grows wheat on about half the land, with large spans of pivot irrigation. In the rainy season, they cultivate corn and soybeans. I had heard that they produced vegetables and raised pigs, poultry, and dairy cows. "We did do this before," Song told me, "but now there is a lot of competition in those areas from local farmers. We decided to give the business to them."

I ask Song about the farm's profits. "It is profitable," he assures me. Every year for almost two decades, China-Zambia Friendship Farm's board of directors meets at CSFAC's headquarters in Beijing, where they scrutinize the farm manager's annual report of expenses and income. "We pay taxes here in Zambia," Song says. "Since I've been here, we haven't sent money back to China. We've been investing in new equipment, new irrigation pivots." Later we walk over to the machinery parked outside the barn. Song wants to show me his purchases. "Our combine harvester is American," he tells me, smiling broadly as he points to a shiny Case 2388. "It's very nice. We also have American John Deere tractors. We buy them locally, but they are made in Brazil."

Zambia is landlocked, thus transportation costs to export overseas are high, and there is a clear local market for the farm's products. Still, I had to ask: "What about exports?" Song laughed. "You mean, are we sending food to China? Every visitor here asks me the same question." Harvard professor Niall Ferguson visited the farm last year, Song tells me, filming for a three-part television series on China. "We had Chinese food together. *He* asked me if our wheat was meant for China. If you grow food in Zambia to send to China, you will lose money. Food in China is very cheap compared to here."

China-Zambia Friendship Farm was among more than a dozen significant Chinese agricultural investments in Africa in the 15 years between 1987 and 2003 (see table 6.1). China State Farm Agribusiness Corporation (and related provincial firms like JSFAC) was one of three major state-owned companies that ventured into agricultural investment overseas in the late 1980s. The other two were primarily construction companies that ended up managing the African government-owned sugar complexes they had earlier built under China's foreign aid program. This chapter focuses on China State Farm Agribusiness Corporation, while in chapter 7 we dive into the complicated world of sugar. We look into this experience in some detail because so far, these investments *still* comprise the majority of actually

Table 6.1. MAJOR CHINESE AGRICULTURAL INVESTMENTS
IN AFRICA, 1987–2003

Country	Year	Name	Original Size (ha)	Company	Former Chinese Aid Project?
Togo	1987	Anié Sugar Complex	1,400	Complant	Yes
Zambia	1990	China-Zambia Friendship Farm	667	CSFAC	No
Zambia	1993	Zhongken Estates Ltd.	3,573	CSFAC	No
Mali	1995	Farako Tea Complex	100	CSFAC	Yes
Guinea	1996	Koba Farm	1,800	CSFAC	Yes
Mali	1996	Sukala Sugar Complex	5,174	CLETC	Yes
Ghana	1997	CALF Cocoa Int'l. Co.	0	CSFAC	No
Madagascar	1997	Morandava Sugar Complex	6,506	Complant	Yes
Gabon	1998	Eastern Agricultural Dev. Co.	300	CSFAC	Yes
Zambia	1999	Zhongken Friendship Farm	2,600	CSFAC	No
Mauritania	1999	Zhongnog/M'Pourié Farm	638	CSFAC	Yes
Zambia	1999	Zhonghua	1,400	JSFAC	No
Tanzania	1999	Rudewa and Kisangata	6,900	CSFAC	No
Sierra Leone	2003	Magbass Sugar Complex	1,280	Complant	Yes
Benin	2003	Savè Sugar Complex	5,200	Complant	No
Togo	n/a	Nongken Ag. Dev. Co.	300	CSFAC	n/a

existing large Chinese agribusiness ventures in Africa (see appendix 1). Yet before we explore CSFAC in Africa, let us detour to the remote outback of Australia, where CSFAC made its first large land acquisition.

"A CHINAMAN IN THE MIDDLE OF NOWHERE"

In April 1989, Australian ranchers in the remote interior of Queensland were startled to find that their new neighbors were Chinese.[2] Ben Lyons, a researcher at the University of Queensland, remembered relatives and friends saying, "Yeah, there's a Chinaman out here in the middle of nowhere." The signing ceremony for CSFAC's purchase of the 30,000-hectare Noella Ranch took place in Beijing and was featured on Chinese television. Clayton Stark, the local stock and station agent who handled the transaction recalled his visit: "Just about every night there was some sort of banquet on."

With Stark's recommendation, CSFAC hired an experienced stockman, Bob Graham, as the on-site manager. The farm encountered problems almost immediately. Their parent company back in Beijing pledged to supply working capital but failed to deliver on the scale required by the farm. He had to sell some of the livestock to cover the farm's growing debts. "We said, 'We've got to sell them, because the Chinese won't . . . they won't send any money to run the place."

Language and cultural differences were challenges for both sides. Groups of Chinese arrived to study Australian farming practice, but they were primarily university-educated scientists and officials, with little farming experience of their own. "They couldn't ride horses . . . motorbikes were an absolute disaster," Clayton Stark recalled. "They were certainly hungry for information," he added. "I think that when they got back to their cottage there at Noella, they would try and analyze what they'd seen for the day and how they could apply it to their own country."

CSFAC had purchased the farm together with a group of private partners from Hong Kong, Indonesia, and Australia. CSFAC held 60 percent of the shares, paying nearly three million Australian dollars (AUD) toward what they thought was an AUD 5.1 million purchase. ("Was it worth 5 million?" the reporter asked. "No, shit, no," Bob Graham said. "It wasn't.") At some point, CSFAC learned that the actual selling price had been AUD 2.9 million. They filed a fraud suit. Documents had been changed, the suit alleged—signatures forged. It was a rude awakening to the dark side of capitalism.

CSFAC still owns Noella Ranch, where five Chinese staff and a group of sheepdogs manage around 11,000 head of sheep, 1,500 cattle, and a small herd of 50 llamas. Presumably they have learned to ride motorcycles. In the scale of Australia's outback where ranches can be a million hectares or larger, Noella Ranch is modest, and its herds relatively small. As we will see, this would be even more the case for CSFAC's pioneering investments on the other side of the world in Africa.

"HAPPINESS COMES TO DIEUK VILLAGE"

In August 1966, as China's Cultural Revolution was raising the cult of Mao to new heights, a team of Chinese technicians arrived in Mauritania to help develop the alluvial soils of the M'Pourié plain for irrigated rice cultivation. Watered by the Senegal River in annual floods, the plain was also subject to incursions of salt water from the Atlantic Ocean. The Chinese team first planted irrigated rice in experimental plots in the flood plains. In the hyperbolic style of the era, *Peking Review* reported on the progress of the project. "Happiness," they said, "comes to Dieuk Village."[3]

According to *Peking Review*, the Chinese technicians were "determined to follow our great leader Chairman Mao's teaching: 'Be resolute, fear no sacrifice and surmount every difficulty to win victory.' " The Chinese did not take a single day of rest. When the annual floods inundated the area, they had to wade through the water to reach the plots.

Their sun-burnt skin peeled and their feet became swollen after long hours in the water. But they still stubbornly went on with the battle. Deeply moved, many local inhabitants took up tools and joined the Chinese technicians in the work. An old worker said with great emotion, "Only China's assistance is genuine. The so-called aid of the imperialists is only meant to rob us more quickly and ruthlessly."

When the experimental plots yielded a plump harvest (helped by the delivery of 10 tons of manure contributed by the villagers of Dieuk and other nearby settlements), the Chinese girded their loins for the next battle: building a 13-kilometer dyke to create a permanent flood barrier. Normally a task like this would take six months, but as *Peking Review* told the story, the Chinese, "guided by the brilliant thinking of Chairman Mao," worked together with the Mauritanians to accomplish it in less than four. The Chinese experts sometimes labored for 30 hours straight. (No doubt the less ideologically driven Mauritanians had no desire to follow Chairman Mao quite that closely.)

According to *Peking Review*, whose Cultural Revolution era reporters knew how to give their tale the right political spin, Mauritanian visitors told the Chinese: "The 'specialists' from imperialist countries never did anything with their own hands; they only ordered others about. They complained about the heat even while shutting themselves up in their air-conditioned offices. If they go anywhere, they go by car. But you work day and night in such hot weather. We have never seen good foreigners like you." As the construction came to an end, *Peking Review* told its readers, the assembled villagers thronged their Chinese friends, shouting with great enthusiasm: "Long live Chairman Mao!"

The dyke protected about 4,000 hectares from flood waters. M'Pourié became a Mauritanian state farm. The Chinese team stayed on to offer extension advice to satellite villages, which were also growing rice. In 1979, a team from the Western-donor supported Club du Sahel visited the project.[4] Mao had been dead for three years, and China was on the verge of its momentous reforms under Deng Xiaoping. The Chinese experts were still at M'Pourié. A riot of yellow canna lilies, and violet, red, and orange bougainvillea now lined the edges of the farm roads, but problems with salinity and an invasion of a water-loving weed called "red rice" had lowered yields and halted plans to expand the rice paddies. Perhaps even more importantly, the Mauritanian government had fixed the purchase price of locally milled rice at a level below the cost of imports. Consequently, the price offered to farms for paddy (unmilled) rice sank below the average cost of production. As we will see, these not-so-small details would become major problems for CSFAC when they decided to invest in Mauritania.

In 1999, the government of Mauritania decided to privatize M'Pourié. CSFAC leased the farm, investing about $800,000 to rebuild the water control system and the dyke.[5] Rice yields rebounded to five tons per hectare, yet the investment did not go well. Under pressure from the IMF to close their budget deficit, the Mauritanian government increased the annual rent on the farm by 20 percent per year and raised the price of imported petrol. The farm's annual expenses went up by over $100,000. To compound CSFAC's problems, the Mauritanian government imposed new price controls on rice. Over three years, CSFAC lost several hundred thousand dollars. They gave up the lease. Later, a CSFAC official would comment that the M'Pourié investment taught them the importance of rigorous feasibility and market studies, although even these might not have anticipated the political risks of sudden changes in African government policy.[6]

An array of similar problems beset many of CSFAC's other early investments. We saw the challenges faced by the Farako tea complex in Mali (chapter 3). In Gabon, CSFAC established the Eastern Agricultural Development Company in 1998 as a joint venture, with the Gabon Ministry of Agriculture holding 25 percent of the shares. The company was able to secure a foreign cooperation loan of $1 million from a joint venture fund set up by the Chinese government and invested another $500,000 of its own funds.[7] They planned to use a plot of 300 hectares to raise vegetables, pigs, and poultry on the site of an old Chinese aid project. In 2001, the company also took over management of an aged cassava-processing plant built under Chinese aid. Six years later, the joint venture still had only been granted 10 hectares of land, which made any economies of scale difficult. However, CSFAC's slowly rusting cocoa-processing project in Ghana was a rockier and more publicly visible outcome.

CALF COCOA AND CARIDEM IN GHANA

In 1997, the Chinese International Cooperation Company for Agriculture, Livestock and Fisheries (CALF), another company owned by the Chinese Ministry of Agriculture, began planning a cocoa-processing factory in the Tema Port export-processing zone, about 24 kilometers from the capital of Accra. The factory would be a joint venture. Caridem Development Company, the commercial wing of the 31st December Women's Movement

(DWM), a politically connected Ghanaian women's group, would own 45 percent of the shares.[8] The company secured a concessional loan from China Eximbank for $8.75 million, guaranteed by the Ghanaian government. Construction began in 2000, the machinery was installed in 2002, and the project was supposed to begin processing cocoa in April 2003. With Ghana's high-quality cocoa, and such high-level political support, CALF expected to "earn handsome returns." Instead, sources in Beijing told me, CALF went bankrupt. Its assets were transferred to CSFAC.

CALF's managers thought their high-level political engagement would be useful for their investment. It proved to be a bad assumption. Between the time when the project was started and the time when it was supposed to begin operations, Ghana underwent a peaceful democratic transition. Jerry Rawlings stepped down as president, and the opposition took power. As first lady, Rawling's wife Nana had been head of the DWM, which was linked to his political party and widely viewed as a vehicle for financing election expenses. After the political transition, Ghana's new minister of finance refused to authorize China Eximbank to release the last $1.8 million tranche of the loan for the factory, saying that he couldn't be sure that DWM could repay the loan. The Chinese company found itself hamstrung by the long-standing Chinese pledge not to interfere in the local politics of their partner countries.

In May 2007, as Ghana's election season began to heat up, the DWM held a press briefing to push again for the release of the loan, offering reporters a tour of the rusting equipment at the factory. Two months later, Ghana's incumbent president John A. Kufuor held his own press conference to launch the start of construction on a state-of-the-art $70 million cocoa-processing factory at the Tema zone—by the American multinational agribusiness firm Cargill. Caridem sued for the release of the last tranche. In May 2008, they won their lawsuit, including damages of $1.75 million. Yet on our research team's last visit, the Chinese-built factory was continuing to rust, while Cargill's factory was employing some 400 Ghanaians. In 2010, reflecting on this experience, CSFAC's deputy manager Xu Jun told *China Daily*, "Now we prefer to talk with government administrators instead of party leaders when it comes to further cooperation."[9]

"A WORN-OUT PIECE OF LAND" IN GUINEA

One hundred and thirty miles northeast of Conakry, the capital of the West African nation of Guinea, Koba Farm became one of CSFAC's largest investments in Africa. A former aid project, Koba had two major components. One, a mixed development of some 300 hectares with poultry, vegetables, and irrigated rice, was built near the hometown of Guinea's late president Lansana Conté. When Swiss journalists Serge Michel and Michel Beuret interviewed Conté in 2006, his face lit up when talking about Koba Farm: "There's no one like the Chinese!" he told them. "I gave them a worn-out piece of land. You should see what they have done with it!"[10] Koba also had a small sugarcane plantation of some 2,000 hectares and a factory. Arriving as investors in 1996, CSFAC was unable to do much with the sugar complex. It was shut down, and some of the land turned over to rice paddies.[11] Koba also had at least 10 other small money-making businesses, including egg production and a factory making bags for the rice produced at Koba and neighboring farms. Nevertheless, a Ministry of Agriculture official in Beijing told me in 2010: "CSFAC did not earn money from this project." It was likely to be wound down.

WHITE GOLD IN TANZANIA

The tropical sisal plant, a type of agave, is indigenous to Mexico. One legend has it that the drought-resistant sisal arrived in Tanzania in 1892 when Dr. Richard Hindorf, an agronomist working for the colonial German East Africa Company, smuggled a thousand small sisal plants from the Yucatan, sewn into the belly of a stuffed crocodile. Others report—probably more realistically—that the plants were ordered directly from a nursery in Florida.[12] However they traveled, the Tanzania sisal industry has its roots in the 62 plants that survived that journey. Britain inherited Germany's possessions in Africa after World War I, including what was then called Tanganyika and its sisal plantations. At independence in 1961, Tanzania had about 487,000 hectares of sisal on more than 70 plantations owned by British, Dutch, Greek, and Indian investors.[13] Sisal farms were the largest employer and brought in more foreign exchange than any other sector.

The socialist government of Tanzania's first president, Julius Nyerere, nationalized most of the sisal estates after famously proclaiming a new strategy of African socialism and self-reliance—*Ujamaa*—in his Arusha Declaration of 1967. This endeared him to the Maoists in China (and also impressed social-democratic Scandinavian donors, who provided ever more foreign aid to support Tanzania's self-reliance). Within two decades, the sisal industry was in crisis. Tanzania's state farms could not compete with synthetic fibers or with the more efficient sisal producers in Brazil. Production of the durable fiber plummeted from 230,000 metric tons a year to just over 20,000 tons. In 1985, *New York Times* reporter Nicholas Kristof wrote about Nyerere's disappointment. "We made a big mistake to nationalize these sisal estates, and then boast that our people would manage them better than their former owners," Nyerere told a public gathering. "If I called the British today to look at their former sisal estates, I am sure they would laugh at us because we ruined their estates."[14]

In 1984, the Tanzanian government owned 34 state farms, covering some 70,000 hectares.[15] Within a decade, the Tanzanian government company that managed the farms had collapsed, and most of the farms were offered to private investors. In some locations, such as the state farm at Mbarali developed by China's aid program, conflicts erupted between the Tanzanian government—which hoped corporations would lease the farms and inject capital into them—and local smallholders, who wanted the state farms broken up and distributed to them.

After four scouting expeditions to Tanzania between 1996 and 1998, CSFAC steered clear of the old aid projects and decided to invest in sisal. The farms they wanted to lease combined two colonial-era estates, Rudewa and Kisangata, a total of about 6,900 hectares. At one point, the former Tanzanian ambassador to France owned at least one of them, at another point, some British investors. CSFAC prepared a feasibility study and applied for a preferential rate investment loan from China Eximbank. In 1999, CSFAC purchased the estates for $1.2 million, securing a 99-year lease.[16]

CSFAC's $9 million investment loan from China Eximbank was approved, but after several early overseas loans went into default, China Eximbank began to tighten its procedures. When the bank's representatives visited the combined estate, they were alarmed by its challenges. Although the farms were accessible by road, there was no electricity or running water. The fields had been abandoned for more than a decade. Small trees pushed up among the dried out husks of old sisal. Thick weeds choked the paths. The sisal would have to be ripped out and replanted, and most of the work would be done manually. Moreover, it would be nearly three years before the earliest of the new sisal plants matured. There would be no income until that time.

Worried by the risks, China Eximbank asked for collateral. The sisal farm had nothing to offer aside from the factory's obsolete, German-made Krupp machinery (installed in 1949). China Eximbank was not sympathetic. In 2001, as *China Business News* reporter Chen Xiaochen found, China Eximbank stopped disbursement of the loan. Starved of funds, the farm went through a series of lean years, surviving in part on funds supplied by CSFAC's farms in Zambia. The first batch of sisal was harvested and processed in 2004 and sold to local buyers.[17] By then, 1,000 hectares had been replanted. Expansion paused between 2005 and 2009, presumably because of a lack of funds. In 2010, the China-Africa Agriculture Investment Company (CAAIC)—the joint venture set up by CSFAC's parent company, China National Agricultural Development Corporation Group, and the China-Africa Development Fund—decided to purchase the sisal farm as one of its first investments. China-Africa Agriculture Investment Company was able to provide a new capital injection.

The farm's fortunes seemed to be finally turning around when I visited in September 2011. The day before, we had gone to see the newly finished agro-technology demonstration center built for the Tanzanian Ministry of Agriculture by Chongqing Academy of Agricultural Sciences, near the old state farms at Dakawa, not far from Morogoro. The center was quiet. Construction was finished, but new activities had not yet started. I learned that the Chongqing company building the farm had already decided against further investment in Tanzania. The basketball court doubled as a drying ground for bright red chili peppers. On the dirt road outside the yellow walls, Masai children were driving hump-backed cattle and thin goats that snatched mouthfuls of dry grass as they passed. A donkey cart kicked up small puffs of powdery soil.

On the last stretch of the five-hour journey to the sisal farm, the driver turned left onto a deeply rutted, winding dirt road. A hundred yards away, roughly parallel to the dirt road, a new paved road was under construction. A sign identified the company building the road: China Civil Engineering and Construction Company (CCECC). Formerly owned by China's Ministry of Railways, CCECC first came to Tanzania in 1970, assigned to help build what is still China's largest foreign aid project: the 1,860-kilometer Tan-Zam (Tazara) Railway, linking landlocked Zambia and Tanzania. According to the sign, the Tanzanian government was footing the bill for the road.

We saw only one Chinese man at the site, overseeing a group of several dozen Tanzanian workers, men and women. None of the workers were wearing uniforms. They were manually preparing a section of packed earth for surfacing. Some had face masks against the dust. Most were wearing flip-flops or, like the Chinese supervisor himself, rubber sandals. At the base of a bridge being built over the Wami River, a Tanzanian worker was operating a drill with bare feet.

Soon we began to pass rows of sisal plants pushing up out of the alluvial plain like the tops of giant pineapples. Blue-sided mountains rimmed the far horizon, shimmering in the heat. Guan Shanyuan, the farm's general manager, was waiting for us at the bungalow that doubled as the Chinese dormitory and dining room. Guan arrived in 2008, transferring to Tanzania from another agricultural joint venture in South Africa. Guan asked Wu, the farm's financial manager, to show us their operation.

In the field, workers were cutting the broad green sisal spears from the plants with machetes, bundling them, and loading the bundles onto trucks.

Sisal fibers are wrenched and beaten from the tough spears through the force of water and powerful machines. Drying on long racks outside the factory, the sisal appeared silky, its color a pale blond. In another section of the factory, a snow storm seemed to be underway. Sisal fibers flew thickly in the air, as a group of women wearing filtered masks packed the sisal into crates for shipping. In some years half the sisal is marketed in Tanzania, where it feeds local factories (none Chinese). The rest is exported, mainly to buyers in China.

Only two of the six Chinese who worked at the farm were on site the day of our visit. Some were on holiday. The chief engineer had flown to China to buy parts for one of the farm's generators, which had recently broken down. With up to a thousand local workers, the farm employed Tanzanians in nearly a hundred senior- and mid-level management positions. Tanzanian managers have housing, healthcare, social security, and results-based bonuses. Four Tanzanian doctors and other medical staff work at the farm's clinic, treating at least 20 cases of malaria daily. Many local managers have brought their families to the farm from surrounding towns, some coming even as far away as the regional capital of Morogoro. Most workers, including temporary hires, belong to the Tanzania Plantation and Agricultural Workers Union.

Studies of the sisal farm by Chinese researchers emphasize the Chinese managers' constant anxiety over labor relations, which are so different in Tanzania compared with China. A 2012 paper by China Agricultural University professors Zhang Li, Xu Xiuli, and Li Xiaoyun argued that the small cadre of Chinese at the head of the managerial hierarchy consciously used a system of patronage and clientelism to smooth threats of strikes and formal legal actions by workers.[18] For example, while the researchers were at the farm, a cook was fired for being absent from work at the end of a holiday. He retaliated by reporting to the police that he had been threatened with a gun. The details of the police report were vague, but the researchers watched the Chinese manager use his personal relations with the cook's family to persuade the cook to drop the charges.

While we toured the sisal operation, Guan, the managing director, was preparing lunch. We ate with him in the small house under a grove of trees on the edge of the farm where all the Chinese managers live. Guan is firmly a part of the new China. He studied plantation agriculture in Hawaii in the early 1990s; his daughter is pursuing a graduate degree in environmental economics in China. After lunch, Guan showed us a proposal he was working on, seeking funds from MOFCOM for a renewable energy project to generate biogas from the sisal waste material.

During his last home leave, Guan searched the Internet to find people who might advise him on corporate social responsibility (CSR). The farm had done some local community work—repairing school build-ings, teaching martial arts, sponsoring a local soccer team—but Guan wanted to explore something with a poverty focus. He decided to visit the International Poverty Reduction Center of China (IPRCC) in Beijing.[19] They put him in touch with Li Xiaoyun, dean of the College of Humanities and Development Studies at China Agricultural University.[20] Professor Li had extensive experience with poverty-reduction projects in rural China and had traveled in Tanzania. He was eager to help guide the sisal farm's experiment.

Several months before our visit, a research group from IPRCC and China Agricultural University had arrived to discuss development plans with community leaders in the village closest to the sisal farm. They were now implementing a pilot poverty-reduction community development project, the first of its kind for a Chinese state-owned enterprise abroad. The sisal farm and IPRCC were helping the village build a community center. They would then help the center offer training courses on subjects determined by the village committee.

The sisal farm only began to make a profit in 2008, *nine years* after CSFAC's arrival. The farm managers were considering adding a new farm in Tanga, the center of sisal production in Tanzania. Yet even after more than a decade growing "white gold" under the blue foothills of the Morogoro Mountains, their company's Beijing headquarters was still not sure about the farm's next steps. The farm planned to continue replanting 300 hect-ares a year until the two former estates were fully rehabilitated.[21] China also grows sisal, accounting for some 12 percent of world output. Wang Lusheng, the farm's chief engineer, told a reporter that if CSFAC grew more sisal in Tanzania, China could save more land at home for vital food crops.[22]

BACK TO ZAMBIA

When they arrived in Zambia looking for investment opportunities at the end of the 1980s, CSFAC and the Jiangsu SFAC were pioneers. Twenty-five years later, as the Hong Kong–based researcher team of Barry Sautman and Yan Hairong noted in a study of Chinese farming in Zambia, the country had six farms with some link to CSFAC.[23] The largest was Zhongken Farm, leased in 1992 with an area of 3,573 hectares. CSFAC asked Wang Chi, a former faculty member at China Agriculture University in Beijing, and now one of the Chinese agricultural experts at China-Zambia Friendship Farm, to develop the new plot of land.

Wang Chi and his wife Li Li, a former nurse, moved to the property in 1994. It "looked like a national park" Li Li told me when I met her in

Zambia in 2008. "No electricity, no running water, trees, and flowers every-where." A slender woman with an angular, serious face, Li Li told me that she and Wang Chi decided to begin by raising chickens because their short production cycle would allow the farm to accumulate working capital more rapidly than field crops. Later, they branched into dairy cows and pigs, and borrowed from a Zambian bank to set up a pivot irrigation system to grow wheat.[24]

Wang Chi was killed in an automobile accident in 2005. Li Li took over running the farm. In the Chinese media, Li Li is a heroine: long hours run-ning the farm, providing a bus to transport Zambian children to school, using her nursing skills to deliver at least 30 local babies. Yet Philip Liu, a scholar from Taiwan, reported that Li Li's husband had spoken of "the pro-cess of tempering her to be less fierce to their employees," suggesting that the farm likely experienced some contentious labor relations.[25]

In 1999, CSFAC invested in Zhongken Friendship Farm, leasing its 2,600 hectares in the Copperbelt, Zambia's economic center. With a large reservoir for irrigation, the farm grew wheat during the dry season and raised vegetables, beef cattle, chickens, and tilapia. CSFAC chose the area, in part, with the goal of exporting to the copper area of Lubumbashi, only 150 kilometers away in the Democratic Republic of the Congo, where fresh produce was scarce and expensive.[26]

Jiangsu SFAC also branched out from their original joint venture on the Friendship Farm. In 1996, they bought Xiyangyang (Radiant Farm) from a local doctor who had inherited it but had no interest in agriculture.[27] The farm, a small investment of 40 hectares in a Lusaka suburb, had two wells, but it had been abandoned for years. The roof of the farmhouse had caved in, and the two parties sat under a mango tree to negotiate the price. In 1999, Jiangsu SFAC also bought a "megafarm" of 1,400 hectares where they planned to raise corn and graze cattle. In 2004, they became part-ners in a smaller investment, the 80-hectare Yangguang (Sunlight) Farm, co-investing with Si Su, a Jiangsu province expert who had been working with them in Zambia for more than a decade.

Si Su brought over two family members to help him run Yangguang Farm and hired several dozen Zambians. They invested in modern irrigation and began growing wheat on what had been scrubby bush. Reporters Joseph Catanzaro and Li Fangchao visited the small farm in 2014, and their story is sobering:[28] "The first time the bandits came, Si Su's wife was home alone. She locked herself in the house and managed to scare them off with a warn-ing shot through the front door. The couple bought guard dogs to prowl their 80-hectare farm at night. They put up an iron gate, but that was not enough."

The farmhouse where Si and his wife live was made of concrete with a patched tin roof. Bullet holes were splashed across the front. Si told the reporters: "They break into your house and rob you. If you don't give them money, they shoot. If you resist, they kill you. My neighbor didn't give them money. They shot two of his Chinese workers, then he gave them the money." In 2011, armed robbers broke into Si's house in broad daylight and tied up his wife, stealing some $75,000 in farm revenues that the couple had hidden in their home. "Chinese have been targeted by criminals in Zambia for at least a decade," Hong Kong University of Science and Technology professor Barry Sautman told the reporters. Although Zhongken Farm is further from Lusaka, Li Li was robbed at least three times along the 18-kilometer dirt road leading to her farm. Despite these challenges, CSFAC's farms have been joined by at least a dozen private Chinese farms, most fairly small, selling vegetables, mushrooms, live chickens, and eggs in Lusaka's outdoor markets.

Toward the end of May in 2013, I met with Dominic Chanda, a senior economist at the Zambia Commercial Farmers Union. We could hear American country western music rolling in from the lobby. *"On the Oklahoma shore of that old Red River, I stand right here and curse my pride. That river runs deep, the current is strong, and the woman I love is on the other side. Red River blue . . . "*

I asked Dominic, "Why do you think there are so many Chinese farms in Zambia?" He leaned back in his chair and put his fingertips together. "We have over forty-two million hectares of land with agricultural potential, and forty percent of the fresh water in southern Africa, and we are only cultivating about one-and-a-half million hectares every year," he said. "It's not just the Chinese. There's been a lot of commercial farming investment in the past few years."

He reminded me of the phenomenal success of Zambeef. In 1991, around the same time that CSFAC began investing in Zambia, Francis Grogan, an Irish immigrant, and Carl Irwin, a white Zambian, went into business together. They started by leasing a small meat-processing operation from Irwin's father, buying cattle on credit and selling in cash. In 1996, they bought the 2,100 hectare Huntley Farm, which became their Zambeef headquarters. Grogan and Irwin had an integrated "farm to fork" business model, and they expanded rapidly, adding milk, poultry, and grain processing.

In 2011, Zambeef purchased three farms in Mpongwe District—46,876 hectares—from Bio-Energy Investments, itself a joint venture between South Africa's Verus Group and a company owned by Kenya's prominent Patel family, investors of Indian origin. Mpongwe joined Zambeef's four other farms, five agro-processing factories, eight abattoirs, and over a hundred retail outlets with more than nine branded products.[29] Between 2010 and 2012, the World Bank's investment arm, the International Finance

Corporation (IFC), sank $40 million into Zambeef, which helped the company expand into Ghana and Nigeria.[30] By 2012, Zambeef had annual revenues of $255 million and was probably the largest agribusiness in Zambia.

China State Farm Agribusiness Corporation and JSFAC were far more cautious investors. They had far less support from Beijing than the support given by the IFC to Zambeef. There were no linkages between the Chinese farms; each operated independently. Some grew feed for the animals they raised, but none of the farms had ventured into agro-industry, and none had developed their own brands. Back in China, the CP Group was building its poultry and feed business into the foundations of a business empire. None of this seems to have inspired CSFAC. The Chinese farms in Zambia have no visible retail outlets, no brand names, no advertising, and so far they have not moved very far up the value chain. There was little sign of the kind of vision that allowed entrepreneurs like Dhanin Chearavanont to help pull China's poultry sector into the 21st century or the team of Irwin and Grogan to do the same in Zambia.

CHINESE LESSONS

In Chinese, as we have seen, CSFAC is known as China *nongken*: which literally means "farm reclamation." In Maoist China, *nongken* conjured up images of heroic pioneers—building farms out of what were seen as wastelands. China State Farm Agribusiness Corporation was China's pioneer in African agriculture—assisting African governments who wanted to carve out their own state farms. Even today, Chinese press reports of CSFAC's African investments reflect an earlier era of reporting: they are nearly always glowing; most reporters seem to be overcome by awe at the sheer difficulty of the task. If the company has formidable challenges, they are presented as technical obstacles to be overcome by heroic effort. Political uncertainty, crime, the problems of logistics: these are almost never mentioned.

More than half of CSFAC's early investments have their origins in a former Chinese aid project, as shown in table 6.1. But we should not make too much of this point. By the late 1980s, China's aid program had built nearly 90 farms across Africa. CSFAC returned to manage or lease only four, and all of these have failed to thrive. There was no master plan to finance farms with Chinese aid so that decades later they could be run by Chinese companies, sending food to China. These farms were set up to provide food for Africans.

Launched in the 1990s, CSFAC's investments in Africa were quite experimental, a learning process. As we will see, the home office expected the farms to be profitable. Chinese teams explored many possible investments before deciding to sink their capital into a particular farm. If an investment did not show profits after a reasonable length of time, they often let it go. Like the sugar companies profiled in the next chapter, CSFAC sometimes partnered with the local government or influential local partners in the belief that this would reduce their risks. However, as we saw in Australia and Ghana, this sometimes *increased* their risks. None of the farms used ordinary Chinese workers, and each farm had only a handful of Chinese managers. At the sisal farm, finance, engineering, and machine maintenance were all overseen by local staff, although other Chinese farms retain Chinese staff in those positions. Finally, so far at least, we see surprisingly little evidence of a strategic vision of moving beyond simple production to developing brand names, retail outlets, or local processing facilities—in short, the kind of efficient and profitable value chain that the CP Group pioneered in China (chapter 3).[31]

In 2000, CSFAC announced that they had launched 11 farming and agro-processing investments in Africa and planned to have 15 or 20 farms plus an additional 10 agro-processing projects by 2010.[32] Instead, in 2010 they were down to only five farms and no factories.[33] We can see the traces of several efforts to invest in other countries: an ostrich venture in South Africa that was never heard from again and failed negotiations in 2005 to enter into a partnership with the Zimbabwe government to manage farms seized from white farmers.[34] (Six years later, as we will see in chapter 8, Zimbabwe would partner more successfully with Anhui province's SFAC.) After nearly 25 years of modest, hesitant, and not terribly successful experiments, had CSFAC run out of steam in Africa? On the other hand, as we saw in chapter 4, in 2014 Chinese policymakers called for giant firms like CSFAC to play a larger role in outward investment. Was CSFAC just getting started?

On a bitterly cold day in December 2013, I traveled through the winding roads of old Beijing to a meeting with CAAIC. Under a startlingly blue sky, a group of small children in puffy, down snowsuits waddled with their teachers toward the entrance of the Beijing Zoo. We passed the summer palace of the last emperor, perched on Longevity Hill, and at last reached a nondescript office district where most of the buildings were still under construction.

We met the CAAIC briefly in chapter 4. It was set up in 2010 by CSFAC's parent company China National Agricultural Development Corporation (CNADC, which owns 55 percent) and the China-Africa Development Fund (CAD-Fund, 45 percent). CAAIC has a young staff of around 30, all with business, legal, and agricultural backgrounds. The company persuaded Li Li from Zhongken Farm to join them in Beijing as a vice president. She finally left the farm where her husband is buried. By the time of my visit,

CAAIC had purchased the sisal farm in Tanzania and Zhongken Farm in Zambia from CSFAC. "We visited 20 farms in Zambia," they told me. "Only Zhongken Farm was a good investment—maybe also China-Zambia Friendship Farm, but CSFAC wouldn't sell it."

The China-Africa Agriculture Investment Company staff hinted that CSFAC was not viewed as a success in Beijing. Yet so far, as we will see in chapter 8, CAAIC's own search for investment projects has been frustrating. "Our plan is to expand our farms in the countries where we're currently investing," a young staffer told me in Beijing. Even Li Li's Zhongken Farm was only cultivating a fraction of its leased land. "We're also looking into agro-processing. Our general manager has had conversations with two African presidents who expressed hope about our contributions to agriculture. We're a little ashamed that we've done so little. Africa needs our investment." He relayed one small victory to me: CAAIC had hired a Chinese cook for the sisal farm. Mr. Guan, the general manager, would no longer have to double as the chef for the farm's growing number of visitors.

CHAPTER 7

Sweet and Sour

Chinese Sugar Investments in Africa

In February 2009, a confidential cable written by a diplomat at the US embassy in Mali blew the lid off of a bitter Chinese-American competition over sugar.[1] Sukala (Upper Kala Sugar Complex), the Sino-Malian joint venture we met in chapter 3, had enjoyed a comfortable position in Mali's protected sugar market since taking over the fields and factories built decades ago under China's aid program. But now, the two factories were antiquated, costs were high, and yields were low.[2] Sukala's output had plateaued at about 35,000 tons of sugar per year, less than a fifth of Mali's annual consumption. There seemed to be ample room for other players.

The first act of this drama happened in 1999 when Dr. Mima Nedelcovych, the energetic managing director of a Louisiana-based consulting firm, Schaffer International, was invited to Mali by the Ministry of Industry to explore its sugar potential. Mima was no stranger to Africa. Born in Yugoslavia, he had accompanied his physician parents to Ethiopia in the 1950s when they went to work in an Ethiopian hospital as part of Yugoslavia's aid program. After nearly a decade in Ethiopia, the family ultimately made their way to the United States. Mima retained his ties to Africa. He worked for the US Agency for International Development (USAID) and the US Trade and Development Agency (USTDA), became the Peace Corps country director in Gabon, and, later, the US executive director to the African Development Bank (AfDB). Drawing on local expertise from the Louisiana sugar sector, Schaffer had built and managed major sugar complexes for governments in Sudan (before sanctions) and several other African countries.

Mima and his team decided that sugar looked promising in Mali. Years later, on a warm October day, I met him in his Washington, DC office. He told me that he had argued for a project that could produce 200,000 tons of sugar: "I'm not going to put up a white elephant that needs import duty protections," he told the Malians. "It has to be the right scale, large enough to compete with sugar imported from Brazil." His government connections helped Schaffer raise almost $2 million in cost-sharing grants from USTDA and USAID for feasibility studies and cane variety trials.

In 2005, the British-owned sugar giant Illovo joined the project, which became known as Sosumar. They began negotiating for a 20,000-hectare land concession near the smaller Chinese venture. This set off alarm bells for the Chinese company. If Mali wanted more sugar to be produced domestically, the Chinese wanted to be part of the plan. Sukala sponsored its own feasibility study and began pressing the Mali government to approve a new Sino-Mali project to produce an additional 100,000 tons of sugar. The Mali government signed off on Sukala's project in April 2007, and Beijing gave it the green light in November of that year. Now *two* projects wanted land in the irrigated region controlled by the government's Office du Niger—and the 20,000 hectare concessions they wanted overlapped. The stage was set for a clash.

GLOBAL SUGAR

Why would an American-British venture collide with a Chinese company over sugar in a remote region of Mali? Over 100 countries produce sugar, and, in most of them, it has long been surprisingly lucrative—and political. The United States has protected sugar producers with high domestic prices, tariffs, and quotas since 1789. Europe has protected its sugar beet farmers and refineries for at least two centuries. Europe's farmers responded by overproducing. In past decades, Europe's huge surpluses were sold (or "dumped") at subsidized prices on the world market, keeping prices artificially low outside its borders. The United States avoided a similar problem by setting quotas for US sugar producers and then requiring them to store—at their own expense—any production over the quota. The resulting artificially low prices in global markets spurred many other countries to protect their own sugar producers by erecting high tariff walls. These provided lucrative opportunities for smuggling and arbitrage.

The global sugar trade thus bears very little resemblance to a free market. Most sugar is consumed domestically, in the countries where it is produced. The bulk of traded sugar travels within a complicated system of quotas, preferential arrangements, and government-mediated prices. A number of developing countries have enjoyed duty-free access to the high-price US and European markets, a form of foreign assistance paid directly by consumers. This has created some perverse incentives. For example, several countries export their own sugar to Europe's protected markets, reaping the high prices, while supplying their own consumers with imported sugar from lower cost producers in Brazil or South Africa. For the residual that *is* traded freely, small changes in supply, demand, or government policy can have large effects on prices. The result is a very unstable market, with trends difficult to predict.

This situation may be changing dramatically. In 2002, a group of the more efficient sugar producers—Australia, Brazil, and Thailand—complained to the WTO that Europe's system of subsidies violated international trade rules. Three years later, the WTO judges agreed. Europe was forced to sharply trim its export subsidies and to lower its protective barriers. In 2006, the last year before reforms kicked in, the EU was one of the world's top sugar exporters, sending out a record 11 million tons of subsidized sugar. A year later, the EU became (and remains) a net importer of sugar.

Complicating the picture further is the role sugarcane plays as a biofuel. Brazil, which has been using ethanol produced from fermented sugarcane juice to fuel its cars since 1975, now has 13 million "flex-cars" that can run on pure ethanol or an ethanol-gasoline mixture. More than 10 states in the United States require 10 percent of gasoline to contain ethanol. In 2008, the EU sent new signals for biofuel producers when it set a target of 10 percent of transport fuel to be made up of renewable energy, by 2020. Most of this would come from biofuels, including sugar. However, turning biofuel targets into laws has been contentious, as critics charged that land in poor countries was increasingly being diverted from food production to biofuels.

How do China and Africa fit into this picture? Africa is a net *importer* of sugar. According to the FAO, in 2012, the continent produced over 10 million tons of sugar, and imported another 10 million tons. At the same time, countries in Africa exported around three million tons, most of it to Europe. The distortions of the global sugar market mean that even though five African countries (Malawi, South Africa, Swaziland, Zambia, and Zimbabwe) are among the world's most cost-effective producers of sugar, they are not able to thrive as exporters. As in Europe and the United States, most African governments protect their local sugar producers. In addition, a number of countries, including Angola, Ethiopia, Malawi, Mozambique, and Zimbabwe have a 10 percent ethanol mandate for their gasoline.

China currently has the world's third-largest sugar output: approximately 12 to 13 million tons of sugar annually. Yet Chinese demand is growing, and, as labor costs rise, China is an increasingly high-cost producer, with its own wall of tariff and quota protections. In 2011, Chinese domestic prices for refined sugar rose as high as $1,150 per metric ton, soaring above European levels ($880 per metric ton).[3] The price gap between high domestic prices and low international prices lured investors to more than double Chinese refinery capacity between 2010 and 2013. The new refineries aim to process imported raw sugar; imports have risen from one million to over three million tons annually. Finally, nine out of the 23 Chinese provinces have a 10 percent ethanol mandate for gasoline.

Does Africa export sugar to China? According to the FAO's trade database, over the past decade, only South Africa and Mauritius have found a sugar market in China, and these exports were both limited and temporary. So far, none of the sugar produced from Chinese investments in Africa goes to China. So why are Chinese companies interested in African sugar? In part, these are legacy investments. As discussed in chapter 3, companies like China Complete Plant Import and Export Corporation (Complant) and China Light Industrial Corporation for Foreign and Technical Cooperation (CLETC) were directed to invest in the 1980s and 1990s in order to bring expensive foreign aid assets back from the brink of ruin. CLETC focused on keeping the Mali venture afloat; there were no exports. However, as we shall see, Complant quickly grasped the attractiveness of exporting from Africa's low-income countries to the protected European market, while CLETC found Mali's protected markets to be quite profitable.

Today, Chinese sugar companies are interested in the profits from building and managing refineries in protected African markets. They are exploring the potential for sugar-based biofuel, and they are watching all possible export markets—even those in neighboring African countries. When the WTO ruling was announced, Complant celebrated. "With the removal of EU export subsidies," a *Xinhua* article noted, sugar prices will rise on international markets. Complant is optimistic about their company's future business prospects."[4]

COMPLANT: "AFRICAN SUGAR KING"

Complant Mansion, the company's Beijing headquarters, sprawls across a small park and is clearly visible from the cars crawling in thick traffic along the Second Ring Road. I have never managed to get inside, although I have interviewed Complant employees in other parts of the world. Like CSFAC and CLETC, Complant is a remnant of the old era of state planning. It was founded in November 1959 as a branch of what is now the Ministry of Commerce, tasked with arranging the setup of "complete plant" turnkey projects as part of China's aid program. Complant would work with the

Ministry of Agriculture to select a provincial company to develop industrial plantations and would delegate factory projects to other state-owned
companies with expertise in a particular sector: textiles, paper mills, ciga-
rettes, and so on. Between 1965 and 1985, China's aid program built at
least a dozen sugarcane plantations and factories around the world, including eight in Africa (see table 3.1). Complant was involved in nearly all of
them.

Substituting locally grown sugar for imports was politically popular
in the new African nations. Not only did it provide employment, having
state-owned factories and plantations that could be staffed with loyal workers from unions controlled by the ruling party created handsome sources
of patronage. Once the Chinese left, the fate of these projects varied, but
very often revenues from sugar sales would disappear into private pockets, depriving the factories of operating funds. In Tanzania, I traveled from
Dar es Salaam to Zanzibar in search of the Chinese-built Mahonda sugar
complex, only to find that it had been closed for more than 20 years. After
the Chinese left, annual sugar production declined from 6,000 tons to
500 tons. Local managers were suspended for embezzlement. In 1998 the
Zanzibar government privatized Mahonda to a local investor, who failed to
resuscitate it.[5]

Lotokila, the sugar complex built by the Chinese between 1975 and
1986 for Zaire (now the Democratic Republic of the Congo) used to produce more than 15,000 tons of sugar annually from its 3,000 hectares. It
collapsed in 1993. Joseph Bassay, a local reporter, visited Lotokila in 2011.[6]
The three factory buildings were nearly lost in a sea of tall grass. Shards
of broken glass clung to the windows, the interior had been looted, and
the sugarcane plantation invaded by weeds. At its peak, Lotokila had 3,000
employees. Crispin Okalamusi, a former worker, told Bassay: "Watching
this factory be destroyed was like being present at a suicide." Complant
now runs three of the Chinese-aided sugar projects, while CLETC runs
the two in Mali. Through privatization, as we will see later in the chapter,
Complant has also invested in three other complexes—one in Benin and
two in Madagascar.

TOGO: "A GOOD BUSINESS"

The Chinese completed building the 1,700 hectare Anié sugar complex
as an aid project for the government of Togo in late 1986. Almost immediately, Togo asked if a Chinese company could be found to operate Anié
with a 10-year renewable lease.[7] The arrangement would help the government of Togo repay the Chinese loan by exporting half the sugar to Europe.

Complant arranged for a Guangdong firm to manage Anié, set up a local company, Sino-Togolese Company, Ltd. or Sinto, secured a loan from the Chinese government, and arranged preferential tax and exchange rate policies from Togo. The complex would pay the Togo government 125 million West Africa francs (about $450,000) in annual rent.

In 1987, China already had several years of experience in breaking through the "iron rice bowl" of cradle-to-grave state employment, but state enterprise reform was novel in Togo. The new Chinese managers sent shock waves through the enterprise. Togo had established separate management teams for the plantation and the factory; the Chinese unified the management, dismissed a number of redundant staff, and replaced many permanent employees with temporary contracts. A version of China's contract-responsibility system was imposed: managers could earn bonuses for exceeding targets and for reducing losses. Hourly wages were replaced by a similar quota-bonus system. The Chinese reforms helped lower production costs by 50 percent while raising output. There were surely worker protests, but the historical record is murky. Thirty years ago, Togo was a single-party state, without a free press. From outside, interest focused on other problems of the era: a series of bombings in the capital city, Lomé, and a coup attempt.

In 1993, Complant took over the management of Sinto from the Guangdong firm. As George Guo, a senior Complant official, would later tell me, "Complant became an independent company, so we had to find commercial opportunities."[8] A Chinese reporter visited the complex in 2011. "Anié used to be a desolate place with only a few farm households scattered over it," he wrote. "Now, Anié has become a thriving small town with more than 10,000 dwellers."[9] A Sorbonne dissertation by French student Frédéric Giraut compared sugar complexes in Africa, noting that the Chinese complex in Anié had the lowest proportion of permanent to temporary employees (one to three) out of six West African sugar firms.[10] In 2011, Sinto employed about 30 Chinese and 450 permanent local employees, hiring more than 2,000 locals during the peak season. They had built and outfitted a primary school and provided clean water to the town of Anié.

In its quiet corner of Togo, the small Anié complex gets little media attention. Yet in late 2007, George Guo had told me that Complant's experience in Togo was critical for his company: "We found that sugar was a good business, especially if it was a former aid project. When we had success with Togo, we went to Madagascar. The government there invited us when they found they couldn't run their factory properly." The big island of Madagascar would be a far different experience. There, Complant would find itself in the midst of violent conflicts, political posturing, and a lively media.

MADAGASCAR: *A SUGAR COMPLEX IN PERIL*

In the summer of 1980, along the drier western coast of Madagascar, Complant began the construction of the last sugar factory they would build under China's foreign aid program. The big island of Madagascar was linked to the colonial French system that began cultivating cane on the nearby Indian Ocean islands of Mauritius and Réunion in the late 18th century. The French group St. Louis Sucre, founded in 1831, came to Madagascar in 1928, dominating the sugar sector throughout the colonial period. At independence in 1960, Madagascar had four sugar refineries. In 1976, after a coup, the Malagasy government nationalized all the private sugar firms and established a sugar monopoly.

The new sugar factory was built to provide employment in the remote town of Morondava, on 6,500 hectares of wetlands and red sands in a region marked by forests of giant baobab trees. The genesis of the Morondava project was marked by unusual cooperation. The Chinese funded the factory, while the African Development Bank and the French aid program co-financed the plantation. Complant completed the factory as a turnkey project in 1984, leaving behind a team of 42 Chinese experts—and two translators—to train the local factory personnel.

The complex reached its peak production in the 1987–1988 season, producing over 21,000 tons of sugar. Each year, as planned, more of the Chinese staff returned home. In 1992, there were only seven, and by 1994 none remained. Production began to plummet; cash from sugar sales disappeared in several rounds of what a local newspaper called "massive embezzlement."[11] Although a visiting evaluation team from the African Development Bank found that local technical skills were adequate to run the factory, the Malagasy managers were handicapped by equipment manuals written in Chinese, making it difficult to order spare parts. The evaluators also warned that the large permanent workforce, now over a thousand people, was pushing up costs.[12] In the 1997 season, the factory processed only 4,213 tons of sugar.

The Chinese were invited to return under a lease-management contract. Complant set up a local company: Complant Sugar Complex of Madagascar (Sucoma).[13] Over the years, Sucoma invested more than $24 million, reduced the permanent local staff to around 500 (including 28 Malagasy managers), and built annual production back to a consistent 16,000 tons. In 2006, Madagascar tried to privatize their four remaining sugar complexes, where output had fallen to a tenth of the production under their French owners. After some hesitation, Complant acquired two (Ambilobe and Namakia); there were no takers for the others. Setting up a new company, Sucre de l'Ouest, or West Sugar, Complant invested more than $90 million, updating the two complexes. Output increased sharply but so did labor complaints. "All benefits have been removed, while wages have not budged one penny," reported one observer, noting that Complant was forcing down the number of permanent employees through a hiring freeze.

For the next few years, Madagascar was wracked by political instability, exacerbated by growing rural tensions and reports that the government had signed an agreement to lease more than three million hectares of arable land to a Korean company, Daewoo. A coup in 2009 brought widespread sanctions from the West. Elections were scheduled—and then postponed again and again. Complant was now managing a group of companies that had become one of Madagascar's largest employers, and many of its decisions would have political as well as economic implications. In 2012, for example, Sucoma's management contract at the Morondava complex was up for renewal, sparking intense debate. Local politicians who were positioning themselves for the elections berated the company's labor relations and asked Sucoma to provide a steady supply of electricity and water to each worker's home.[14]

The Chinese wanted to shift from pivot irrigation to a drip system at Morondava. However, the company had allowed some of their seasonal cane-cutters to set up small farms and graze a few zebu cattle on the periphery of the fields and between the circular pivots. By 2005, the farm in Morondava hosted 500 of what the local media called "squatters." Encouraged by local politicians, the cutters had invited their relatives to join them. By 2012, five thousand people had settled on the plantation, diverting water from the company's irrigation system to grow rice and allowing their cattle to feed on the young sugarcane.

These issues mixed with a highly volatile political situation. Violence accelerated in Madagascar after the 2009 coup. Supporters of the ousted president fought political rivals. Sucoma called in the police periodically to raid the encampments, and the squatters retaliated by setting fire to the cane. Presidential and parliamentary elections were finally scheduled for October and December 2013.

Gilbert Romain, the administrative head of the region, told a reporter that five rounds of dialogue with the Chinese had failed to calm the situation. "Many squatters are ready to go because of the rise in insecurity but politicians encourage them to stay." A Malagasy official pointed to the risks local politicians were taking. Did they want to drive the Chinese investors away? "We should not let people destroy what little remains of the sugar industry in Madagascar for private or political interests," he warned. "Certainly the Chinese approach is not entirely satisfactory, but if the plant were run by other investors, they would have packed up long ago. How many people may be unemployed because of the greed of a corrupt politician?"

The squatter issue fell back to a simmering resentment after the 2013 elections. The following year, Madagascar produced nearly 100,000 tons of sugar—all at aging factories managed by Complant. The Chinese were hold-ing up their end of the bargain, but what kind of bargain was it? And was it sustainable? Madagascar consumed around 167,000 tons of sugar annually, yet customers preferred the more expensive, refined white sugar imported from South Africa, India, and Brazil. Complant's factories mainly produced the unrefined brown sugar still desired by European refineries. "We cannot compete with imports," a Chinese manager said.[15] So Madagascar ended up importing over 100,000 tons of refined sugar, mainly from Brazil, while its Chinese-run factories were exporting raw sugar to the protected markets of Europe. Their profits depended on the politics of protected sugar markets in Europe, a risky situation for long-term sustainability.

Furthermore, real and politicized grievances continued to shake the complex at Morondava.[16] In late November 2014, the Chinese and Malagasy managers were hastily evacuated by local police after striking workers broke into the compound with sticks and stones. Two Chinese staff and a Malagasy colleague were injured; the complex was later looted. When seven of the alleged looters were arrested in mid-December, protests exploded into deadly riots. Angry men stormed the local police compound with machetes, seeking to liberate their colleagues; police shot two dead. Others attacked the sugar complex again, setting fire to some buildings, while opportunists commandeered trucks to steal more than a thousand tons of sugar, stored in 50-kg bags.

The looting continued well into the new year. By February 2015, a witness reported that 95 percent of the complex was in ruins; tractors and trucks had been stripped of their engines: "Day and night the robbers come and even steal the roofs of buildings on the site." Public opinion in Madagascar was polarized. A Chinese spokesman told reporters that Sucoma was con-tributing enormously to the local economy: "Each year Sucoma has paid $2.6 million in wages and benefits, plus taxes and rents to the government of over $1.3 million." The workers are unreasonable, asking for more than twice the minimum wage, he added.

The minister of Labor and Social Legislation explained that the workers had real grievances: "It is rather difficult to work with the Chinese," he told the media, without giving details. An editor elaborated: Chinese entrepre-neurs in Madagascar were "greedy, hard businessmen—overly concerned with profits and productivity." They lived in isolation in their compounds, watching CCTV, and had few local connections.

On the other hand, an editorial in the local *Gazette de la Grande Île* fumed: "It is absolutely unacceptable for employees to impose their will on managers of a private company with the support of some corrupt politicians. True, the Chinese are not models of correct behavior. But what happened in Morondava crosses the line. No investor will come in such an atmosphere with such risks," he added. "The workers have spat into their own soup." As this book went to press in the summer of 2015, the factory at Morondava remained closed.

SIERRA LEONE: "THE FACTORY WAS ALMOST FULLY DESTROYED"

When Sierra Leone's 10-year civil war ended in 2002, Complant was one of the first companies to return to the battered country. Complant had been managing the Magbass sugar complex since its completion as a Chinese aid project in 1982. "The factory was almost fully destroyed," George Guo, the Chinese manager, told me when I met him in Sierra Leone in 2007.[17] "Everything that could be moved was gone."

The Sierra Leone government was eager to have a highly visible employer return to a former rebel stronghold. They offered Complant an attractive deal for a 30-year, renewable lease, at an annual rent of about $185,000.[18] The government promised to rebuild the road to the complex, exempt Magbass from all import duties and local sales taxes, and provide a 10-year corporate tax holiday. Sierra Leone also negotiated a duty-free quota for sugar exports to Europe. Although China Eximbank provided a loan for the project, Complant also wrote into the contract a request that Sierra Leone "do its best" to help Magbass get loans from the World Bank or the African Development Bank, if needed.

In 2007, the year I visited Sierra Leone, Magbass was exporting nearly 7,000 tons of sugar to Europe and employing 437 unionized workers, with up to a thousand working there during the high season. Labor relations were not particularly antagonistic. The contract vaguely stated that employees on the complex should be "mainly Sierra Leoneans" and that former employees would have priority in recruitment, but it also said the Chinese could "recruit or dismiss its employees at its own discretion." Although the Sierra Leone Labour Congress was unhappy that the Chinese were not required to apply existing rules on severance, they had freely organized the Magbass workers. When I met the union leaders in their second-floor office on the outskirts of Freetown, they were pleased with the results of their latest collective bargaining agreement, covering salary, uniforms, and safety issues.

The politics of patronage and access to land were far more contentious. Some of the annual rent the Chinese paid was supposed to be distributed to the landowners, but the villagers complained to me that the money never reached them once politicians had taken a share. The lease contract required Sierra Leone to deliver another 800 to 1,000 hectares to the project within a year, "unencumbered." Nearly five years and one election later, this had still not been done. Two competing local landowners' committees had aligned with the two major parties, quarrelling about the rents and compensation, and disputing earlier agreements on the land. "The landowners committee has to be responsible," Sama Monde, the former minister of agriculture told me in his office in Freetown in December 2007. "The land lies fallow for years because they don't have the wherewithal to develop it."

By 2013, some of the quarrels had been resolved, and Complant had slowly expanded to 1,845 hectares. Sierra Leone president Ernest Bai Koroma visited Magbass in June 2013.[19] When the general manager admitted that Magbass was one of Complant's smallest sugar investments, Koroma urged him to expand. Why not become the biggest? He pointed to the $352 million Addax Biofuels project nearby, where a Swiss company had painstakingly negotiated the lease of 57,000 hectares from hundreds of individual local farmers and was already planting sugarcane on 10,000 of them. Addax had committed to pay $12.50 per hectare in annual rents directly to the farmers and planned to produce ethanol for the European market. They were also sponsoring local people to grow food crops in the areas between the circular irrigation pivots and had committed to independent, external monitoring. Koroma urged Complant to work with outgrowers, to "teach Sierra Leoneans how to grow sugar cane so as to help reduce land tensions."

At a ceremony marking the 10th year of renewed production at the plant, the new Chinese manager Yang Cheng noted that Magbass had built schools and a clinic, and trained many skilled workers. Two local staff had been promoted to management, and Magbass had paid out 18 billion leones (about $4.2 million) in salaries. But smooth operations continued to be elusive, as we can see from the local paramount chief's comments at the ceremony: "I have advised my people to be law abiding and desist from setting fire to the sugar cane and stealing the company's equipment."[20]

BENIN: SAVÈ OF THE HILLS

In 2011, a researcher reported that "in Benin, as in other countries, China has acquired considerable amounts of farmland for the production of fuel crops."[21] That's not exactly what happened in Benin. What the Chinese did have was a lease-management agreement for a troubled 5,200-hectare sugarcane complex in Savè. Most of the sugar from this complex was exported, mainly to Europe, as raw sugar.[22] Complant arrived in Benin in 2003.

The story of Complant's investment in Benin foreshadows the difficulties African societies and interested Chinese investors would face as the land rush heated up later that decade. It is also a window into Complant's new thinking about its African investments.

Savè des Collines (Savè of the Hills) lies in the east of Benin. The picturesque Ouémé river winds through the region, but travelers are most struck by the Oke Shabe hills—large rounded granite domes, shrouded by low-lying clouds, and sometimes draped by the ropes of Benin's rock-climbers. In 1975, Benin asked its neighbor Nigeria, newly flush with oil revenues, to cofinance a sugar complex. The two governments brought in the London multinational Lonrho to develop a 5,200 hectare plantation, while a Belgian firm built the factory.

The complex was designed with an annual capacity of 40,000 tons and completed in 1983. A 1989 review by the United Nations Economic Commission for Africa reported that the complex produced only 123 tons of sugar during its first season. Worse, the reviewers wrote, "the situation remained practically unchanged" over the next five years: very low production and a very large workforce. "Everything seems to indicate that right from the onset, the complex was to operate at a loss," they concluded.[23]

Nigeria's former president Olusegun Obasanjo had negotiated the investment before stepping down in 1979. In 1988, Obasanjo visited the complex and was shocked to find it closed, the factory "rotting away."[24] The World Bank was pressing for the complex to be privatized. Obasanjo offered to lease the factory together with a local businessman. They invested nearly $600,000 to get the factory going again—and fired nearly a thousand workers. "With a rifle at our backs," a former worker testified more than 20 years later, "we were dismissed from the sugar company."[25] The Savè workers refused to simply go away. Their plight would become the problem of the Chinese.

The complex went through two more changes in management before Complant arrived in May 2003 as the only company to bid on a new lease-management contract at the troubled complex.[26] Complant agreed to invest $3.4 million to rehabilitate the complex and to keep about 250 of the former workers. The annual rent paid by the Chinese would be used by Benin to gradually pay off the construction debt, salary arrears, and severance payments to workers.[27] Complant set up a local company to take over the lease: Complant Sugar Complex of Benin, or Sucobe.

About three-quarters of the formal sector is unionized in Benin, including the workers at the sugar complex. Labor grievances were frequent—some directed at the Chinese and some at the Benin government, which was slow to provide the promised severance payments. "Sometimes [the Chinese] yell, or kick, or even spit on the workers," a striking protester claimed. A team of French researchers who studied the complex in 2013 reported that both sides had complaints.[28] A Benin worker gave an example of the lack of respect some of the Chinese displayed: "One day, my brother had a fatal accident on the way to the factory. According to the labor law, the employer has to bear the [funeral] costs because the travel was linked to work. The Chinese have refused to pay anything more than a flimsy cardboard coffin. They haven't given a penny more, they are so stingy." Another complained: "They don't treat us well. In the morning, they come to pick us up in a livestock trailer. They should buy a bus."

On their side, the Chinese expressed surprise that the workers had so little appreciation for the role the Chinese had played in bringing the sugar complex back to life. The Chinese human resources manager told the French research team that Sucobe had agreed to hire hundreds of the former workers, even though they were "no longer very young." The worst thing for the Chinese staff was the regular threat of strikes. "For the three months campaign of the high season, we need to run the factory 24 hours a day. This is when the workers go on strike. Their claims are often unreasonable," she said. In 2011, the Savè complex was paralyzed for over a month by protests organized by former workers, still pressing for retirement benefits and unpaid salaries dating from the Obasanjo period in the 1980s—before the Chinese had arrived. "We have paid more than the minimum wage from the beginning," she said, "and they always want more. We have studied the labor code, translated it for the Chinese staff who don't speak French, but the workers don't always follow their own rules." She added: "It's really hard for us to work here."

We will return to Benin in a moment, but first we need to take a detour. As fuel prices began to rise sharply in the mid-2000s, Complant went to the noisy, bustling, urban financial center of Hong Kong to begin implementing a transformative vision for its African plantations.

HUA LIEN AND HONG KONG

In the first decade of the 21st century, Complant's African sugar was heading for export markets, mainly Europe. All four countries had quotas to sell sugar to Europe's protected market, where, as we have seen, prices could be up to 300 percent higher than world market prices. But after the WTO decision, Europe's internal prices were scheduled to fall, and its attractiveness began to decline. At the same time, fuel prices were rising. With Brazil in the lead, countries around the world began expanding their use of biofuels for transport. As we saw earlier, Europe and the United States were establishing fuel standards for gasoline that would incorporate a percentage of ethanol. Officials at Complant became excited by the idea of producing biofuels with sugar. Yet Beijing was putting the squeeze on old state-owned enterprises like Complant. Where would they find the money to build distilleries and secure new land?

In 2008, Complant forged a deal with Hua Lien, a private Chinese leather firm with a Hong Kong stock exchange listing.[29] Complant would transfer three of its African sugar investments to Hua Lien, accepting payment in Hua Lien stock. The Hong Kong listing would allow Hua Lien (and Complant) to raise money through the issue of shares and bonds. (It would also force unprecedented transparency on the company.) Two years later, Hua Lien's leather business had been jettisoned, Complant had become the controlling shareholder, and the leather company was now a biofuels firm. Hua Lien and Complant brought in an important third player, China-Africa Development Fund, and the three agreed to explore biofuel investments in Africa, together. An article in the *South China Morning Post* noted that the goal was to sell ethanol mainly in Africa and Europe. Although China did not have enough feedstock for its own ethanol factories, "high transport costs to move the materials from Africa and mainland fuel price control policies meant that it would not be lucrative to export them to China."[30]

Now we can return to Benin. The Benin government was strongly encouraging biofuel investors, having stated a hope of supplying 1 to 2 percent of Europe's growing biofuel demand by 2020.[31] In 2011, according to the Hong Kong stock exchange disclosures, Benin signed an agreement to give the Chinese investors a 25-year lease on 4,800 hectares of land at an annual rent of $25 per hectare. (In Benin, a false rumor spread that the government would provide the land to the Chinese rent-free for 99 years). On the strength of this, the Chinese began building a medium-sized ethanol distillery—but once again, they were in for a surprise.

As they would have done in China, Complant left the details of the land allocation to the local government. The Chinese appear to have been unaware that in 2007 Benin's National Assembly had passed a law granting customary land-tenure equal status with civil law property rights. They were unlikely to know that international donors had been helping Benin citizens to register their land and providing customary tenure certificates in the years since then. They probably had a better idea of these developments in January 2013, when, with much fanfare, Benin's National Assembly passed a strict new law limiting all land transfers to a maximum of 1,000 hectares.[32]

A month after the law was passed, the chairman of Complant visited Benin to discuss what the new law meant for the project. The answer was not encouraging for the Chinese. Complant and Hua Lien consulted their lawyers and suspended construction of the distillery. In March 2014, Hua Lien announced in Hong Kong that their Benin ethanol project had suffered what they referred to vaguely as "disturbance events."[33] The project's long-term profitability "had been seriously hit by the unlikelihood of being granted the 4800 hectares of leased land." While they could purchase cassava from local farmers as ethanol feedstock, feasibility studies showed that without a core plantation, the project would probably not break even.

MALI: "A SPOONFUL OF CHINESE SUGAR"

Meanwhile, back in Mali, things seemed to be going better for the Chinese than for the Americans. In 2011, Schaffer International cooperated with a US antipoverty group to produce a documentary about their attempted investment, Sosumar.[34] I watched the film. While sympathetic to Schaffer and the benefits of their innovative public-private partnership that promised to include smallholder farmers and the community, the filmmakers gave equal time to villagers and civil society groups who opposed the project, describing how protestors burned some of the pilot project's sugarcane plots and attacked the project's security guards. The Chinese project was not specifically mentioned, but the narrator invoked China when framing the issue, intoning: "Rich, land-hungry nations like China and Saudi Arabia are leasing Mali's land to turn large areas into agribusiness farms."

The Sosumar project had lined up a total commitment of over $600 million in financing from 17 separate lenders, including the Korea Import-Export Bank, Islamic Development Bank, and the African Development Bank. Yet the banks would not release funds for the projects until Mali's parliament ratified the loan agreements.[35] Schaffer hoped to have the groundbreaking for the factory before President Touré left office, after the April 2012 elections.

The Chinese were also having trouble. A frank analysis published in the MOFCOM newspaper *Guoji Shangbao* commented on the "low efficiency" of the Mali government.[36] For example, the Chinese project team had to visit the minister of finance 36 times on 27 separate days before they could get the minister's signature as required for the Chinese loan. The article portrayed the *Chinese* project's land requests as "obstructed by the Americans," illustrating the sharp differences between the views held by both parties. But finally, CLETC managed to secure a loan package from China's Eximbank for the joint venture, which would retain the 60:40 shares of the first investment. They began pushing hard to complete their factory before the 2012 elections.

Instead, both projects were in for a shock. On the night of March 21, 2012, a group of disgruntled Malian soldiers attacked the presidential compound and took control of the country. "The government simply melted away," one report said. For Schaffer, this was the last step. That May, Illovo announced a $21 million write-off of the money it had advanced.[37] "Sosumar is a white man's project," a villager explained to the filmmakers, "and they don't like conflict."

More than a year later, I met with the head of CLECT in Beijing. I asked him how the coup had affected his company. "There was no impact on our older company," he said, "but it affected construction on the new Sukala project (N-Sukala)." Some staff returned to China and the installation of machines was delayed by several months, but the Chinese factory opened in November 2012.[38] However, it was still operating below capacity because the Mali government had only contributed 3,570 hectares of land. Mali's new minister of rural development visited the project in October 2013, and the Chinese officials pressed him again on the land issue. The factory had "a critical shortage of land in its immediate vicinity. The parcels proposed were far from the factory, increasing costs."[39] Meanwhile, Mima Nedelcovych told me, although the company set up by Schaffer and Illovo was liquidated, and he had himself moved on to new challenges, the land in the Office du Niger allocated to the company was still being held in reserve for the project. Mima remained on the board of Schaffer, ready to assist the government of Mali to revive the project when requested. The Chinese may have won the skirmish, but it wasn't clear they would win the sugar war.

SWEET BUSINESS

Sugar appears to be an increasingly sweet business in Africa. The British-owned company Illovo has investments in Malawi, Mozambique, Swaziland, South Africa, Tanzania, and Zambia, with at least 64,000 hectares of its own sugarcane fields. Illovo has 16 processing factories that also take sugarcane from outgrowers on another 112,000 hectares. Over the past few years, investor interest in sugar has been trumpeted in dozens of African headlines. Tanzania plans to triple its annual sugar production by 2016 with nine new complexes. Firms from India, Egypt, Sweden, and Dubai have all explored sugar production investments there. Brazilian, Japanese, and Portuguese companies have been in discussions with the Angolan government to build three sugarcane-based biofuel complexes that would require nearly 100,000 hectares. British, French, Indian, South African, and Mauritian sugar firms have advanced plans to invest in Mozambique. Ethiopia hopes to build 10 major complexes across the country, while Sudan is expanding its sugar output.[40]

In this land rush, so far, the Chinese remain very small players. China Light Industrial Corporation for Foreign Technical Cooperation is cultivating less than 10,000 hectares on its three Mali complexes, although it plans to expand when circumstances allow. Its parent company, Sinolight, has explored the feasibility of establishing a 100,000-ton sugar factory for the government of Mali's neighbor Niger, but finance for the project remains elusive. As we saw in chapter 5, the Ethiopian government agreed to provide Hunan Dafengyuan with 25,000 hectares for a sugar complex, but the venture never went forward.

As I write this, Complant still holds just 22,000 hectares of cultivated sugarcane land across its six African sugar complexes, all leased between 1987 and 2008. Complant explored investing in Sudan's sugar sector when Kenana Sugar Company, Sudan's large state-owned firm, was seeking partners for at least four sugar projects in its ambitious 2020 Investment Plan. Complant conducted several rounds of talks regarding a direct equity investment in the Red Sea sugar refinery near Port Sudan (jointly with the China-Africa Development Fund), which would refine raw sugar and sell much of it to the Italian sugar company Eridania. They have also expressed interest in a joint venture in another of Kenana's proposed flagship projects: the Al-Redais sugar complex.[41] Yet the loss of oil revenues, and renewed fighting in the region after the secession of South Sudan in 2011, began frightening off agricultural investors, Complant among them.

Complant is no longer as optimistic as they were before the problems in Madagascar, Benin, and Sierra Leone brought them face to face with the realities of acquiring land for African investments. They seem to be turning back to their core business, construction. In November 2011, I met with officials at the China-Africa Development Fund office in Addis Ababa. I knew that Complant had been pursuing a construction contract for one of the Ethiopian government's 10 proposed sugar projects, and I asked whether the CAD-Fund might invest in a sugar complex in Ethiopia with Complant. "We have discussed this," the officials said, "but at present, Complant prefers to be a contractor rather than an investor." He added: "We wish Complant would change their mind." Several years later, there was still no Chinese equity involved, although both China Eximbank and China Development Bank were providing loans to Ethiopia for sugar complexes. At least one—the $123 million Afar sugar factory in northeastern Ethiopia—would be built by Complant.[42]

Let us end this chapter with another look at Magbass, the small sugar complex in the hinterlands of war-torn Sierra Leone. In December 2013, I had tea with a Chinese expert who had worked at Magbass in the 1990s. Now based in Beijing, he told me: "Sugar is a good business if it is managed correctly. You need economies of scale. There are a lot of costs. Everything has to be imported, it's all expensive. Landownership is not clear. You might negotiate with one person and then another will come and say, 'That land belongs to me!'" I asked him what was likely to happen to Complant's African projects. "We are still exporting about ninety percent of the sugar to Europe," he said. "Prices are still high there, but at some point this is going to end." He paused, took a sip of the strong *tieguanyin* we were drinking, and continued. "Maybe when that happens Complant can export sugar to China, and Chinese sugar farmers can plant something else."

In these two chapters, we have seen the outcome of China's earliest agricultural investments in Africa. While some investments have their origins in foreign aid, this was neither necessary nor sufficient. China's state-owned companies experimented with different ways to keep old aid projects afloat. In some cases they chose joint ventures with local governments, expecting that this would help protect their joint interests. Yet these governments had competing goals, including employment, patronage, and political stability, things that contentious labor relations could jeopardize. Sometimes, as in Mali, the Chinese firms enjoyed long stretches of protected markets. In others, as in Zambia, they did not have the field to themselves but competed with other foreign investors and local farmers for a share of a lively local market.

In 2011, Complant and Hua Lien made a surprise bid to purchase three loss-making sugar complexes owned by the government of Jamaica. As had so often been the case in Africa, they were the only bidders. "There were not scores of companies waiting to buy our decrepit sugar assets," a Jamaican government official admitted. The Chinese would gain three antiquated factories and a 50-year lease on 32,572 hectares of sugarcane for $9 million but committed to spend another $127 million to modernize the complexes. Jamaica had traditionally supplied raw sugar to British refineries. The new Chinese manager told the Jamaican *Gleaner* that he wasn't worried about selling the sugar. Lucrative markets were waiting—in China *and in Africa*, where countries, like Sudan, were planning to build factories to refine imported raw sugar.[43]

Complant's purchase of the sugar assets in Jamaica could mark more of a global vision for the firm, steps in building the kind of integrated value chain that agribusiness requires in order to be efficient and profitable. On the other hand, it could be a quixotic effort by a fading state-owned enterprise to try to reinvent itself in a complex global business that its leaders do not really understand. In the next chapter, we will meet the new generation of firms—private entrepreneurs and listed companies with a mix of private and government shares—that are the latest face of Chinese investment in rural Africa.

CHAPTER 8

Unfinished Business

Risks and Realities of China's African Harvest

In March 2009, Tyson Chisambo, the executive director of the Biofuels Association of Zambia, traveled to a biofuels conference in South Africa. "China," he told a Reuters reporter, "has approached the Zambian government to plant 2 million hectares of jatropha. We are still waiting for more details."[1]

This bit of news made a big splash in the media, circulating around the world as a Chinese government "request" for land. Although jatropha is grown as a biofuel and cannot be consumed by people, a report published by IFPRI included the 2 million hectare figure in a table of "government to government" investments "to secure food supplies."[2] It was also featured in an article in the *Economist* which spun the story to imply that the Chinese government was putting intense pressure on Zambia to approve the project: "In Zambia, the main opposition leader has come out against China's proposed 2m-hectare biofuels project—and China has threatened to pull out of Zambia if he ever came to power."[3]

The Wuhan Kaidi Zambian biofuel project was more than a rumor, although the story unfolded quite differently from the way it was just described. Along with the other projects and business ventures analyzed in this chapter, it contains many lessons. Like the proposed ZTE palm oil project in the Democratic Republic of the Congo discussed in chapter 5, it illustrates the sometimes surprisingly unrealistic scale of ambition of entrepreneurial Chinese with little or no experience in Africa—but not an organized attempt by the Chinese government to acquire land. It shows the practical difficulties of achieving even the first step of those ambitions. And it highlights the key roles played by Africans. As we will see, although the project appeared to come out of nowhere as a "request" from the Chinese government, it was actually conceived by two Zambian businessmen, who were also on a steep learning curve. Ultimately, its fate would depend on two Zambian presidents.

In 2008, as global interest in biofuels began to soar, a young Zambian, Kumbukilani Phiri, was working in China, in the international business division of Wuhan Kaidi, a private, renewable energy company listed on the Shenzhen stock exchange. Phiri had just earned a civil engineering degree from Guangxi University on a Chinese government scholarship. He was in love with the Chinese woman who would later became his wife, and he wasn't about to leave China quite yet. Wuhan Kaidi's hard-driving CEO Chen Yilong was looking for opportunities to go global. They hadn't thought of Africa, but Phiri suggested Africa—and Zambia, in particular—would be worth a visit.

Wuhan Kaidi's goals would be music to the ears of another Zambian, Thomson Sinkala, a former professor of engineering at the University of Zambia, president of the Biofuels Association of Zambia, and an entrepreneur with his own biofuels company. I met up with Sinkala in the Zambian capital, Lusaka, in June 2013.[4] We sat in the garden cottage that serves as his home office; its pale green walls reflected the strong afternoon light. Outside, a woman was hanging laundry on a line stretched in front of a late blooming frangipani. Red bougainvillea spilled over the fence.

Sinkala told me that Kumbukilani Phiri had come to see him in 2008. Their meeting went well, and Sinkala was invited to visit Wuhan Kaidi's headquarters in China. "Someone from the Zambia Development Agency [ZDA] came with me," Sinkala said. "We made a presentation on Zambia's biofuel potential. And then we decided to invest together." Sinkala and Phiri began working with ZDA to put together a large land concession for their joint venture.

Investment trends come and go, and at that point, African governments had many options for agribusiness investment. George Schoneveld, a researcher at CIFOR, wrote his doctoral dissertation on large-scale farmland investments in Africa.[5] He found that between 2008 and 2009, African governments signed dozens of large project agreements of various kinds. The Zambia Development Agency had an MOU with the German firm MAN Ferrostaal for another Zambian biofuels project of 150,000 hectares. Schoneveld documented biofuel-related lease agreements of 452,500 hectares in Madagascar by a UK company, Hunter Resources, and a concession of 303,750 hectares signed by a Norwegian company, ScanFarm, in Ghana. A Texas-based firm signed a lease agreement with a local government in South Sudan for a 600,000 hectare concession, while an Italian company, Nuove Iniziative Industriali, claimed to have a 710,000 hectare biofuel concession in Guinea.

As Tyson Chisambo had reported, Wuhan Kaidi's initial ambitions were large but also rather vague. In 2009, as feasibility studies were underway, Zambian officials described the project as a $3 billion investment seeking to lease 700,000 hectares of land and create 50,000 jobs.[6] Michael Sata, then the leader of the opposition and a sharp critic of Chinese investment, told a radio audience that he opposed the project, saying that he expected Chinese workers to be employed on the plantation.[7]

Now we can return to the *Economist* editorial quoted earlier, which implied—quite wrongly, as it turns out—that the Chinese government was deeply concerned about then-opposition leader Michael Sata's antagonism toward the biofuels project. These threats had actually happened three years before anyone had envisioned a giant Chinese biofuels investment in Zambia. In Zambia's 2006 elections, Michael Sata, known popularly as "King Cobra," had pledged to give diplomatic recognition to Taiwan if he was elected. China regards Taiwan as a renegade province—which is also the official position of the United States and most of the rest of the world. The threat referred to here was the Chinese ambassador's warning that his government would be forced to break diplomatic relations if Sata carried out his promise to recognize Taiwan as the "Republic of China." Sata lost that election, but his attacks on Chinese investment continued.

When I met Kimbukilani Phiri for breakfast in a Lusaka restaurant in June 2013, he told me that Wuhan Kaidi was prepared to invest substantial resources in biofuels, but the scale would depend on how much land they could acquire, how much loan financing they could raise from Chinese banks, and the development of an organized market for biofuels in Zambia. (Later, at the Chinese embassy in Lusaka, a senior diplomat would express skepticism about the untested company's ability to carry out an investment on the scale under discussion, saying dryly: "Wuhan Kaidi tends to do very sensational news conferences.")

The project planned to use a mixed plantation (70 percent) and out-grower (30 percent) system, Phiri said, with a large factory. The company would provide seedlings and inputs to local contract farmers, and take a share of their harvest at the refinery. Nearly 94 percent of Zambian land is under customary tenure, vested in rural chiefs who are supposed to hold it in trust for their people. At the ZDA, an official walked me through the steps in acquiring a concession on customary land. "We negotiate with the chief, to take ownership of the land. It is then converted to statutory land, and once we get the business plan, we lease it to the investor, up to ninety-nine years at a fixed rent." Consultations were not legally required, but the company held multiple public hearings with the chiefs and villagers. "We kept going back and forth," Phiri recalled, "first the chiefs, then the government, then the chiefs, then the government. It was all open, transparent."

Chiefs in northern Zambia seemed to favor the investment, pointing to the employment it would generate (according to the investors, there was no plan to bring in Chinese workers). "I am from that area," Thomson Sinkala told me. "I looked after my parent's cattle as a boy. The area was forest. But over the years, it has gotten degraded. The trees were cut to export charcoal to Tanzania. There are too many cattle now. The forest is receding." A writer on a Zambian blog devoted to chiefdom issues expressed worries that Zambians in the project area might not be making the best choices. Farming on acidic soils with low fertility, increasingly desperate to grow enough food to feed their families, they could be "susceptible to the blandishments of snake-oil salesman bearing samples and seeking concessions."[8] The risks were high. Plundering Zambia's lands might not raise living standards, he said, but create greater poverty, keeping life expectancy "at pre-industrial revolution levels."

Sinkala disagreed. "I believe this project was well designed," he said. The biomass power plant would bring electricity to the area. The factory would process biofuel from a lot of different inputs: cassava, sweet sorghum, sugar beet. Local people could choose to participate at the level they could handle. Local firms would build the plantation workers' housing. "We've been very open from day one," he told me. "There have been no secrets—it must be one of the most highly investigated investments ever in Zambia."

By mid-2011, ZDA had obtained signed agreements from traditional chiefs for 79,300 hectares, and Wuhan Kaidi had pledged to invest $450 million. They had to go all the way up to the president's office for approval of the conversion of such a large area of customary land. But Zambia was in election season and, given the polarization of Zambian politics around the issue of Chinese investment, President Banda postponed a decision.

On September 20, 2011, opposition leader Michael Sata won Zambia's presidential election. In office, Sata became more pragmatic toward Chinese investors, but he was reluctant to approve the land conversion. He decreed that the project could begin with a 2,000 hectare pilot phase. Yet starting gradually was out of the question for Wuhan Kaidi—it was too risky and would ruin the financial projections. "It was like a proposal," Phiri told me. "You pursue a woman, you knock on her door, you do everything, but she doesn't respond. Now it's up to the Zambian people to go and fight for this investment." With the project postponed indefinitely, Phiri decided to apply to business school and was offered a scholarship in the UK.

Several months after my last trip to Zambia, I had an opportunity to speak with Chen Yilong, the CEO of Wuhan Kaidi (rebranded as "Sunshine Kaidi"), at the September 2013 Asian World Economic Forum in the Chinese coastal city of Dalian. We met in a stylish espresso bar at the convention center. On the plaza outside, a water sculpture shot jets of white spray into a brilliantly blue sky. Why couldn't you start on a smaller scale? I asked. "The local infrastructure is very backward," he said, leaning forward to make his point. "Even for a pilot project, we would have had to make a huge investment in an irrigation system, roads, worker housing, the processing plant—everything. We need to have a large enough scale to recover the investment."

Chen told me that he was looking for investment opportunities closer to home, in Myanmar and other Asian countries. "But we are still working with Professor Sinkala to do research on fast-growing local plants and trees that might be good biofuel candidates," he added. "Zambia imports all of its oil. The price of oil in Zambia is three times higher than in the US. We would supply the Zambian market—we promised to do this—and if there was a surplus, it could be exported to the region, to Europe. We have put a lot of investment in Zambia already. We will look for opportunities to restart this project." In October 2014, Phiri finished his degree (with distinction) in the UK. That same month, Michael Sata died in office, after an undisclosed illness. "Kaidi is still interested," Phiri confirmed in an e-mail. The moribund project might have a second life.

SEEDS AND SERVICES: THE RICE CLUSTER OF HUNAN

We turn now to a business cluster in Changsha, capital of China's rice-growing province of Hunan, where Chinese expertise and intellectual property are both considered assets in the march to succeed as global agribusiness players. I traveled to Changsha late in 2013 to learn more about their African business. Rice was clearly a theme in the brightly lit Longhua International Hotel where I ate breakfast on a rainy December morning. Each table was decorated with an artificial sheaf of rice. An abstract sculpture with thousands of golden glass rice grains hung from the ceiling. Outside, a dark bank of smog pressed heavily on the city.

Changsha has been a major rice market since the end of the Ming dynasty. It is also the home of Professor Yuan Longping, the revered rice scientist who was one of the main draws of my visit. Changsha also hosts the Hunan Academy of Agricultural Sciences, China National Hybrid Rice Research and Development Center (CNHRRDC), Longping High-Tech, and other research institutes and companies that together own considerable intellectual property. Some Changsha experts got their start in Africa doing rice variety trials at CSFAC's Koba Farm in Guinea during the 1990s.[9] More recently, the rice cluster has offered high-yielding seeds, consulting and technical assistance, and, increasingly, capital for joint ventures, with projects in at least seven African countries, including in Ethiopia, Liberia, Madagascar, Mali, Nigeria, Zambia, and Zimbabwe. The rice cluster in Hunan is the vanguard of China's agribusiness development *and* its economic diplomacy.

Longping High-Tech and the Father of Hybrid Rice

Professor Yuan, winner of the 2004 World Food Prize, was the first researcher to break the code for the production of hybrid rice. His patent was the first agro-technology patent registered to China in the United States. Today, Yuan Longping's name and reputation support China's commercial and political hopes for hybrid rice and other high-yielding seeds. The company set up in 1999 that bears his name—Longping High-Tech Agriculture (LPHT)—is a multinational, public-private partnership. A listed company with shares held by several public Hunan research institutes and a number of private individuals (including Professor Yuan), it is dominated by the private Xindaxing Group, which since 2007 has been partly owned by French multinational agribusiness giant Vilmorin, the world's fourth-largest seed company. Longping High-Tech Agriculture controls 20 percent of China's hybrid seed market.

I grew up in Wisconsin, America's dairy land. As children, we played hide and seek in the tall cornfields that bordered our neighborhood, dodging signs for hybrid seed companies like Pioneer and DeKalb. Hybrid corn was released for commercial use in the United States in the 1930s; American farmers tripled their yields. However, to ensure a good harvest, hybrid seeds must be purchased anew each season, ensuring a steady supply of customers. Today, the global seed business is estimated to be worth some $50 billion. Pioneer grows, markets, and sells hybrid seed corn in nearly 70 countries. Their signs appear in fields across Africa, from Algeria to Zambia. Longping High-Tech and China's other hybrid rice seed firms would like to duplicate this success.

My first stop in Changsha was at the LPHT International Training Center, which offers a three-month technical course popular with African agriculturalists. I watched a video. "The international food crisis is a battle faced by the entire human race," the narrator intoned against a background of stirring music. "One child dies of starvation or related diseases every six seconds." The export volume of hybrid rice seed is increasing by 30 to 50 percent annually, I learned.

After a discussion with LPHT's young but well-traveled staff, I met with Professor Yuan. In his mid-80s, very thin, with deep creases on his sun-weathered face, the professor spoke excellent English. I asked him if he was still riding a motorcycle to the research fields, and he laughed. "No, now I drive a car." He explained that the Chinese government had asked him to help develop hybrid rice in Africa, but he seemed more excited about prospects in America, where some 500,000 hectares were planted with LPHT rice. He smiled broadly: "The Americans pay royalties to us."

China's agricultural business model for Africa is "not easy," another LPHT official added. "We are just at the start of exploring this." He pointed out that the ATDCs being built by the Chinese aid program should improve Africa's weak agricultural research support systems. Longping High-Tech won a competitive tender to build and manage the Liberian ATDC. As noted in chapter 4, the centers were fully funded by the Chinese government, which also provided three years of operational support. After that, the companies and their hosts negotiate future steps. In Liberia, LPHT agreed to finance and manage the center for 12 years, funding training and research out of its own revenues and creating "a viable commercial farm that can be emulated or modeled by local entrepreneurs."[10]

Longping High-Tech tried to use the ATDC as a platform for other business. They had leased the old Kpatawee rice seed farm built for the Liberian government under China's aid program in the 1980s. I remember it well from my PhD dissertation fieldwork: the farm is located in a scenic valley, fed by a waterfall tumbling out of the mountains. "This was a long negotiation," a member of LPHT's staff told me. Some African governments were clearly making informed demands, even though increased rice production would ease their own shortages. "The Liberian government has asked us to do a lot, with our own money," he commented. "We have a twenty-year lease, and we will pay a portion of the crop as rent." Their long-term plan is to build the China-Liberia Kpatawee National Agricultural Zone: a 2,000-hectare, high-tech agricultural park, with demonstrations, seed production, training, and tourism. Longping High-Tech also embarked on a joint venture with the Dunbar family, one of Liberia's elite dynasties, to revitalize their 380-hectare vegetable farm, once the largest in Liberia. "The local partner should provide the funding for this," one of the LPHT staff explained, "but it hasn't happened yet."[11]

In Zambia, LPHT had co-invested with a Jiangsu entrepreneur in the 380-hectare West Xing Farm, setting up a maize seed business and partnering with the United Nations Environment Program to demonstrate water conservation techniques. Longping High-Tech was also invited to conduct trials in a rice-growing region in the north of Ethiopia. "This is not an investment," LPHT vice president Zhou Dan explained. "It is for Ethiopia, a kind of economic diplomacy." In 2011, according to FAO statistics, Ethiopia spent over $50 million importing rice from abroad. Yuan Longping's youngest son, Yuan Ding'an, has his own Changsha company,

Yuan Hybrid Rice International Development. They have launched a joint venture with the China Africa Agricultural Investment Corporation (CAAIC) in Madagascar—also in hybrid rice.[12]

Green West Africa

Longping High Tech's largest project in Africa is a joint venture in the northwestern Nigerian state of Kebbi: Green West Africa. Their partner is China Geo-engineering Construction Corporation (CGCOC). Yang Jiao, a University of Florida anthropology student, visited the project in April 2014 with a grant from our China Africa Research Initiative, while I met with their managers in Beijing in March 2015.[13] We found that CGCOC obtained a lease on the 2,025-hectare Warra Farm in 2006 and formed Green West Africa with LPHT two years later, becoming a registered seed producer in Nigeria.[14] CGCOC also has partnerships with other Chinese research institutes on hybrid maize and is working with Hebei province's "father of hybrid millet" Zhao Zhihai, to develop hybrid millet. At Warra, they grow foundation seed on about 400 hectares of their farm, but their major business is seed multiplication. Green West Africa provides foundation seed to more than 5,000 Nigerian contract farmers across three states, who grow and harvest the seed, selling it back to the company. Green West Africa cleans and packages the seed, selling it to the Nigerian government, which markets it to local farmers (although heavily subsidized).

"The Chinese firm buys up our harvest at N6,500 per bag," a participating farmer told a visiting journalist, comparing this favorably with the N4,000 offered by local middlemen. But a local critic said the farmers were "compelled" to sell their rice, adding: "This is the highest form of exploitation and domestic slavery Nigerians are exposed to."[15] Although the land allocated for the project was a government reserve, local farmers had been using it informally since Nigeria's independence, more than 40 years. "We were made to sign some papers," a local farmer complained, noting that each farmer only collected between $178 and $300 in compensation and had to find new land on their own. The Kebbi government negotiated with the displaced farmers, allowing Green West Africa to concentrate on the project. Although they were not joint investors, the role of the local government proved crucial to CGCOC's relatively successful venture in Nigeria.

In Beijing, Green West Africa's general manager Wang Miao told me, "This is just the beginning. The big business is not seeds, but agro-processing. This is the bottleneck in Nigeria. They are importing more than three million tons of rice. We would like to start this as soon as possible." What about sending the rice back to China? I asked. Wang looked at me and laughed. "Impossible," he said. "It would cost too much. Many African countries are importing rice from Vietnam, Thailand, and India. If we want to import rice, we'll go to those countries too."

NEW TRENDS: "COMPANY + FARMER MODE"

Green West Africa is another in a growing number of examples of contract farming, or what the Chinese call "company + farmer mode." Contract farming has benefits and risks for both sides.[16] For the purchasing company, contract farming allows a steady supply of a commodity produced by farmers who know their land and its quirks, and who take on all the production risks. Take China-Africa Cotton, for example, a joint venture set up in 2010 between the China-Africa Development Fund and two private companies from the coastal city of Qingdao—better known to beer drinkers as "Tsingdao"—in Shandong province. China-Africa Cotton operates across the postharvest value chain, purchasing cotton in seven African countries—Chad, Malawi, Mali, Mozambique, Togo, Zambia, and Zimbabwe—and using a contract farming system in many. As we saw with Datong's sesame debacle in Senegal (chapter 5), contracted farmers can be tempted to "side-sell" their output to competing firms. Green West Africa, China-Africa Cotton, and the Chinese tobacco firm Tianze in Zimbabwe are, so far, more successful.[17]

Until recently, some 6,000 commercial farms in Zimbabwe—mainly white owned—cultivated over 12 million hectares of the best land in the country. By 2010, after a violent land reform, just 725 white-owned commercial farms remained.[18] More than 162,000 rural households gained plots of land but without titles, so they were unable to borrow from banks. They also lacked credit and training to finance and grow the technically demanding crop. Tobacco output plummeted from 237,000 to 67,000 tons, creating a sharp drop in foreign exchange.

In 2004, the Zimbabwe government started a contract farming scheme, effectively privatizing extension services, input supply, and credit to commercial companies. British American Tobacco and other buyers began working directly with farmers. In 2005, the state-owned China National Tobacco Import and Export Group Corporation joined them, setting up a local firm, Tianze. By 2011, 40 percent of Zimbabwe's tobacco was going to China (half through Tianze), with Europe taking another 40 percent.

"Tianze has been very positive for Zimbabwe," Rodney Ambrose, the patient CEO of the Zimbabwe Tobacco Association told me when I visited his office in July 2013. "Chinese demand has led to good prices for our tobacco." Zimbabwe's marketing board helped control side-selling. "Tianze doesn't charge interest, and they don't require farmers to buy inputs from them," Ambrose said. "You can borrow their money and buy inputs at the best price you can find." At the Commercial Farmers Union, I learned that some of Zimbabwe's remaining white farmers were also planting tobacco under contract with Tianze.

Yet there were also complications. By 2014, Zimbabwe had 91,000 registered tobacco growers, representing perhaps a million dependents. With prices high for tobacco and low for maize, many small farmers expected to use their tobacco earnings to buy the staple foods they had formerly produced themselves. Profits were higher, but food security had become more precarious. This led Zimbabwe to pursue joint ventures with Chinese agribusiness firms. A company from Anhui province would play a controversial role.

ZIMBABWE: FINDING A GOOD PARTNER

Just after dawn one morning in the summer of 2013, a friend and I set off from Harare in search of Zim-China Wanjin Agricultural Development Company (Wanjin)—the largest Chinese agricultural investment in Zimbabwe. With the sun still low on the horizon, we drove through the long ridges and mineral-rich hills of the Great Dyke of Zimbabwe. Goats browsed in the dry grass by the side of the road. In the distance, a pivot irrigation tower moved slowly across a green field. After managing to overtake a precariously leaning green and yellow bus with the motto "Judgment Day" painted across the back, we arrived in the university town of Chinhoyi and eventually found Wanjin's headquarters in a small cluster of newly built cottages at the far end of a series of fields.

Earlier in the week I had interviewed the Chinese economic counselor in Harare. Two large white lions guarded the red entrance gate outside his office. "Investment in agriculture is difficult here because they do not allow land to be sold or leased to foreigners," he told me. "For the Wanjin project, the local partner provides the land, the Chinese partner provides the technical services and the finance." The Chinese partner in this case was the Anhui province State Farm Agribusiness Corporation.[19] Their primary local partner was the Zimbabwe Ministry of Defense.

Zimbabwe had tamed inflation and reinvigorated its economy with the adoption of the US dollar in 2009. Anhui SFAC came to Zimbabwe for the first time in 2010, at the invitation of Zimbabwe's Ministry of Defense, which had taken the lead in spearheading joint-venture projects with the Chinese (they had a notorious joint venture in the Marange alluvial diamond fields with another Anhui company: Anhui Foreign Economic Construction

Group). As Major General Douglas Nyikayaramba later told an audience of potential Chinese investors: "A hungry nation is an angry nation," adding that food security was the "top concern" of his government: "a vast area of idled fields is waiting for cultivation."[20]

The two partners established Wanjin and designed an ambitious five-year business plan. There were indeed many idled fields. For example, Chinhoyi University of Technology (CUT) had been allocated the 2,000-hectare Hunyani Farm to meet the needs of its agriculture sciences program but was unable to put it to use. By 2015, Wanjin planned to have invested $240 million across 50,000 of those idled hectares, building a complete value chain for soybeans, wheat, and maize with production, processing, logistics, and storage. When I visited in 2013, Wanjin had joined CUT in a joint venture to cultivate winter wheat, maize, and soybeans on the university's Hunyani Farm. They were also managing two other farms, had leased a total area of about 5,000 hectares, and had secured an $8 million preferential loan from China Eximbank.

As we sat in the whitewashed cottage that housed the Wanjin office, the Chinese manager told me: "We are here because of the relationship between our two countries." Gesturing at the fields outside the window, he continued. "A lot of land has been abandoned. We have come here to help Zimbabwe produce." By 2014, the joint venture had expanded to include seven farms with about 10,000 hectares in total, overseen by 16 Chinese experts, several dozen Zimbabwean managers, and 800 local workers. Other companies from Anhui were starting to follow Wanjin's path. In 2014, a private Anhui company, Wanjin Tianrui, decided to invest $30 million to grow and process maize.

BIG RUBBER

So far, the largest Chinese-owned agricultural investment in operation in Africa is a group of rubber plantations that lie mainly in Cameroon. In the mid-1990s, GMG Global, a Singapore company, bought an older 45,000-hectare concession, Hévéa du Cameroun (Hevecam) and several smaller rubber concessions being privatized by the governments in Cameroon and Côte d'Ivoire. A decade later, Sinochem, a large state-owned Chinese firm, took control of 51 percent of GMG Global. Sinochem left the existing structure in place. For example: Hevecam's CEO is a Canadian, Alain Young.

In 2010, GMG Global added another 41,000 hectares in a new subsidiary, Sud-Cameroun Hévéa. According to their website, in 2014 GMG Global held 106,135 hectares of rubber and palm oil concessions in West

Africa, including a small plantation in Côte d'Ivoire. For comparison, just one European conglomerate, Bolloré, holds 373,164 hectares of oil palm and rubber concessions across West Africa.[21]

GMG Global recruited experts from Hainan province to manage the replanting at Hevecam. Sinochem's website described their new venture in romantic terms reminiscent of Maoist China's efforts to develop China's Great Northern Wilderness:

> In Cameroon, there is a group of people, staying far away from [their] hometown with the resolve to spread the natural rubber seeds of Sinochem Group far and wide. Since stepping onto the bleak land studded with wild mountains and jungles in 2008, this group of people has worked hard against all odds to conjure up a miracle—to turn the wasteland overgrown with weeds into a vast stretch of rubber plantation. The magic changes have not only amazed both local governments and residents, but added a splendid chapter to the rubber development of Sinochem Group in African continent![22]

Led by an expert named Li Hong, the Hainan technicians trained over 150 local villagers, drawing charts to overcome language barriers. According to the glowing accounts on the Sinochem website, the Chinese managers began work at 5:00 a.m. "Shocked upon the discovery that their 'Chinese bosses' started work much earlier than them, local staff felt inspired to work hard."

The intrepid researchers at CIFOR conducted a field study of GMG Global's Hevecam project.[23] Would changing ownership (first the Cameroon government, then a private firm from Singapore, now a Chinese state-owned firm as majority owners) change the nature of the investment and, in particular, the social investments? The CIFOR researchers found a legacy of problems that could be traced to the first owner, the government of Cameroon. These continued and even intensified when the company was privatized to the Singaporean group. Interviews with local communities and plantation employees revealed long-standing feelings of injustice due to inadequate compensation for land and perceptions that workers were poorly paid and treated unfairly.

Yet perhaps surprisingly, under Sinochem's majority ownership, the situation seemed to be changing for the better. After 2008, Hevecam began holding dialogues with local communities, new insurance policies were established for employees, new safety equipment provided, and (following a strike) the company paid a bonus and transferred 3 percent of its shares to local employees. Hevecam's manager Alain Young seemed determined to reduce conflicts. These hopes for a higher level of CSR will be put to the test when GMG Global begins to develop its new concessions.

Another vast rubber plantation investment has been under negotiation for several years in Sierra Leone. In June 2013, China Hainan Rubber Industry Group, a listed provincial company, signed an MOU to build and operate a 100,000-hectare rubber plantation and 35,000-hectare rice farm. The Sierra Leone government would hold 10 percent of the shares.[24] In November that year, China's official aid program paid for 20 agricultural technicians from Sierra Leone to visit Hainan Rubber for three weeks of training. Few details have emerged about the possible design of the project, and, as of mid-2015, no land had been acquired. The investors had applied to China Eximbank for a loan. The bank's decision was pending at the time the Ebola epidemic began to expand across Sierra Leone, but in Beijing, Ministry of Agriculture officials seemed confident that Hainan Rubber would be successful: "they will mortgage assets they hold in Hainan to secure the loan."[25]

GAZA-HUBEI FRIENDSHIP FARM IN MOZAMBIQUE: "DARE TO EAT CRAB"

The Limpopo River winds across southern Africa for more than a thousand miles before spilling into the Indian Ocean near the Mozambican town of Xai-Xai. The 19th-century British poet Rudyard Kipling was a frequent visitor to South Africa, and it was in his *Just So* children's stories that I first encountered "the great, grey-green, greasy Limpopo River, all set about with fever trees." In chapter 1, we left the Chinese company Hubei Lianfeng in charge of the Gaza-Hubei Friendship Farm, a small concession of 300 hectares along the Limpopo River. In 2007, a Chinese newspaper had described Hubei Lianfeng's venture as "daring to eat crab"—referring to a Chinese saying *Gan chi pangxie, cai you huibao,* meaning those who have the courage to be first to try something new will reap the rewards.[26]

Friendship Farm was primarily a political venture, a Hubei manager noted a year later.[27] Mozambique had asked Hubei province to help the country meet its food needs. Friendship Farm "will be growing grain and vegetables for a relatively long time," he said. "We will mainly sell in Africa, in Mozambique." Yet, he added, "We are, after all, a business. While we are working to settle Mozambique's food supply, we will consider other kinds of crops, and develop other markets, for example, Europe or even China. If China has a food shortage, we are prepared to deliver part of our harvest." However, he said, "China's food problem is not about rice or wheat—it's mainly about oil crops—soybeans, sesame, or rapeseed."

Gaza province had promised to provide additional land if the company was successful in its pilot project of 300 hectares. Yet three years later, Hubei Lianfeng had developed only 40 hectares. Mainly, they conducted variety trials: rice, but also cotton, soybeans, watermelon, and vegetables. The contract with Gaza province also required Hubei Lianfeng to train local farmers and transfer technology.[28] Hubei Lianfeng charged local farmers for plowing and other services, which surprised many Mozambicans. Was Friendship Farm an aid project or a business? This would become clear in June 2011, when Hubei Lianfeng announced that the Wanbao Group—a large, private grain-processing firm from Hubei—would join the project as a major investor.

"She Never Saw the Big Tractor Coming"

The rain was gently falling when Sérgio Chichava, Sigrid Ekman, and I crossed the Limpopo just west of Xai-Xai in November 2014. A flat delta of rich, black soil extended to the horizon. This was the Wanbao project. In July, several months earlier, *National Geographic* had begun an article on the rise of agribusiness in Africa with a story about Wanbao:

> She never saw the big tractor coming. First it plowed up her banana trees. Then her corn. Then her beans, sweet potatoes, cassava. Within a few, dusty minutes the one-acre plot near Xai-Xai, Mozambique, which had fed Flora Chirime and her five children for years, was consumed by a Chinese corporation building a 50,000 acre farm. . . . "No one even talked to me," the 45-year-old Chirime says, her voice rising with anger. "Just one day I found the tractor in my field plowing up everything."[29]

As we drove along the raised road at the edge of the giant project, Sigrid and Sérgio debated why this had happened to Flora Chirime and other farmers, and how Mozambique's land laws, resettlement, and compensation provisions played out in projects like this. The violence of forced eviction had poisoned relations between the project and the town.

"The law is ambiguous," Sigrid said. "It says that people who have been working the land for more than ten years have a legal right to use the land."

"That's not exactly true," Sérgio said. "There was a state farm here, but it collapsed. People began to use the land, but it's like if this road collapsed and someone built a house right here. They couldn't expect the government to compensate them when they come to rebuild the road. Those people knew that the land belonged to the state."

Sigrid was quick to reply. "But the state farms collapsed at the end of the 1980s. People have been farming here for more than a generation." We looked out at the vast empty fields on the left, while on the right, an area not yet developed by the company, we could see a scattering of small *machambas* (local farmers' fields) and groups of cattle grazing in the distance.

"This has created a negative perception of the Chinese, that they came and destroyed the machambas." Sigrid continued. "There could have been mediation, consultation. This has hurt Wanbao."

Like every other Chinese investor in Africa, Wanbao had wrongly assumed that they could simply follow the local government's assurance that the land was now theirs, and they could evict farmers who were now seen not as local citizens with contestable rights but as simple trespassers. Resettlement was an internal affair of the leasing government. This assumption is likely to continue to poison community relations as Chinese investments increase.

The headquarters of the Friendship Farm lie down a muddy lane, a short walk from the center of Xai-Xai. The general manager, Lu Haoping, smiled broadly when I asked where he had learned his good English. "In Hawaii," he said. "In 1986, I went to Hawaii under the World Wide Farmer's Exchange program. I worked on Mr. Watanabe's farm in Maui, growing vegetables." In 2012, when they became the largest shareholder, Wanbao retained Lu Haoping and the rest of the Hubei Lianfeng staff. "The conditions for rice production are good here," he told us. "Gaza province wanted the project to be big, but Hubei Lianfeng didn't have the money to invest. We needed a partner." If you want to be big and make profits, he continued, you have to be vertically integrated. You need to control the whole value chain. "Planting is risky, but marketing is zero risk. Processing and storage can also be profitable, but you need scale."

Wanbao was a grain-processing business. Their entry into the project was brokered by Liu Jianxin, head of the Mozambique working group in China Development Bank's Hubei branch. In May 2011, Liu Jianxin sent a text message to Chai Shungong, the president of Wanbao: "Mozambique is rich in agricultural resources, and political stability. Hubei State Farm's Friendship Farm in Gaza province has three years of trials with good results. Come and see."[30] Chai Shungong was skeptical. "Africa means hunger, poverty, war, risky investments," he thought.[31] Liu Jianxin sent another text: Mozambique was importing 450,000 tons of rice annually.

By early June, Chai was on a plane to Mozambique. The vast marshland of the Lower Limpopo impressed him. Friendship Farm could be the foundation for a major project. A month later, containers with construction equipment began to arrive in the Maputo harbor. By November that year, Friendship Farm finally had its full 300-hectare concession under cultivation. Despite his enthusiasm, Chai Shungong was prudent. Wanbao did a market survey and an environmental impact study, as required by Mozambican law.[32] They also explored other options: Angola, Malawi,

Zambia, and Zimbabwe. They learned that the southern region of Africa had an annual rice deficit of over two million metric tons, but Xai-Xai seemed to be the only place where an existing irrigation system covered such a large expanse of fertile land. In 2012, Wanbao formally took over the project, promising to develop 20,000 hectares over five years, bring in modern rice mills, and train local farmers.

On November 17, we spoke with Armando Ussivane, the US-educated head of Regadio do Baixo Limpopo (RBL), the government office tasked with managing the Lower Limpopo irrigation system. "The land belongs to the state," Ussivane said.[33] "RBL has the official DUAT, the right to use the land. Our agreement with Wanbao covers infrastructure and technology transfer. They will provide a guaranteed market for our local farmers, a place to sell and process the rice. Without a buyer, the farmers can't get credit."

Wanbao had agreed to complete this work across 20,000 hectares in the Lower Limpopo system in just three years. The project moved quickly. One night in Xai-Xai we met labor leaders in a local bar. Over glasses of whiskey, they complained about Wanbao's poor safety practices: "Nobody had insurance," one leader pointed out. "There were accidents, and they just gave the injured workers 30,000 meticals [about $800]. So many conflicts between the Chinese and the Mozambican workers! We were always going back and forth, back and forth." More than 2,000 local people worked at the project in the first phase of construction, but only around 1,200 were registered for official benefits. Wanbao also brought in over 500 Chinese construction workers.

"The early years are the hardest," Armando Ussivane said. "The Chinese have to level the land and build the canals. When the areas are good, ready, the Mozambican farmers can be introduced," he added. Friendship Farm was still providing training. "Technology is not something magic. It can be learned. Over time, local farmers will be able to get up to twenty hectares in the irrigation system, perhaps buy a tractor, and sell services to other farmers."

In the meantime, the Mozambique government had allowed Wanbao to bring in four Chinese teams—about 162 people—as contract growers until enough Mozambicans could be trained. Wanbao contracted with state-owned farms in Hubei province (including one *junken* farm) and in Heilongjiang to send the teams on renewable one-year contracts.[34] The Chinese experts remained employees of their companies in China; their families stayed home. They lived in simple one-room dormitories, worked seven days a week, and sold the rice they produced to Wanbao at a fixed price. With high yields, each team member can earn a substantial profit, but they also shoulder some of the risks.

"Growing rice and corn is not the company's ultimate goal in Africa," Chai Shungong told *China Daily* in 2014. "We are a private company, and we believe our strength is in grain processing. Once the local farmers learn the new techniques, we will shift back to our competency of processing grains." He added: "We are confident that Mozambique will be able to overcome its food problems in the long run."[35] As noted in chapter 4, Wanbao's website stated that "in the long run the farm will also become one of China's sustainable grain and oil production bases overseas, serving to consolidate the food security of our country."[36] They had not given up on soybeans.

"You Have to Be Lucky"

Almost from the start, Wanbao was hit with challenges. As we drove to Xai-Xai, Sérgio had pointed out the high-water mark from the historic flood in 2000: Mozambique's worst natural disaster in a hundred years. In January 2013, days of torrential rain pushed the Limpopo over its banks. Water flooded the entire farm, even spilling into the streets of Xai-Xai. All the young rice seedlings drowned or were swept away; the entire harvest was lost. The company rebuilt the polders and dykes of the irrigation system and prepared the 7,000 hectares for the 2013–2014 season. Again, some areas were flooded, but in 2014 the farm managed a modest harvest. Still, they were bleeding money, paying more than $1 million monthly in wages for Chinese and local workers.[37]

Furthermore, although Wanbao had built a couple of schools and provided some donations to local groups, there was considerable local opposition to the giant project. Early one evening, we visited the bungalow where Fórum das Organizações Não Governamentais de Gaza (FONGA), a local NGO platform, has its headquarters. FONGA had charged that at least 1,000 families and possibly as many as 80,000 people will be hurt by Mozambique's decision to lease land in the government's Lower Limpopo irrigation system to the Chinese company. "These people have no place to graze their cattle. Some lost their homes, the graves of their ancestors," an activist told us. "The government keeps insisting it is a good project. But we only see a small group benefiting."[38]

"No one was planting anything there before Wanbao," a Chinese official had told me in Maputo, but this was clearly not the case. When we raised these issues with RBL, Armando Ussivane sighed and then said: "We know that when these government schemes collapsed during the war, people started using them for grazing their cattle. But this can't continue. We need to use the land inside the irrigation scheme more intensively."

Sérgio wrote about an incident in late 2013, when around 400 local farmers armed with hoes marched to the farm in protest, threatening a team of Chinese working there.[39] Because FONGA had provided several different figures for the total number of families affected by the project, it was possible, Sérgio wrote, "that FONGA is exaggerating the numbers in order to focus public attention on this issue."[40] Still, the issues were very real.

We met with several of the project's Mozambican trainee farmers. One, the matriarch of a family, lived down a narrow clay path on the edge of town. Walking to her home, we passed a tree heavy with purple mangos hanging like ornaments. At the end of the lane, a wall of *caniço* reeds surrounded two round clay huts—one painted bright turquoise—along with several animal pens and concrete-block buildings. Two turkeys and half a dozen ducks pecked at the bits of grain in the dirt. Our hostess sat outside on a stool, shelling a bowl of wild peas under a lime tree with electric wires twisting up its branches, connecting to an outdoor light.

"Before Wanbao came," she said, "I was farming in the old irrigation system. I had about five hectares—I grew corn, sweet potatoes, cassava. One day the RBL came and told me that there was a new project with the Chinese. They invited me to join as a trainee. I knew I was going to lose that farm and there was not going to be any compensation, so I decided to join."

As she spoke the sun dipped lower in the sky. We heard a commotion outside her gate, and then five spotted cattle trotted into the yard, followed by a laconic teenager wearing a green Celtics T-shirt.

"Many people refused to join because of the violent way in which they were evicted. They thought they would have to work for the Chinese, for free, like the old *chibalo* system. They didn't trust them. But now they see that those who joined have some potential for a future. Those who didn't join now have some regrets." As she spoke, a black pig ran across the yard, squealing as a small boy chased after it with a long stick.

"There is potential with this new system," she said after describing the difficulties they had experienced with floods and the slow arrival of credit from government banks. "But you have to be lucky, and you have to use your head."

Wanbao's Risks

Drive two hours north along the Limpopo River and you will reach Chokwe, another of the old Portuguese irrigation systems. A British company, Mozfoods, has been operating a contract farming scheme to grow its popular Tia Rosa brand of rice in Chokwe since 2004. Unpredictable weather, high freight costs, and competition with imported rice mean that as of 2012, they had not yet made a profit.[41] Mozambique provides little protection for local rice growers. In 2010, they removed even the relatively low tariff on rice imports to help counter urban protests because of a rise in the price of bread. At the same time, the Mozambican currency began to appreciate against the US dollar, which made imports even cheaper. [42]

Mozfoods supplied inputs and services to local farmers, deducting the cost at harvest. "The problem was we were basically taking 100 per cent of the risk and each year we were being hit by problems—early rains, late rains, problems with birds, it's very risky," Mozfoods' chief financial officer told a reporter.[43] "There is a lot of land here that has great agricultural potential, but it is about money and it is about knowledge." Other companies reported similar risks. As of early 2015, ProSavana, a giant plan for the commercial development of 35 million hectares of Mozambique's savannah using capital and technical assistance from Japan and Brazil, appeared stillborn.

During our visit, the risks of Wanbao's more modest venture became very clear. Wanbao had applied for $79 million from China Development Bank, while CAD-Fund and its sister vehicle, the China-Portuguese-Speaking Countries Cooperation and Development Fund (CPD-Fund), had joined the project as equity investors. So far, CDB had only disbursed $20 million. When the project was hit by two successive floods, CDB decided to reevaluate the risks. Wanbao was still waiting for a decision at the time of our visit.

On our last day in Xai-Xai, an official from RBL drove with us around the giant farm. We stopped at the spot on higher ground where Wanbao is building its new headquarters. At the edge of the complex, just before the land sloped sharply down to the rich delta, the company had built two large villas with views of thousands of hectares of farmland. "Those are for Wanbao's owner, when he visits," the official told us. Behind the houses stood two rows of large storage warehouses and a half-built shell for an enormous rice mill, which had still not arrived. Dozens of large construction machines were parked in the yard. The planting season was about to start, but there was almost no activity.

Back in Maputo, a Chinese embassy official told me that he was confident that the project was experiencing only a temporary setback, something common in large farming investments.[44] Wanbao had enough seed to plant just over 3,000 hectares this season. "Their original plan was to do about seven thousand hectares, but three thousand hectares—that's not bad." He looked outside at the light layer of clouds building in the east and smiled slightly. "Wanbao is lucky," he said. "The rainy season has been delayed by one month. They still have time."

When I asked him about rumors in Xai-Xai that Wanbao was planning to ship the rice back to China, he shook his head, saying, "No, no, no! Even if you consider the entire area of the Lower Limpopo, they still won't be able to produce enough to meet local demand. We still have a long way to go to solve African countries' food supply. This is a very big task. That's why we pay a lot of attention to Wanbao's farm. This will be a big example of what is possible for African countries. Let them focus on grain. Even in China, our government is still focused on basic food security, our domestic grain production. Africans need to produce their own food."

"PROCEED WITH CAUTION"

"Proceed with caution," two Chinese analysts advised in a 2012 article outlining the risks that had led to the bankruptcy of many Chinese agricultural projects in Africa.[45] Foreign farming can bring great profits—but it is also full of challenges. In 2013, the *Economist* newspaper profiled two contrasting examples.[46] The Horita family emigrated from Japan decades ago, opening a 500-hectare farm in Brazil's fertile, temperate south. Their youngest son, Walter, left the farm in 1984 to join other pioneer farmers in the virgin lands of Brazil's northeastern *cerrado*. "There was nothing," he told a reporter. "No roads, no schools, no health care, no electricity, no water supply, no phone." Yet new technologies were creating a grain miracle on the region's poor, acidic soils. Within three decades, he and his older brothers were growing soybeans, cotton, and corn on 150,000 hectares.

On the other hand, a group of 18 experienced white farmers from Zimbabwe had a far less successful experience in Nigeria's Nasarawa State where, in 2006, they had been invited to settle by the then governor.[47] Seven years later, only one family remained, living on a farm that lacked electricity, running water, and paved roads. The entire agricultural support system they enjoyed in Zimbabwe was simply absent. Seed and fertilizer were poor quality, and there were no extension or research facilities, trained labor, or local accountants. When their tractors broke down, there was no local spare parts distributor, and Nigeria had no organized marketing boards with guaranteed, preannounced prices. "In Nigeria you're on your own," they said. Chinese investors would have the same reaction.

This chapter provided the last set of case studies of the handful of significant agricultural investments that actually exist (or, as in the case of Wuhan Kaidi, came very close to existing). We learned about the challenges and the risks. Land has many claimants, and local governments cannot always deliver land "unencumbered" as promised. Contract farmers might side-sell to other competitors. Coups and changes in government affect investors whose ties are too close to a previous regime.

Chinese analysts repeatedly say that China's overseas agricultural investment is still "in its infancy." In particular, we see a growing number of agro-processing investments like Wanbao's, most planning to operate with African contract farmers. In December 2013, as we were leaving the Longping High Tech training center in the Hunan province capital of Changsha, Zhou Dan told me about her last trip to Liberia. "There are so many obstacles to overcome: disease, accidents. I had to take a motorcycle taxi to the airport—with all my luggage! There was a traffic jam. I was so scared. I never had to do this in China. It took an hour. I held on to the driver. I was trembling. He kept saying, 'Don't be afraid.'"

I asked her: In the face of all this, do you think Africa has potential for Chinese agribusiness investment? "Yes," she nodded firmly. "Yes, yes."

CONCLUSION

LESSONS, RUMORS, AND CHALLENGES

As global food prices soared in the first decade of the 21st century, China's rising prosperity and shortage of arable land seemed destined to clash with the needs of vulnerable rural Africans whose own food security was often precarious. Many feared that a ravenous China had embarked on a state-sponsored quest to lock up vast tracts of African land to grow food to send home to feed its people. This book argues that the realities on the ground in rural Africa do not match the conventional wisdom regarding China's role. The Chinese are not building a new empire on the continent.

As I write this, numerous reports proclaim that Africa is "on the move." Indeed, growth rates and measures of well-being have been improving. Despite continued conflict in Somalia, Sudan and South Sudan, parts of Nigeria, and the Democratic Republic of Congo, much of Africa is at peace. Although there are setbacks from time to time—the Ebola crisis in West Africa, for example—the current generation of African citizens is healthier, better educated, and enjoys far more open, democratic governance compared with the past. The continent boasts an expanding middle class, a telecommunications revolution, and the world's fastest rates of urbanization. Yet these signs of modernization are not reflected in African food security. Low and decreasing crop yields, high population-growth rates, and the impact of climate change could mean that by 2050 Africa will be able to meet no more than 13 percent of its food requirements.[1] Rapid price increases in staple foods have already led to deadly urban riots in Algeria, Cameroon, and Mozambique. Increasing local food supplies is a political and humanitarian imperative. As Tegegnework Gettu, former director of the United Nations Development Program's Africa bureau, wrote in 2013: "Africa must stop begging for food."[2]

Halfway around the world, Chinese concerns about food security are also very real and still provoke intense debates within the country. After the 1995 publication of Lester Brown's book *Who Will Feed China?*, Chinese leaders drew a red line to try to manage the relentless disappearance of farmland under urban sprawl. They set targets for self-sufficiency in basic grains: China would feed China. Yet over the past two decades, the Chinese have also moved gradually, carefully, in the direction of enmeshing their food system with global markets and modernizing their agriculture with foreign investment.

China's food security is being assured on multiple fronts; it no longer rests only on the backs of millions of Chinese peasants toiling in rice paddies and wheat fields. Today a Thai company, Charoen Pokphand (CP) Group, has become China's largest producer of animal feed. American firms taught Chinese peasant farmers how to be part of integrated supply chains for restaurants like McDonald's. International grain and oil seed companies—Cargill, Archer Daniels Midland, and others—entered China in the 1990s, and China's state-owned companies had to learn to compete. Global giants DuPont and Monsanto are key players among more than 70 foreign high-tech seed companies doing business in China. In 2014, China was the largest single destination for US agricultural exports, consuming over \$24.6 billion in American soybeans, maize, and other products.[3] The country's confidence about its own food security is matched by its role as a supplier of food aid. According to the World Food Programme, China became the world's third-largest food donor in 2005.[4]

By contrast, African food security looks ever more precarious, with chronic hunger affecting some 227 million people—the only region where the number of hungry people is on the rise.[5] Africa already depends on global markets and foreign assistance to feed its people, making its food security a function of scarce foreign exchange and charity. What do we now know about the role Chinese agricultural investment has played—or might play—in this picture?

MYTHS AND REALITIES

In the introduction, I outlined four widespread beliefs about Chinese agricultural engagement in Africa: (1) the Chinese have acquired large areas of farmland; (2) the Chinese government is leading this effort through its state-owned firms and sovereign wealth funds; (3) the Chinese are growing grain for export to China; and (4) the Chinese have sent (or plan to send) large numbers of Chinese farmers to settle on the continent. The chapters of this book explored the evidence for and against these beliefs.

Have the Chinese Acquired Large Areas of Farmland in Africa?

No—or at least, not yet. If Chinese companies had actually acquired all the land they were alleged to have acquired since 2000, they would have "grabbed" around six million hectares, just under 1 percent of all the arable land on the continent.[6] Yet, as we have seen, Chinese agribusinesses have, so far, acquired very little land in Africa (appendix 1). Even including all the farms leased in the 1990s, and the GMG Global plantations in Cameroon, Chinese companies at the end of 2014 held around 240,000 hectares of African land, roughly equivalent to twice the size of New York City.[7] Discouraged by poor infrastructure, political instability, and the sober realization that profits were likely to prove more elusive than hoped, Chinese firms came, explored, and then often went elsewhere—most often to countries in China's border regions: Russia, Central Asia, and Southeast Asia.

I suspect that the widespread idea that the Chinese were leading the land grab in Africa stems from just two widely circulated stories: ZTE's oil palm project in the Democratic Republic of the Congo (chapter 4), and Wuhan Kaidi's biofuels project in Zambia (chapter 8). Both companies arrived in Africa as novice agribusiness investors, albeit with global ambitions. Their vague but large-scale visions were embraced by African governments, business associations, and investment agencies, who then boasted to the media about the potential size of these investments. However, when the excitement died down and the companies began negotiating formal agreements, the amount of land at stake turned out to be far from the initial reports of a combined 4.8 million hectares, shrinking to a more realistic total of 179,000 hectares, and then to practically zero, as neither project has ever been implemented.[8]

Although these projects never made it beyond the stage of grandiose ideas, the initial reports were extraordinarily persistent. In writing this chapter, I checked the IFPRI website and found that it still contains an interactive map titled "Land Grabbing by Foreign Investors in Developing Countries." The map is marked by large dots, each of which is supposed to represent foreign land grabbing. Clicking on the Zambia dot brings up this information: "2 million hectares requested by China for jatropha"; clicking on the DRC reveals: "2.8 million hectares secured by China (ZTE International) for biofuel oil palm plantation."[9] These megaprojects live on, rising from the dead, again and again, like Count Dracula.

There is little investigative reporting on Chinese agricultural investment in Africa, and visiting reporters often do not spend the time needed to dig deeply into these issues. For example, a journalist who visited Mozambique's northern Nampula province to look into Chinese migration was told by a local activist that many Chinese were "now looking for places to grow rice" and that Chinese were "farming in almost every district."[10] Nampula province has 18 districts, so this would have meant "almost 18" Chinese farms. Or perhaps the activist meant all 128 districts in Mozambique? In any case, the statement was reported without question, as though it was an accurate representation of the facts.

On the other hand, in 2014, Sigrid Ekman and Filipe Di Matteo spent four months in Mozambique creating an inventory of agribusiness investment from emerging economies for CIFOR.[11] They were able to confirm only three operating Chinese farms, including the Wanbao investment in Xai-Xai. Sigrid and Filipe found *one* Chinese farm in Nampula province—but it was no longer in operation. They also visited China-Africa Agriculture, a farm with 300 hectares in Maputo province. Other researchers have found a medium-sized private Chinese farm producing a mix of crops in Inhambane, and identified two new Chinese farming investments about to be launched in Sofala province, where Wen Chen Liao rice farm was being operated by a South African of Taiwanese origin.[12] It was possible that they had overlooked some small chicken or vegetable farms run by Chinese who were borrowing land from official leaseholders, yet, "I went out of my way to try to find these Chinese guys," Sigrid said. "They are just not there."[13]

Sigrid pointed out that civil society activists also rely on information gathered from the Internet that may not be accurate. She compared the rumors about widespread Chinese investment with those about Brazilian investment in Mozambique. "Everyone will tell you that Brazilians have loads of landholdings in northern Mozambique now," she said, "but if you ask them, 'Can you tell me exactly where they are and who they are?' few can give you one single concrete example."[14]

Is the Chinese Government Leading an Effort to Acquire Land Through Its State-Owned Firms and Funds?

Not in the sense implied by the question. Another persistent belief involves the role of the Chinese government—the notion that Beijing has a "grand plan" to acquire land in Africa and has set up major funds and invested "immense sums" toward this goal.[15] Informed Chinese observers would scoff at this notion. As Zhu Xinkai, an agricultural economist at Beijing's Renmin University complained in 2013, "We do not have a unified national policy on agriculture 'going out.' "[16]

In exploring the role of the Chinese government in fostering agricultural investment and land acquisition in Africa, we traced the evolution of policy support over the past three decades. Chinese companies first moved to invest in Africa in the 1980s, and this has slowly increased over the decades. Overseas farming was not newly added to the agenda when global food prices rose around 2007. Agriculture has been included in the activities supported by government incentives ever since the "going global" policies took off in 2001. We saw that in 2006 and 2008, China's two major policy banks, China Eximbank and China Development Bank, signed strategic cooperation agreements with the Ministry of Agriculture, making available more than $8 billion in lines of credit to support an expansion of the global business of China's agriculture, forestry, and fishing companies.[17]

These funds could be seen (as in the conventional wisdom) as strong support for land acquisition in Africa and elsewhere. Indeed, Anhui State Farm drew on these funds for its Anjin farming ventures in Zimbabwe, and Wanbao's loan from CDB for its Mozambique project could also have come from these lines of credit. Yet a closer look shows that these funds were not set up to acquire land overseas: China Eximbank's loan program specifically excluded land purchases from the list of acceptable projects. The loan programs support a wide range of agribusiness activities: boosting Chinese exports of agricultural machinery, upscale food products, and patented seeds; securing overseas construction contracts; allowing fishing companies to upgrade their boats; subsidizing efforts to acquire foreign patents and license intellectual property to move up the value chain; marketing activities to build global brands; and so on. In other words, these funds are part of the portfolio of multiple and varied tools employed by an active Chinese government, a developmental state trying to jump-start its firms' global agribusiness prospects. So far, both China Eximbank and CDB appear to have been far more active in providing project finance for *African* governments to invest in their own new state-owned farms (as in Angola), agro-processing factories (as in Mozambique), and sugar refineries (as in Ethiopia) than in providing support for *Chinese* farms or even agro-processing investments.

What about the China Africa Development Fund, described (in error) as a $5 billion fund for agricultural investment?[18] As we have seen, in its first five years of operation, the CAD-Fund invested only $57 million in agricultural projects in Africa—and this included not just farms but also several agro-processing factories.[19] In 2010, the CAD-Fund and China National Agricultural Development Corporation did set up a joint Africa agricultural investment vehicle, the RMB 1 billion ($161 million) China Africa Agricultural Investment Corporation (CAAIC). Germany has established a fund with very similar goals: the $135 million Africa Agriculture and Trade Investment Fund, set up in 2011 on behalf of Germany's federal Ministry for Economic Cooperation and Development.[20] China's fund should be seen as a parallel tool, not something focused on "land grabbing."

China Africa Agricultural Investment Corporation's first investments went toward refinancing China State Farm Agribusiness Corporation's aging sisal farm in Tanzania and Zhongken Farm in Zambia. However, as an official at CAAIC told me, their search for projects has been frustrating: "The investment environment gives us challenges: labor, water, electricity. African governments are willing to allow foreign investment in agriculture, but it's hard to find good opportunities. Chinese companies have had a lot of difficulties. It's pretty bad, actually. We've talked to Brazilian and European companies, only a few seem to be actually investing."[21]

Globally, Chinese agricultural investment appears to be pausing. Between 2006 and 2010, Chinese overseas agricultural (including farming, forestry, fisheries, and animal husbandry) investment worldwide grew at an annual rate of over 34 percent, then it stabilized between 2011 and 2013 at around $2 billion annually.[22] This is still less than 2 percent of all outbound investment from China, which is why Chinese experts repeatedly note that China's overseas farming is still "in its infancy." We will undoubtedly see more Chinese farming in Africa. But the difficulties described in this book suggest that we are not likely to see the rapid expansion of large, new Chinese farms on the continent. This has more to do with the difficulties presented by African realities than a lack of interest by Chinese firms.

"The Chinese Want to Grow Food in Africa to Send Back to China"

No, or—at least—not yet. The details of investment and attempted investment so far reflect three general patterns: small- and medium-scale farms producing mainly for African markets (vegetables, wheat, maize, rice, beef, poultry), large-scale industrial farms growing traditional industrial commodities, primarily for export (rubber, sugar, sisal, oil palm) and contract farming with African growers (tobacco, cotton). This pattern is likely to be followed by other investments in the pipeline. In 2014, for example, Julong Group, China's largest palm oil trader, set up an office in Ghana to explore investments in West Africa. "We sell according to market demand globally," their vice president told a China Daily reporter. Noting that African countries were already big importers of palm oil, he said: "There's no need to sell our palm oil back to China."[23]

The trade data also support the conclusion that Africa is not feeding China, at least not yet. The most recent data on agricultural trade collected by the United Nations Commodity Trade show that Chinese imports of agricultural commodities from Africa continue to be headed by raw cotton, natural rubber, sesame seeds, tobacco, and cocoa beans (see appendix

2).[24] Except for rubber, most of these crops are grown by African farmers or non-Chinese multinationals. Sesame seeds and cocoa are rising in importance, but, between 2004 and 2014, the data show no Chinese imports of rice or wheat from Africa, and only tiny amounts of maize, soybeans, and cassava.[25]

Several African countries are already food exporters and would very much like China to be a market for their food commodities. For example, Nigeria has been determinedly marketing its dry cassava chip exports. Most go to nearby Niger and to the United States, but in 2013, Nigeria secured an agreement to export significant quantities of cassava chips to China for animal feed.[26] South Africa is the world's fifth-largest exporter of maize, with markets in Mexico, Kenya, and South Korea. After mounting what one analyst called a "vigorous marketing campaign" to secure Asian buyers for the country's crops, South Africa has begun exporting maize to China.[27] Still, despite its agricultural strengths, South Africa is likely to remain a minor player. In 2012, the United States exported 5.4 million tons of maize to China. Between 2010 and 2012, as the US Department of Agriculture has noted, the United States accounted for 97 percent of China's maize imports "and will continue to be a key supplier" as Chinese demand for maize increases. In 2004, South Africa sent a sample of its soybeans to China but was unable to secure further exports. In 2014, Brazil exported 32.8 million tons of soybeans to China. For the foreseeable future, China's food is likely to continue to come from the Americas, not Africa.

Could this change? Some Chinese companies investing or exploring investment in Africa have spoken openly about the hope that their African investments might one day supply Chinese markets. These examples of provincial interest are still rare but could increase, especially if—as a Chinese analyst suggested to me—some companies believe that framing an investment as boosting provincial food security might increase their chances of securing support from overseas economic cooperation funds controlled by the province.

As noted above, the trade data show that, over the past decade, several African countries have sent very small amounts of maize, cassava, and soybeans to China: Thirty kilograms here, 200 kg there.[28] These might be research samples, or they might be samples for trade. However, supplying Chinese food from Africa will require more than provincial interest—or even political will. The key to sustainable modernization of Africa's agriculture and the production of surpluses that can be exported lies in the hands of African governments. Nearly everywhere across the continent, investment environments would have to become far more stable and attractive. Zimbabwe's own history offers some lessons here. Before Zimbabwe's agricultural sector collapsed in Mugabe's violent land reform, commercial farmers used to export significant amounts of maize and wheat.[29] They supplied green peas to the UK, milk to Botswana, oranges to Germany, and wheat to Spain. In 1989, Zimbabwe exported nearly 300,000 tons of wheat to Indonesia, Malaysia, and China before the tables turned, and it became a major food importer.

In December 2013, during lunch in the Chinese city of Changsha with Zhou Dan, vice president of Longping High Tech, I asked: "Will Africa ever become a major grain supplier for China?"

"It's possible, from a technical point of view," she said, pausing with her chopsticks close to the steamed fish in the center of the table. "But there are a lot of other factors. It needs the right policies from African governments. They need to build up their own internal markets. From our side, we can only analyze the technical aspects. The potential is there. They can be locally self-sufficient and export, too."

At the handover of the Chinese-financed ATDC in Liberia in July 2010, Chinese ambassador Zhou Yuxiao echoed this message. Noting that Liberia was only using 10 percent of its arable land for agriculture, he said: "Rainfall is abundant, and its sunshine is plenty and its labor force is more than adequate. All this tells us that Liberia's agricultural potentials are enormous. I hope this center will play a positive role in tapping the potentials and making Liberia self-sufficient in food in the not too distant future. Let's look forward to a day when Liberia exports grain to China."[30]

"Beijing Plans to Send Its Displaced Farmers to Africa"

No. There is no plan to export large numbers of Chinese farmers to Africa. We saw that Li Ruogu, the president of China's Eximbank, noted in a 2007 speech in the city of Chongqing that many rural Chinese would be displaced as China urbanized. He seemed to encourage the Chongqing government to organize groups of Chinese farmers to invest in agriculture in Africa. However, despite his support of the idea, there have been no programs set up to foster this immigration. In practice, it would be nearly impossible for a group of Chinese peasants without significant collateral to obtain an overseas investment loan from the China Eximbank.[31]

The proposal by NPC delegate and agricultural scientist Zhao Zhihai that China adopt an official strategy to send up to a million unemployed Chinese to solve Africa's food shortages was never officially endorsed, but it stimulated considerable discussion on Chinese websites.[32] Some liked the idea. "Many people from my province are going to Russia to grow vegetables," a reader from Jilin said. "And they earned a lot of money. Farming in Africa can also make money." Others were critical. "Better to increase our own food output and export it to Africa, to earn foreign exchange," a reader from Zhejiang wrote. "This is the funniest proposal of 2009," someone from Shanghai commented. From Chongqing: "If Africa doesn't work, how about going to the moon?" And from Shandong: "I have one word for this: *bullshit*."

No one knows how many Chinese have settled in Africa as farmers, but the number is both constantly changing and almost certainly smaller than many people believe. Zambia—with fertile soil, friendly policies, and a long history of Chinese agricultural investment—probably has the largest number of private Chinese farmers. Researchers Solange Guo Chatelard and Jessica Chu researched this issue extensively during fieldwork for their PhD dissertations. They reported in late 2014 that they had found approximately 30 private Chinese farms in Zambia, nearly all had fewer than 250 hectares, and some were as small as two hectares.[33] The operators of these farms were not displaced Chinese peasants, Solange and Jessica reported, but people from a variety of backgrounds who entered farming as a business venture.

High-productivity farming on a major scale requires expertise. Yet a study on the progress in going out in agriculture conducted by a working group organized by the Chinese Ministry of Agriculture found that a major problem for Chinese agribusiness investors was a shortage of Chinese agricultural technical experts willing to work overseas.[34] In Africa and Southeast Asia, where agriculture is less advanced than in China, local agricultural experts are in short supply. "Companies have to send Chinese experts to these African countries," the report found. "But Chinese experts are not willing to go."

Work permits for Chinese experts are an additional difficulty. In 2007, the deputy director of Hubei State Farm Agribusiness Corporation told a reporter, "If the development is good, we can transfer some of the excess workforce in Hubei's state farms to Africa."[35] Wanbao's Mozambique investment was able to secure temporary work permits for two teams of Chinese experts from Hubei's state farms, and another two from state farms in Heilongjiang, about 162 people, to operate the first phase of its contract farming scheme in Xai-Xai. Other Chinese agricultural investments—the Tanzania sisal farm, for example—have fewer than a dozen Chinese technicians and rely on African managers for their large African workforce. Farming in Africa has not proven to be an El Dorado for China's labor exports—and this is unlikely to change.

INTERNATIONAL HARVESTER

What does the research presented here say about China's actual commercial farming footprint in Africa—as opposed to the myths? And what does the past and the present suggest about the future? First, mixed farms growing food for local consumption are likely to continue. In Zambia, CSFAC developed or leased several mixed farms, similar to the farms operated by Zambeef. However, while founders Francis Grogan and Carl Irwin were able to develop Zambeef into a modern, vertically integrated operation with retail stores and a strong brand, the Chinese farms have not been able to move beyond the live supply of generic chickens in open markets, where they compete with indigenous farmers. Indeed, Solange Gou Chatelard and Jessica Chu reported that the Chinese farmers in a major Lusaka market are only allowed to sell their chickens between 2 a.m. and 8 a.m. in order to reduce competition for local poultry farms.[36] In this regard, it is interesting that the Thai firm CP Group—profiled in chapter 3—has entered the poultry market in Africa, launching operations in Kenya and exploring the markets in Tanzania and Nigeria. CP Group may play the catalytic role in Africa that it played in China—a role that does not appear to be on the agenda of the Chinese companies.

More controversially, in Zimbabwe, Anhui province's State Farm branch now operates at least seven mixed soybean, maize, and wheat farms out of the thousands seized over the past decade, mainly from white farmers, as part of Zimbabwe's fast-track land reform, and then left idle. Run as joint ventures with the Zimbabwe military, the Chinhoyi University of Technology, and perhaps cronies of the Mugabe regime who supply the land, the Chinese supply financing, machinery, and inputs as well as management. While bringing idle farmland back into production can be seen as positive, Anhui's close relationship with a controversial government is obviously risky—and the fortunes of these investments could be quite vulnerable to political change.

Aside from mixed farms, we have also seen growing Chinese interest in a second type of farming, the kind of plantation agriculture that has long been practiced by European and American firms in Africa. Today, the West African rubber plantations owned by Singapore-based GMG Global (majority owned by the Chinese state-owned firm Sinochem) comprise together the largest concession (106,135 hectares) held by any existing Chinese-owned agricultural company operating in Africa. Other Chinese firms have begun serious negotiations over new plantation investments: a rubber and irrigated rice project in Sierra Leone (China Hainan Rubber Industry Group), an oil palm plantation in Ghana (Julong Group). When this book was going to press, these major new plantations remained in the planning phase; no land was yet acquired. Yet when these or others like them move forward, we are likely to see further conflicts with villagers and subsistence farmers who have their own claims to fertile land. Chinese companies have not generally accepted that corporate responsibility requires more than unquestionably accepting a local government's word that the land they have been allocated is "owned by the state" or that it is unencumbered. Building this awareness will take time and should be an urgent priority. Until this happens, Chinese investors will continue to be confronted by protests and local resistance.

Third, we see the rise (again) of the kind of build-operate-transfer (BOT) state farm package that characterized China's very early foreign aid program. The ATDCs being built with Chinese aid funding in 25 African countries use this model on a small scale. Once the centers are built, they are operated for three years (with Chinese subsidies) and then transferred to local ministries of agriculture. African governments are also employing Chinese companies directly to clear, level, and prepare virgin land for planting by African state-owned plantations and farms. The ill-fated Zimbabwe contract undertaken at Nuanetsi Ranch by a Chinese firm in 2003 was a harbinger of these arrangements, but Chinese engineering firms have secured similar contracts in Angola, Chad, Guinea, and (with Libya) in Mali. The government of Chad held a tender in 2012 for Chinese companies to compete for a contract to build three large irrigation schemes totaling 20,000 hectares in Chad, drawing on the depleted waters of Lake Chad, Lake Fitri, and the Bahr Salamat River. These projects were to be financed by a $2 billion oil-secured line of export credit provided by China Eximbank.[37] Contracts like this have not generally involved ownership shares for the Chinese firm. However, some governments—Sudan, for example—have been interested in contracting with Chinese firms to build, manage, and perhaps even co-own their new state-owned sugar complexes, and CITIC is negotiating with Angola on a major new project that might involve CITIC's own capital.

Finally, a growing trend in Chinese agricultural engagement is the outgrower model, or contract farming. Expanding this mode was one of the primary recommendations of the Ministry of Agriculture's "Going Out" Research Working Group, which noted that companies should minimize the purchase of land and instead use contract farming to foster technological change, higher standards, and skills transfer.[38] In Mozambique, Wanbao's business model at the Friendship Farm involves contract farming through what might be called an "in-grower" scheme: independent Chinese teams and individual Mozambican farmers are allocated areas within the perimeter of the irrigation scheme, and the farm will supply inputs and plowing, and buy their products. In Zimbabwe, Tianze holds no land, but it contracts with local Zimbabwean farmers. China-Africa Cotton operates contract farming schemes in seven African countries. The company claims to be involving 200,000 African farmers while using Chinese experts to provide advice and training.[39] Tianli Spinning, a Chinese company based in Mauritius, is opening a cotton contract farming project in Madagascar. Contract farming comes with risks for both sides; yet, as in China, it may be a way for foreign investment to boost incomes and productivity of local farmers, provide credit in countries with weak banking systems, and move from subsistence farming to activities with higher income potential.

More than a decade after "China in Africa" began to hit the headlines, there continues to be an enormous gap between what many in the West imagine Chinese intentions in Africa to be and the realities. For example, in the West, it appears to be widely believed, as an editorial in the *Economist* stated, that the Chinese are deliberately "secretive" about their overseas land acquisitions.[40] The Chinese government is far from transparent, and overseas land acquisitions are recognized as a politically sensitive area. However, other interpretations are possible. A reporter for the *China Economic Herald* concluded in 2013, after interviewing a number of Chinese experts about the agricultural going out strategy: "How much land have Chinese firms purchased? What are these pieces of land for? No one is coordinating and regulating these investments.... There is not even a credible statistical database!"[41] Large land transactions now require approval at the highest levels of government, as we saw in chapter 4. In the future, at least this kind of data will be tracked. Whether it will be public is another matter. As far as I know, the United States does not collect this data for our own firms' agricultural investments abroad. Yet China does collect and publish official data on other sensitive topics, like protests in the Chinese countryside or the number of Chinese workers sent abroad each year, country by country. Perhaps we will see more transparency here.

Many fears have been raised about the Chinese as a new colonial power in Africa, and the land issue is a central factor stoking these concerns. These fears about Chinese intentions in rural Africa have surprisingly deep roots.[42] In the late 19th century, Chinese traders arrived in southern Africa, settling in European colonies that are now Mauritius, Madagascar, South Africa, and Zimbabwe. In most of these colonies, Chinese were not allowed to own land, which is one reason why they worked as petty traders and tailors or set up small laundries. Philip Snow's remarkable book *The Star Raft* noted that when 63,500 Chinese indentured workers were imported to work (temporarily) in South Africa's gold mines between 1904 and 1910, white South Africans were "terrified" that the Chinese would settle in the colony, "buy their land, [and] capture their businesses and jobs."[43] These fears were reignited during the Cold War. For example, the first president of Congo-Brazzaville wrote in 1966 that Africa was under threat of a Chinese communist colonization: "coherent, logical, and terribly effective, which would in due course turn the entire continent into a gigantic rice field."[44]

Of course this did not happen, and it is not happening now. There is no evidence to support the notion that Chinese firms in rural Africa are the beachhead of a rising imperial power. Rather, they are part of a new wave of globalization that began in the 1980s. Chinese firms are going out in the footsteps of companies like Swiss seed giant Syngenta, US tractor manufacturer John Deere, and French commodities firm Louis Dreyfus. The rise of transnational corporations like these in Africa is seen as a hopeful sign by some, including the US government. In 2012, President Obama initiated a new program to involve private sector companies like DuPont, PepsiCo, and Walmart in "Feed the Future," the US government's signature program in support of global food security.[45] Activist organizations like GRAIN and Food First are more skeptical of the role agribusiness can play in food security. Chinese companies are at the start of their learning curve as global businesses. But the rules these companies play by and the corporate social responsibility issues their investments raise are very different from the military conquests and political domination that occurred during the 19th century. No Chinese in Africa plays a role remotely like that played by the English businessman and financier Cecil Rhodes or Belgium's King Leopold.

Throughout my research, I have met many thoughtful Africans who recognize that China's newfound interest in their rural areas presents opportunities as well as risks. The challenge of engaging with China and its companies is their task. Late one morning on the green campus of the University of Zambia, I met with Dr. Mick Mwala, a US-educated agronomist and dean of the School of Agricultural Sciences. At the end of our discussion, Dr. Mwala told me that China's agro-technology demonstration center in Zambia was not well-located. "It's too close to Lusaka, too far from the farmers. They put it up in a very short time. It won't be a white elephant, the university will use it, but we would have benefited more if they had engaged in the construction of ideas, not just buildings. There's a lot we don't know. They are buying tractors, but who will maintain them? Where is the budget line for this?"[46]

He told me that the Chinese seemed to have come to Zambia like a whirlwind, a flood. "I've asked myself: Is this flood a blessing or a curse? In the western provinces of Zambia, we have floods during the rainy season. All the ponds fill with water, alluvial soils are deposited. When the floods recede, we can plant. These are good floods. I believe the Chinese flood is going to be positive, but we have to work on it." The commercialization of agriculture in Africa is all but inevitable, yet the fate of the continent's own farmers is not yet sealed. China's agricultural modernization could offer useful ideas for African leaders and lessons on how foreign skills and talents can be channeled into positive outcomes for their people. But Africans themselves must make these decisions. Will their continent continue to be fed by China (as well as Brazil, the US, and Europe) or will Africa, one day, feed itself . . . *and* China?

Chinese Agricultural Investments in Africa, 1987–2014

Country	Farm Name	Reported Location	Reported Chinese Investors	Reported in Year	Largest Reported Size (ha)	Actual Land Acquired (ha)	Year Cultivation Began, if known	Planned Crops
Angola	Pedras Negras	Malange	CITIC Construction	2011	12,580	0	n/a	grains
Angola	Sanza Pombo	Uige	CITIC Construction	2012	9,433	0	n/a	rice, cattle
Angola	Manquete	Cunene	CEIEC	2014	45,000	0	n/a	rice
Angola	Kamacupa	Bie	CAMC Engineering	2012	4,500	0	n/a	grains, fish
Angola	Longa	Cuito Cuanavale	CAMC Engineering	2012	1,500	0	2014	rice
Angola	Cuimba	Zaire	CAMC Engineering	2014	3,000	0	n/a	grains
Angola	Camaiangala	Moxico	CEIEC	2013	16,000	0	n/a	grains
Benin	Sucobe	Savè	Complant	2003	6,000	5,200	1983	sugar
Benin	"Bioenergy Project"	n/a	Complant	2010	4,800	0	never	sugar
Cameroon	Sud-Cameroun Hevea	Meyomessala	GMG Global/Sinochem	2010	45,198	45,198	2011	rubber
Cameroon	Hevecam	Niete	GMG Global/Sinochem	2008	40,992	40,992	1991	rubber
Cameroon	Hevecam	Kribi	GMG Global/Sinochem	2012	18,365	18,365	n/a	rubber
Cameroon	"Chinese Farm"	Nanga-Eboko	Shaanxi SFAC/Sino-Cam IKO	2006	10,000	100	2006	grains, rice
Côte d'Ivoire	Tropical Rubber	Anguededou	GMG Global/Sinochem	2008	1,580	1,580	1995	rubber
DR Congo	No name	Equateur province	ZTE Agribusiness/Zonergy	2007	3,000,000	200	never	oil palm
DR Congo	N'Sele-DAIPN	N'Sele	ZTE Agribusiness/Zonergy	2010	540	540	1967	mixed
Ethiopia	No name	Gambella	Hunan Dafengyuan	2010	25,000	0	never	sugarcane
Ghana	n/a	n/a	Jiangxi Yu Sheng Food	2013	500	500	n/a	soybeans
Guinea	Koba	Faranah Region	CSFAC	1996	2,400	2,400	1979	mixed

Country	Project	Location	Company	Year	Area	Value	Year	Crop
Madagascar	Liangguangfeng	n/a	n/a	2013	100,000	n/a	n/a	castor
Madagascar	Siranala	Morondava	Sucoma (Complant)	1997	6,506	6,506	1984	sugarcane
Madagascar	Namakia (West Sugar)	Namakia	Sucoma (Complant)	2007	8,900	8,900	1935	sugar & rice
Madagascar	Ambilobe (West Sugar)	Ambilobe	Sucoma(Complant)	2007	14,064	14,064	1953	sugarcane
Madagascar	Chengsheng	Ambatondrazaka	Hunan WinMa Resources	2013	7,000	n/a*	2013	cassava
Madagascar	No name	n/a	Hunan Yuan Int'l	2011	6,000	1,000*	2013	rice
Mali	Malibya	Office du Niger	CGCOC/CNHRRDC	2008	100,000	0	n/a	rice
Mali	N'Sukala	Office du Niger	CLETC/Mali govt.	2009	20,000	20,000	2013	sugarcane
Mali	Sukala/Siribala	Office du Niger	CLETC/Mali govt.	1996	3,520	3,520	1962	sugarcane
Mali	Sukala/Dougabougou	Office du Niger	CLETC/Mali govt.	1996	1,654	1,654	1970	sugarcane
Mali	M'Béwani	Office du Niger	COVEC	1998	1,000	1,000	1998	rice
Mali	Farako	Sikasso	Shimen State Farm	1995	500	0	1973	tea
Mauritania	M'Pourié/Zhongnog	Rosso	CSFAC	1999	638	0	1969	rice
Mozambique	Friendship	Xai-Xai	Hubei Lianfeng/Wanbao	2006	20,000	20,000	2007	rice
Mozambique	n/a	Chokwe	Wanbao	2014	6,000	6,000	n/a	rice
Mozambique	Not Chinese	Malanga	Luambala Jatropha	2008	8,789	0	n/a	not Chinese
Mozambique	n/a	Inhambane	Hao Shengli	200	2,024	2,024	n/a	stevia, mix
Mozambique	Sunway	Nampula	Rizhao Sunway	2010	500	500	n/a	oilseeds
Mozambique	Lianhe	Sofala	Hubei Hefeng Grain & Oil	2012	2,000	2,000	2013	rice, cotton
Nigeria	Green West Africa	Kebbi state	CGC/LPHT	2006	2,025	2,025	2008	rice seed
Nigeria	n/a	Kwara state	ZJS International	2008	5,000	0	n/a	not Chinese
Nigeria	n/a	Ondo state	Wems Agro	2014	25,000	0	n/a	not Chinese
Senegal	n/a	Dakar area	Datong	2008	60,000	0	n/a	sesame
Sierra Leone	n/a	Tonkolili	Hainan Rubber	2012	135,000	0	n/a	rubber, rice
Sierra Leone	Magbass	Tonkolili	Complant	2003	8,100	1,845	1974	sugarcane

Country	Farm Name	Reported Location	Reported Chinese Investors	Reported in Year	Largest Reported Size (ha)	Actual Land Acquired (ha)	Year Cultivation Began, if known	Planned Crops
Sudan	n/a	Merowe	ZTE Energy	2009	10,000	60	n/a	mixed
Sudan	None	Al-Rahad Scheme	Shandong IETC/H. Shuofeng	2012	6,667	1,667	2013	cotton
Tanzania	Rudewa & Kisangata	Morogoro	CSFAC/CAAIC	2000	6,900	6,900	1930s	sisal
Togo	Sucriere d'Anié	Anié	Complant	1987	1,700	1,700	1987	sugar
Uganda	Hebei Hanhe	n/a	Qiu Lijun [Hebei Hanhe Ag. Inv. Co.]	2010	41,000	160	2010	mushrooms
Uganda	n/a	n/a	Liu Jianjun [Baoding]	2009	4,000	0	n/a	mixed
Zambia	n/a	Nakonda, Isoka	Wuhan Kaidi	2009	2,000,000	0	n/a	biofuel
Zambia	Zhongken Estates	Chisamba	CSFAC/CAAIC	1993	4,100	3,573	1994	mixed
Zambia	Zhongken Friendship	Kitwe	CSFAC	1999	2,600	2,600	1999	mixed
Zambia	Zhonghua	n/a	Jiangsu SFAC	1999	1,400	1,400	1999	mixed
Zambia	Ch-Zam Friendship	Lusaka area	CSFAC	1990	667	667	1990	mixed
Zambia	China Harvest	Ndola area	China Yong Group	2009	612	612	n/a	mixed
Zimbabwe	Nuanetsi Ranch	Masvingo Prov.	China Intl. Water, Elec. Corp.	2003	100,000	0	2005	maize
Zimbabwe	Zim-China Wanjin Ag.	Chinhoyi, other	Anhui SFAC	2010	50,000	10,000	2011	wheat, soy
Zimbabwe	Wanjin Tianrui	Chinhoyi	Anhui Tianrui Env. Tech.	2014	5,000	3,228	2014	maize
Zimbabwe	Grey Monkey Farm	n/a	Hubei Liangfeng (JV)	2012	685	685	2013	tobacco
				Totals	6,001,074	239,365		

Note: Includes only cultivation (farming) projects, not forestry, animal husbandry or aquaculture. According to Chinese sources, at the end of 2013, the stock of Chinese investment in cultivation projects in Africa came to $540 million. (Ministry of Agriculture, International Cooperation Service Center and Foreign Economic Cooperation Center, eds. Zhongguo duiwai nongye touzi hezuo baogao 2014 [Report on China's Agricultural Foreign Investment Cooperation 2014], Beijing: China Agriculture Press, 2014.)
* Company also has contract farming arrangements that involve farmers on their own land. This is not leased.
Sources for this table and further information available at sais-cari.org.

African Agricultural Exports to China, 2004–2013

	2004	2005	2006	2007	2008	2009	2010	2011	2012	2013
Nuts						KEN (6)				ZWE (6)
Citrus		ZAF*** (7)					ZAF (6)	ZAF (34)	ZAF (23)	ZAF (52)
Grapes									ZAF (37)	ZAF (30)
Tea								KEN (6)		
Groundnuts										SEN (5)
Sesame and castor seeds		ETH (67) TZA (14)	MLI (7) MOZ (5) ETH (110) TZA (9)	MOZ (10) ETH (65) TZA (10)	MLI (6) MOZ (25) ETH (57) TZA (12)	NGA (7) UGA (8) MLI (11) MOZ (37) ETH (118) TZA (38)	NGA (8) TGO (5) UGA (12) MLI (22) MOZ (24) ETH (233) TZA (48)	NGA (19) TGO (12) UGA (15) MLI (32) MOZ (24) ETH (223) TZA (63)	NER (5) SDN (32) TGO (23) UGA (11) MLI (48) MOZ (33) ETH (253) TZA (85)	SOM (16) NER (14) SDN (115) TGO (69) UGA (30) MLI (29) MOZ (47) ETH (258) TZA (115)
Pharmaceutical, cosmetics, insecticidal, etc.*							GHA (14)	GHA (8)		
Groundnut oil										
Sugar		ZAF (6)	ZAF (10)	SEN (10)		SEN (28) ZAF (11)	SEN (31)	SEN (36)	SEN (19)	
Cocoa	GHA (16)	CIV (15) GHA (27)	CIV (13) GHA (24)	TGO (6) CIV (13) GHA (25)	CIV (30) GHA (71)	TGO (6) CIV (11) GHA (24)	TGO (9) CIV (13) GHA (37)	TGO (20) CIV (20) GHA (63)	TGO (5) CIV (10) GHA (38)	CMR (6) CIV (23) GHA (65)
Peaches and nectarines					ZAF (6)	ZAF (5)	ZAF (7)	ZAF (8)	ZAF (12)	ZAF (14)
Wine						ZAF (5)	ZAF (9)	ZAF (20)	ZAF (22)	ZAF (22)

Product	Source	1	2	3	4	5	6	7	8	9	10
Oil cake extraction waste/residue**	ETH							5			
	SDN										11
Tobacco	ZWE	117	126	94	91	119	94	111	281	369	490
	ETH										9
Animal hides	ZAF			13	34	39	61	115	97	82	131
Wool	ZAF			24	54	66	93	88	119	171	186
	LSO										8
Cotton	GHA	8		5							
	NGA			6						7	7
	UGA	9	12	7							
	CAF									13	5
	ZAF								8	14	
	SDN										44
	MWI							10	24	28	14
	MOZ		6	10					15	6	18
	TCD	25	20	30	7	8			12	24	
	TGO	43	26	15	12			8	6	21	15
	TZA	8	37	37			6	12	35	32	44
	SEN		6	7	10		6	10	11	12	10
	ZWE	18	16	14	13	9		14	69	63	58
	ZMB	22	31	39	8	10	7	8	46	64	37
	MLI	107	79	107	32	56	24	44	106	260	106
	CMR	55	43	89	57	38	41	64	90	173	132
	CIV	92	63	40	15	18	19	37	51	81	63
	BFA	123	163	193	155	62	15	117	176	231	187
	BEN	109	126	82	81	82	69	55	65	141	84

* Likely *Griffonia simplicifolia* seeds, *Fadogia agrestis* seeds, or *Fadogia agrestic* bark, all used in pharmaceuticals.

** Groundnut, rape seed, or cola oil extraction waste/residue for animal fodder.

*** Table applies United Nations ISO ALPHA-3 country codes: Benin (BEN), Burkina Faso (BFA), Cameroon (CMR), Central African Republic (CAF), Chad (TCD), Cote d'Ivoire (CIV), Ethiopia (ETH), Ghana (GHA), Kenya (KEN), Lesotho (LSO), Malawi (MWI), Mali (MLI), Mozambique (MOZ), Niger (NER), Nigeria (NGA), Senegal (SEN), Somalia (SOM), South Africa (ZAF), Sudan (SDN), Tanzania (TZA), Togo (TGO), Uganda (UGA), Zambia (ZMB), Zimbabwe (ZWE).

Source: United Nations Comtrade Database, 2015, retrieved February 24, 2015.

Chinese Agro-technology Demonstration Centers in Africa, 2006–2014

Country	Chinese Company or Institute	Province/ Municipality
Angola	Xinjiang Beixin Road & Bridge Group Co.	Xinjiang
Benin	China National Agricultural Development Co.	National
Cameroon	Shaanxi Nongken & Shaanxi Overseas Inv. & Dev. Co.	Shaanxi
Central African Republic	Shanxi Int'l. Ec. & Tech. Coop. Co.	Shanxi
Congo (Brazzaville)	Chinese Academy of Tropical Agricultural Sciences	Hainan
Congo (DRC)	ZTE Energy	National
Côte d'Ivoire	TBD	TBD
Equatorial Guinea	Jiangxi Ganlian Industrial Co.	Jiangxi
Eritrea	TBD	TBD
Ethiopia	Bagui Agricultural Tech Co.	Guangxi
Liberia	Yuan Longping High-Tech Co.	Hunan
Madagascar	Hunan Academy of Agricultural Sciences	Hunan
Malawi	Ruichang Cotton Industry	Shandong
Mali	Redbud Textile Technology Company	Jiangsu
Mauritania	Mudanjiang Yanlin Zhuangyuan Sci. & Tech. Co.	Heilongjiang
Mozambique	Hubei Lianfeng Overseas Ag. Dev. Co.	Hubei
Rwanda	Fujian Agriculture and Forestry University	Fujian
South Africa	China National Agricultural Development Co.	National
Sudan	Shandong Academy of Ag. Sci. and Shandong Int'l Ec. & Tech. Coop. Group	Shandong
Tanzania	Chongqing Academy of Ag. Sci. & Zhongyi Seed Co.	Chongqing
Togo	Jiangxi Huachang Infrastructure Engineering Co.	Jiangxi
Uganda	Huaqiao Fenghuang Group (Fisheries)	Sichuan
Zambia	Jilin Agricultural University	Jilin
Zimbabwe	Chinese Academy of Agricultural Mechanization Sciences	National

Sources: Tang Xiaoyang, "Zhongguo Dui Feizhou Nongye Yuanzhu Xingshi De Yanbian Jiqi Xiaoguo" [The transformation and effects of Chinese agricultural aid to Africa], *Shijie Jingji Yu Zhengzhi*, May 2013, pp.4–18; and Deborah A. Bräutigam and Tang Xiaoyang, "China's Engagement in African Agriculture: 'Down to the Countryside,'" *China Quarterly*, September 2009, pp. 686–706.

NOTES

INTRODUCTION

1. Mthuli Ncube, "The Expansion of Chinese Influence in Africa—Opportunities and Risks," *Inclusive Growth* (blog), African Development Bank, August 14, 2012, http://www.afdb.org/en/blogs/afdb-championing-inclusive-growth-across-africa/post/the-expansion-of-chinese-influence-in-africa-opportunities-and-risks-9612/.

2. The quotations in this paragraph, in order, are from Stephen Leahy, "Agriculture: Foreigners Lead Global Land Rush," Inter Press Service, May 5, 2009, http://www.ipsnews.net/2009/05/agriculture-foreigners-lead-global-land-rush/; Barry Sautman and Hairong Yan, "Chinese Farms in Zambia: From Socialist to 'Agro-Imperialist' Engagement?," *African and Asian Studies* 9, no. 3 (2010): 322, citing "Between Bin Laden and Zambia: The Result of Land Privatization," Land News, July 22, 2009; Robert O'Brien, "China's Africa Play," CBS News, January 18, 2010, http://www.cbsnews.com/news/chinas-africa-play/; Andrew Malone, "How China's Taking over Africa, and Why the West Should Be VERY Worried," *Daily Mail*, July 18, 2008, http://www.dailymail.co.uk/news/article-1036105/How-Chinas-taking-Africa-West-VERY-worried.html; Howard W. French, "The Next Empire," *Atlantic*, May 2010, http://www.theatlantic.com/magazine/archive/2010/05/the-next-empire/308018/; Carl Rubinstein, "China's Eye on African Agriculture," *Asia Times*, October 2, 2009, http://www.atimes.com/atimes/China_Business/KJ02Cb01.html. One hectare equals 2.47 acres.

3. The quotations in this paragraph are from "China's Engagement in African Countries: A Rockefeller Foundation Exploration," New York, Rockefeller Foundation, 2009, http://www.issuelab.org/click/download1/chinas_engagement_with_african_countries_key_findings_and_recommendations; Henning Mankell, "A la différence de l'Afrique, l'Europe est devenue un continent de bavards" *Le Nouvel Observateur* May 7, 2013, http://bibliobs.nouvelobs.com/actualites/20130523.OBS0465/henning-mankell-a-la-difference-de-l-afrique-l-europe-est-devenue-un-continent-de-bavards.html; Camille Saiah, "Le plaidoyer du syndicat béninois Synergie Paysanne sur les questions foncières," 2013, http://dumas.ccsd.cnrs.fr/dumas-00948184/document, citing an interview with Simon Bodéa, secretary general of SYMPA (Synergie Paysanne) of Benin, at the UN Conference on Sustainable Development, Rio+20, Brazil, June 12, 2012, http://www.wat.tv/video/agrobusiness-met-sous-pression-1o5f0_2h1z5_.html.

4. These two paragraphs' quotations are from "Cornering Foreign Fields: Land Deals in Africa and Asia," *Economist*, May 21, 2009; P. Fandio, "Razzia chinoise sur terres camerounaises," ARTE, September 12, 2009, http://www.arte.tv/fr/razzia-chinoise-sur-terres-camerounaises/2837674,CmC=2837676.html; "Ce qui me révolte, par Henning Mankell," *Le Nouvel Observateur*, January 8, 2008, http://bibliobs.nouvelobs.com/romans/20080108.BIB0580/ce-qui-me-revolte-par-henning-mankell.html; Jay MacDonald, "Interview with Henning Mankell," Bookpage.com, March 2010, http://bookpage.com/interviews/

8567-henning-mankell#.VKAvaF4AA; Howard W. French, *China's Second Continent: How a Million Migrants Are Building a New Empire in Africa* (New York: Knopf, 2014), p. 172.

5. The data on China-Africa food trade is from the UN's Commodity Trade Database, http://comtrade.un.org/data/, accessed March 2, 2015, summarized in appendix 2.

6. GRAIN, "Seized: The 2008 Land Grab for Food and Financial Security," GRAIN Briefing, Barcelona, October 24, 2008, http://www.grain.org/article/entries/93-seized-the-2008-landgrab-for-food-and-financial-security.pdf.

7. "Germany Blames Chinese Land Buys for Africa Drought," Agence France-Presse newswire (AFP), July 28, 2011. The original German story was "Hungersnot in Afrika: Das ist auch menschengemacht," *Frankfurter Rundschau*, July 28, 2011, http://www.fr-online.de/politik/hungersnot-in-afrika--das-ist-auch-menschengemacht-,1472596,8719210.html.

8. Paul Ehrlich, *The Population Bomb* (New York: Ballantine Books, 1968), p. xi.

9. Lester Brown, *Who Will Feed China?* (New York: W. W. Norton, 1995), p. 32.

10. Robert Paarlberg, review of *Who Will Feed China?*, by Lester Brown, *Foreign Affairs* 75, no. 3 (May/June 1996), p. 127.

11. Richard McGregor, "Foreign Investors Eye Chinese Farming," *FT*, September 30, 2003.

12. Bryan Lohmar, Fred Gale, Francis Tuan, and Jim Hansen, "China's Ongoing Agricultural Modernization," USDA, Economic Information Bulletin No. 51, April 2009, p. 34. This book will use "maize" and "corn" interchangeably, with a preference for maize.

13. Shenggen Fan, "Toward Food Secure China," *China Daily*, January 21, 2014.

14. See, for example, "China to Maintain High Grain Output in 2014–2023," *China Daily*, April 21, 2014; "GM Food Faces Hurdle of Fears," *China Daily*, October 27, 2014.

15. "Feeding 1.36 billion People: Daily Bread," *Economist*, October 26, 2013.

16. Jikun Huang, "China's Food Supply: Enough for Everyone," *China Economic Quarterly*, September 2014, pp. 20–23.

17. Gbemisola Oseni, Kevin McGee, and Andrew Dabalen, "Can Agricultural Households Farm Their Way out of Poverty?" (Policy Research Working Paper 7093, World Bank Development Research Group, Poverty and Inequality Team, Washington, DC, Nov. 2014), http://documents.worldbank.org/curated/en/2014/11/20356662/can-agricultural-households-farm-way-out-poverty.

18. Huang, "China's Food Supply."

19. Steve Wiggins and Sharada Keats, "The End of Cheap Rice: A Cause for Celebration?," Overseas Development Institute, ODI Briefing 83, London, August 2013, http://www.odi.org/sites/odi.org.uk/files/odi-assets/publications-opinion-files/8516.pdf.

20. Deborah Brautigam, *Chinese Aid and African Development: Exporting Green Revolution* (New York: St. Martin's Press, 1989).

21. Solange Guo Chatelard and Jessica M. Chu, "Chinese Agricultural Engagement in Zambia: A Grassroots Analysis," SAIS-CARI Policy Brief No. 4/2015, Washington, DC: Johns Hopkins University, SAIS-CARI, January 2015.

22. Political scientist James Scott described this well in his book *Seeing Like a State: How Certain Schemes to Improve the Human Condition Have Failed* (New Haven, CT: Yale University Press, 1998).

23. Hem Socheth, "Foreign Investment in Agriculture in Cambodia: A Survey of Recent Trends," International Institute for Sustainable Development, TKN Report December 2012, http://www.iisd.org/sites/default/files/pdf/foreign_investment_ag_cambodia.pdf.

CHAPTER 1

1. All quotations in this section are taken from Henning Mankell, *The Man from Beijing* (New York: Knopf, 2010), English translation. Originally published in Swedish as *Kinesen* (Stockholm: Leopard Förlag, 2008).

2. Loro Horta, "China, Mozambique: Old Friends, New Business," International Relations and Security Network (ISN), Zurich, Switzerland, August 13, 2007, http://www.isn.ethz.ch/Digital-Library/Articles/Detail/?lng=en&id=53470.

3. Loro Horta, "The Zambezi Valley: China's First Agricultural Colony?," Center for Strategic and International Studies, Washington, DC, May 20, 2008, http://csis.org/publication/zambezi-valley-chinas-first-agricultural-colony.

4. Emphasis added.

5. Joachim von Braun and Ruth Meinzen-Dick, " 'Land Grabbing' by Foreign Investors in Developing Countries: Risks and Opportunities," IFPRI Policy Brief 13, Washington, DC, April 2009.

6. Matthias Görgen, Bettina Rudloff, Johannes Simons, Alfons Üllenberg, Susanne Väth, and Lena Wimmer, *Foreign Direct Investment (FDI) in Land in Developing Countries*, (Eschborn, Germany: Deutsche Gesellschaft für Technische Zusammenarbeit [GTZ], December 2009). The GTZ is now known as the GIZ (Gesellschaft für Internationale Zusammenarbeit).

7. Todd Amani, "Mozambique: China's Rice Basket?," Wikileaks cable, August 30, 2008, https://www.wikileaks.org/plusd/cables/08MAPUTO784_a.html.

8. Lorenzo Cotula, Sonja Vermeulen, Rebeca Leonard, and James Keeley, *Land Grab or Development Opportunity? Agricultural Investment and International Land Deals In Africa*, (London/Rome: IIED/FAO/IFAD, 2009), p. 55.

9. International Rice Research Institute, "Rice in Mozambique," Los Baños, Philippines, http://irri.org/our-work/locations/mozambique, retrieved June 12, 2015 (emphasis added).

10. Unless otherwise stated, all FAO statistics in this book were retrieved from FAOSTAT, http://faostat3.fao.org/home/E between January and June 2015.

11. Simon Freemantle and Jeremy Stevens, "List of Products Enjoying Zero-Tariff Treatment for African Least Developed Country (LDC) Exports to China," Standard Bank, April 7, 2010. By 2013, the duty-free product list would swell to 7,831 products, and rice would still be excluded. "Haiguan zongshu gonggao 2013 nian di 34 hao" [General Administration of Customs of the PRC, 2014 Announcement 2014, No. 34], General Administration of Customs of the PRC, June 28, 2013, http://www3.customs.gov.cn/publish/portal0/tab399/info436004.htm.

12. While researching *The Dragon's Gift*, I e-mailed the author, who was unable to provide any sources in support of the tale. Loro Horta, e-mail message to author, September 10, 2009.

13. Otto Roesch, "Migrant Labour and Forced Rice Production in Southern Mozambique: The Colonial Peasantry of the Lower Limpopo Valley," *Journal of Southern African Studies*, 17, no. 2 (June 1991), pp. 239–270. See also Ana Sofia Ganho, "'Friendship' Rice, Business, or 'Land-grabbing'? The Hubei-Gaza Rice Project in Xai-Xai" (Working Paper 32, Land Deal Politics Initiative, International Institute of Social Studies, The Hague, Netherlands, 2013).

14. Alessandro Alasia, Francesco Goletti, Tim Purcell, Paulo Mole, Celestina Jochua, Stuart Higgins, Bui Thi Kim Khanh, and Mario Souto, "Development Strategy for the Rice Sector in Mozambique," Draft Final Report, Agrifood Consulting International for Cooperazione Italiana, Maputo, Mozambique, September 8, 2005, emphasis added.

15. Republic of Mozambique, "Plano de acção para a produção de alimentos 2008–2011," Maputo, June 11, 2008, http://fsg.afre.msu.edu/mozambique/caadp/MINAG_PAPA_FoodCommoditiesStrategicPlan2008.pdf.

16. "Chinese, Mozambican Presidents Vow To Further Relations," Xinhua, September 15, 2005.

17. "Mosangbike nongye ziyuan, nongye zhengce he xiyin waizi de youhui zhengce" [Mozambique's agricultural resources, agricultural policies, and incentives to attract foreign investment], MOFCOM (Ministry of Commerce, People's Republic of China), March 28, 2006 (translation by author), http://mz.mofcom.gov.cn/aarticle/wtojiben/wtojieshao/200603/20060301771650.html, accessed October 10, 2014. The document is no longer on the original website, but a version can be found here at http://www.agri.cn/V20/ZX/sjny/201312/t20131225_3724106.htm.

18. Ibid.

19. Interview, Maputo, June 17, 2009. See also "Company Set up in Mozambique to Attract Chinese Investment," Macauhub, April 17, 2006, http://www.macauhub.com.mo/en/2006/04/17/865/.

20. Deborah Brautigam and Sigrid-Marianella Stensrud Ekman, "Rumours and Realities of Chinese Agricultural Engagement in Mozambique," *African Affairs* 111, no. 444 (July 2012).

21. The wording is from Joseph Hanlon, "Land Moves up the Political Agenda," Mozambique Political Process Bulletin 48, February 22, 2011, citing Sigrid-Marianella Stensrud Ekman, "Leasing Land Overseas: A Viable Strategy for Chinese Food Security?" (MA thesis, Fudan University, Shanghai, 2010).

22. Ana Cristina Alves, "Chinese Banking Interests in Mozambique," South Africa Institute of International Affairs, China in Africa Project, Policy Briefing 37, November 2011, pp. 2–3. All quotations in this paragraph are from this source. See also "Company Set Up in Mozambique to Attract Chinese Investment," Macauhub, April 17, 2006, http://www. macauhub.com.mo/en/2006/04/17/865/; and "Geocapital Focus on the Development of the Zambezi Valley in Mozambique," *AgroNotícias*, December 10, 2005. There had been similar rumors about Chinese settlers associated with Geocapital's efforts to invest in Angola, Alves noted. Ana Cristina Alves, e-mail message to author, October 19, 2014.

23. Interview, Maputo, November 19, 2014.

24. Sérgio Chichava, "Chinese Rice Farming in Xai-Xai: A Case of Mozambican Agency?," in *China and Mozambique: From Comrades to Capitalists*, ed. Chris Alden and Sérgio Chichava (Aukland Park, South Africa: Fanele, 2014), pp. 140–141. I very much appreciate the assistance from Dr. Chichava, who confirmed the dates of this investment story in a meeting with Momade Valá, agricultural provincial director in Zambezia province, 2006–2011. Sérgio Chichava, e-mail message to author, February 27, 2015.

25. Joseph Hanlon, "Understanding Land Investment Deals in Africa: Country Report Mozambique," Oakland Institute, 2011, http://www.oaklandinstitute.org/sites/oaklandinstitute.org/files/OI_country_report_mozambique_0.pdf.

26. Wu Juan, "Zhongguo ren Feizhou chuangye: Mosangbike zhong di, zai wan yu gongli wai de Feizhou" [Chinese entrepreneurs in Africa: Farming in Mozambique, thousands of kilometers away], June 15, 2007, *Changjiang Ribao* [Yangtze River Daily News], reposted at http://news.sina.com.cn/o/2007-06-15/063512026411s.shtml, (translation by author and Hanning Bi).

27. Zhang Yu, "Zhongguo Nongken haiwai tuohuang" [China State Farm Agribusiness Corporation overseas pioneer farming], *Oriental Outlook*, June 12, 2008 http://www. lwdf.cn/oriental/business/20080612144232666.htm, (translation by author and Hanning Bi).

28. Wu, "Zhongguo ren Feizhou chuangye" [Chinese entrepreneurs in Africa].

CHAPTER 2

1. Xiaogang Ren, "Gengyun zai Kamailong de tudi shang: Shaanxi nongken shishi 'zou-chuqu' zhanlue jishi" [Plow the land in Cameroon—Shaanxi Nongken's going out strategy] (blog), *China Value*, January 24, 2007, http://www.chinavalue.net/General/Blog/2007-1-24/4044.aspx. Shaanxi State Farm Agribusiness Corporation (SSFAC) is known as "Shaanxi Nongken" in China.

2. Zilin Zhang, "Now Is the Best Time to Invest in Africa," *China Economic Herald*, June 18, 2010, http://www.focac.org/eng/mtsy/t712495.htm. The second quotation is also from this source.

3. Mark W. Rosegrant, Jawoo Koo, Nicola Cenacchi, Claudia Ringler, Richard Robertson, Myles Fisher, Cindy Cox, Karen Garrett, Nicostrato D. Perez, and Pascale Sabbagh, *Food Security in a World of Natural Resource Scarcity: The Role of Agricultural Technologies* (Washington, DC: IFPRI, 2014).

4. Lester Brown, *Plan B 2.0: Rescuing a Planet under Stress and a Civilization in Trouble* (New York/London: W. W. Norton, 2003). A kilo is 2.2 pounds.

5. Klaus von Grebmer, Derek Headey, Tolulope Olofinbiyi, Doris Wiesmann, Heidi Fritschel, Sandra Yin, Yisehac Yohannes, Connell Foley, Constanze von Oppeln, Bettina Iseli, Christophe Béné, and Lawrence Haddad, *2013 Global Hunger Index—The Challenge of Hunger: Building Resilience to Achieve Food and Nutrition Security* (Bonn/Washington, DC/Dublin: IFPRI, Concern Worldwide, Welthungerhilfe, and Institute of Development Studies, October 2013).

6. UN Millennium Project, *Halving Hunger: It Can Be Done*, Task Force on Hunger (London: Earthscan, 2005), p. 10.

7. Liz Alden Wily, "Enclosure Revisited: Putting the Global Land Rush in Historical Perspective," in *Handbook of Land and Water Grabs in Africa: Foreign Direct Investment and Food and Water Security*, ed. T. Allen, M. Keulertz, S. Sojamo, and J. Warner (London: Routledge, 2013), p. 17.

8. Mark Overton, "Agricultural Revolution in England 1500–1850," BBC History, February 17, 2011, http://www.bbc.co.uk/history/british/empire_seapower/agricultural_revolution_01.shtml.

9. See John Wong and Yanjie Huang, "China Food Security and Its Global Implications," *China: An International Journal* 10, no. 1 (March 2012); and Simon Freemantle and Jeremy Stevens, "China's Food Security Challenge: What Role for Africa?," in *Agricultural Development and Food Security in Africa: The Impact of Chinese, Indian and Brazilian Investments*, ed. Fantu Cheru and Renu Modi (London: Zed Books, 2013), p. 175.

10. Ministry of Agriculture, *Agriculture in China* (Beijing: Ministry of Agriculture, People's Republic of China, 2013). Unless otherwise stated, all statistics on Chinese agriculture and rural development in this section are from this source.

11. Duncan Freeman, Jonathan Holslag, and Steffi Weil, "China's Foreign Farming Policy: Can Land Provide Security?" Brussels Institute of Contemporary China Studies, BICCS Asia Paper 3, no. 9 (November 2008), p. 8.

12. Jimin Wang of the Chinese Academy of Agricultural Sciences, quoted in Lucy Hornsby, "China Scythes Grain Self-Sufficiency Policy," *FT*, February 11, 2014.

13. Kerry Brown, ed., *China and the EU in Context: Insights for Business and Investors* (London: Palgrave Macmillan, 2014), p. 262.

14. "Findings from Landesa's Survey of Rural China Published," Landesa, February 6, 2012, http://www.landesa.org/news/6th-china-survey/.

15. Steve Wiggins, "Can the Smallholder Model Deliver Poverty Reduction and Food Security for a Rapidly Growing Population in Africa?," from the Expert Meeting on How to Feed the World in 2050 Forum, FAO, Rome, 2009, p. 5, http://www.fao.org/3/a-ak542e/ak542e17.pdf; Manitra A. Rakotoarisoa, Massimo Iafrate, and Marianna Paschali, *Why Has Africa Become a Net Food Importer?* (Rome: FAO, 2011), p. 66, http://www.fao.org/docrep/015/i2497e/i2497e00.pdf.

16. Hans P. Binswanger-Mkhize, "Challenges and Opportunities for African Agriculture and Food Security: High Food Prices, Climate Change, Population Growth, and HIV and AIDS," from the Expert Meeting on How to Feed the World in 2050, FAO, Rome, 2009, p. 4, http://www.fao.org/3/a-ak542e/ak542e16.pdf.

17. Deborah Potts, "Land Alienation under Colonial and White Settler Governments in Southern Africa: Historical Land 'Grabbing,' " in Allen et al., *Handbook of Land and Water Grabs in Africa*, pp. 34–35.

18. "Kenya: Opening the Highlands," *Time*, October 26, 1959.

19. Niels Hahn, "The Experience of Land Grabbing in Liberia," in Allen et al., *Handbook of Land and Water Grabs in Africa*, p. 75; Martin Lowenkopt, *Politics in Liberia* (Stanford, CA: Hoover Institution Press, 1976).

20. Kenneth F. Kiple and K. C. Ornelas, eds., *The Cambridge World History of Food* (Cambridge: Cambridge University Press, 2000). The story of Lever also draws on Lorenzo Cotula, *The Great African Land Grab? Agricultural Investments and the Global Food*

System (London: Zed Books, 2013), p. 18, and Fred Pearce, *The Land Grabbers: The New Fight Over Who Owns the Earth* (Boston: Beacon Press, 2013).

21. Facts and quotations in this paragraph come from Victoria Bernal, "Colonial Moral Economy and the Discipline of Development: The Gezira Scheme and 'Modern' Sudan," *Cultural Anthropology* 12, no. 4 (1997): 447–479.

22. Alex De Waal, *Famine Crimes: Politics and the Disaster Relief Industry in Africa* (Bloomington: Indiana University Press, 1997).

23. Rakotoarisoa, Iafrate and Paschali, *Why Has Africa Become a Net Food Importer?*

24. Christoph Seiler, "Africa's Challenge in the 21st Century—Food Security," Celsias, September 23, 2013, http://www.celsias.com/article/africas-challenge-21st-century-f ood-security/

25. Rakotoarisoa, Iafrate, and Paschali, *Why Has Africa Become a Net Food Importer?*, p. 7.

26. World Bank, *World Development Report 2008: Agriculture for Development* (Washington, DC: World Bank, 2007), hereafter *WDR 2008*. Unless otherwise stated, all statistics on agriculture in the rest of this chapter are from this report.

27. Rakotoarisoa, Iafrate, and Paschali, *Why Has Africa Become a Net Food Importer?*

28. World Bank, "Missing Food: The Case of Postharvest Grain Losses in Sub-Saharan Africa," Report No. 60371-AFR, Washington DC, 2011, http://siteresources.worldbank. org/INTARD/Resources/MissingFoods10_web.pdf; Dana Gunders, "Wasted: How America Is Losing Up to 40 Percent of Its Food from Farm to Fork to Landfill," Natural Resource Defense Council, Issue Paper 12-06-B, August 2012, http://www.nrdc.org/ food/files/wasted-food-IP.pdf.

29. Rakotoarisoa, Iafrate, and Paschali, *Why Has Africa Become a Net Food Importer?*, p. 66; FAO, *Statistical Yearbook 2012* (Rome: FAO, 2013), p. 56.

30. Ben Barber, "Interview with Shenggen Fan, Global Food Policy Leader," *FrontLines*, USAID, July 2010, p. 2, http://pdf.usaid.gov/pdf_docs/PNADS955.pdf.

31. Josef Schmidhuber, Jelle Bruinsma, and Gerold Boedeker, "Capital Requirements for Agriculture in Developing Countries to 2050," from the Expert Meeting on How to Feed the World in 2050, FAO, Rome, 2009, http://www.fao.org/3/a-ak542e/ak542e09.pdf.

32. ReSAKSS, "Africa: CAADP 10% Expenditure Target," Regional Strategic Analysis and Knowledge Support System, July 2013, http://www.resakss.org/region/africa-wide/ growth-options; Samuel Benin and Bingxin Yu, "Trends in Public Expenditures in Africa," ReSAKSS Issue Note no. 22, November 2013, http://www.resakss.org/sites/default/ files/pdfs/IB22%20-%20ATOR%202012.pdf.

33. Nathan Nunn and Nancy Qian, "The Determinants of Food Aid Provisions to Africa and the Developing World" (NBER Working Paper 16610, 2010).

34. Carl Eicher, "Flashback: Fifty Years of Donor Aid to Agriculture" (revised version of a paper presented at the InWEnt, IFPRI, NEPAD, CTA Conference: Successes in African Agriculture, 2003), p. ii, http://www.ifpri.org/sites/default/files/pubs/events/ conferences/2003/120103/papers/paper16.pdf.

35. Ibid.

36. Independent Evaluation Group, *World Bank Assistance to Agriculture in Sub-Saharan Africa: An IEG Review*" (Washington, DC: World Bank, 2007), https://openknowledge. worldbank.org/handle/10986/6907.

37. Klaus Deininger and Derek Byerlee, "The Rise of Large Farms in Land Abundant Countries: Do They Have a Future?" (Policy Research Working Paper 5588, World Bank, Development Research Group, Agriculture and Rural Development Team, March 2011). Unless otherwise stated, the statistics on large farms come from this source.

38. Ibid.

39. Paul Collier, "The Politics of Hunger: How Illusion and Greed Fan the Food Crisis," *Foreign Affairs* (Nov./Dec. 2008): 71. Others have been sharply critical of this perspective, including Scott, in *Seeing Like a State*.

40. See also Deininger and Byerlee, "The Rise of Large Farms," pp. 19–20, 31–32.

41. Rebecca Smalley, "Plantations, Contract Farming and Commercial Farming Areas in Africa: A Comparative Review," Future Agricultures Consortium (FAC), (FAC Working Paper 15, April 2013), p. 4.

42. Klaus Deininger and Derek Byerlee with Jonathan Lindsay, Andrew Norton, Harris Selod, and Mercedes Stickler, *Rising Global Interest in Farmland: Can It Yield Sustainable and Equitable Benefits?*" (Washington, DC: World Bank, 2011), p. 20. The other examples in this paragraph come from Yujiro Hayami, "Plantation Agriculture," in *Handbook of Agricultural Economics*, ed. P. L. Pingali and R. E. Evenson (North Holland: Elsevier, 2010); IFAD, "Rural Poverty in Mauritius," Rural Poverty Portal, http://www.ruralpovertyportal. org/country/home/tags/mauritius; and Eleni Z. Gabre-Madhin and Steven Haggblade, "Successes in African Agriculture: Result of an Expert Survey," IFPRI, September 2001, http://www.ifpri.org/sites/default/files/publications/syn04_survey.pdf.

43. For discussions of this, see Philip McMichael, "The Land Grab and Corporate Food Regime Restructuring," *Journal of Peasant Studies* 39, no. 3–4, (2012): 681–701; and Kim Burnett and Sophia Murphy, "What Place for International Trade in Food Sovereignty?" *Journal of Peasant Studies* 41, no. 6 (2014): 1065–1084.

44. Andreas Mayer, Anke Schaffartzik, Willi Haas, and Arnulfo Rojas-Sepúlveda, "Patterns of Global Biomass Trade—Implications for Food Sovereignty and Socio-environmental Conflicts," EJOLT Report 20, n. 106 (March 2015), http://www.ejolt.org/wordpress/ wp-content/uploads/2015/03/150312_EJOLT-20-Biomass-FINAL-VERSION.pdf.

45. Adam Robert Green, "Growing Africa's Land," *This Is Africa*, July 2, 2012, http://www. thisisafricaonline.com/News/Growing-Africa-s-land?ct=true.

46. World Bank, *Growing Africa: Unlocking the Potential for Agribusiness* (Washington, DC: World Bank, January 2013).

47. Nathan Childs, Rice Outlook: July 2014," USDA ERS Rice Outlook No. RCS-14G, July 2014, http://www.ers.usda.gov/publications/rcs-rice-outlook/rcs14g.aspx#. U86KbPldVlo.

48. The quote is from Roger J. Swynnerton, *The Swynnerton Report: A Plan to Intensify the Development of African Agriculture in Kenya* (Nairobi: Government Printer, 1954), cited in Wily, "Enclosure Revisited," p. 19 (emphasis added).

49. "Country Profile: Senegal, Property Rights and Resource Governance," US Agency for International Development, http://usaidlandtenure.net/sites/default/files/ country-profiles/full-reports/USAID_Land_Tenure_Senegal_Profile.pdf, retrieved June 15, 2015.

50. Wily, "Enclosure Revisited," p. 14.

51. Unless otherwise stated, this story draws on these sources: GRAIN, "Unpacking a Chinese Company's Land Grab in Cameroon," October 22, 2010, http://farmlandgrab.org/16485; Jacques Bessala Manga, "Production: Le Cameroun abandonne ses sociétés rizicoles," *Le Jour Quotidien* (Cameroon), April 22, 2008, http://www.bonaberi.com/ar,production_ le_cameroun_abandonne_ses_societes_rizicoles,4150.html; "China-Cameroon Cooperation Posts Steady Growth," Xinhua, January 20, 2007; Ren, "Plow the Land in Cameroon"; Jean Bruno Tagne, "Enquête sur la riziculture chinoise à Nanga-Eboko," *Le Jour* (Cameroon), August 13, 2010, http://cameroon-info.net/stories/0,27126,@,enquete-sur- la-riziculture-chinoise-a-nanga-eboko.html; Charles Ngorgang, "Chinese in Cameroon: An Agricultural Misunderstanding," *Vita Società Editoriale S.P.A.*, December 30, 2009, http://www.afronline.org/?p=2908; Mireille Fouda Effa, "Cameroon—Joseph Fa'a Embolo: Emprisonné pour avoir défendu ses terres," Centre Pour l'Environnement et le Développement, May 12, 2012, http://www.nkul-beti-camer.com/ekang-media-press. php?cmd=article&Item=3891&TAB=-1&SUB=0; Mohamadou Houmfa, "Cameroon: Jail Time for Not Ceding Land to the Chinese," Radio Netherlands Worldwide, March 1, 2012, http://www.cameroon-info.net/stories/0,32144,@,cameroon-jail-time-for-not-ceding- land-to-the-chinese.html; Fandio, "Razzia chinoise sur terres camerounaises," Jean-Bruno Tagne and Simon Gouin, "Quand le Cameroun Nourrit la Chine," Politis, October 21, 2010, http://www.politis.fr/Quand-le-Cameroun-nourrit-la-Chine,11909.html.

52. In 2010, when most of these articles were written, rice was selling in China for about US$ 0.43 per kilogram, while in Cameroon, it sold for US$ 0.86 a kilo. FAO, *Rice Market Monitor*, 13, no. 3 (Nov. 2010), p. 30, http://www.fao.org/docrep/013/am016e/ am016e00.pdf.

53. "Rice Imports Rise by 8.9% in Cameroon," Business in Cameroon, December 11, 2013, http://www.businessincameroon.com/trade/1112-4527-rice-imports-rise-by-8-9-in-cameroon; Economist Intelligence Unit, *Cameroon: Country Report,* March 2012, EIU, p. 13.

54. Greenpeace, "Herakles Farms in Cameroon: A Showcase in Bad Palm Oil Production," March 5, 2013, http://www.greenpeace.org/usa/global/usa/planet3/pdfs/forests/heraklescrimefile.pdf.

CHAPTER 3

1. Jan S. Prybyla, "Communist China's Economic Relations with Africa 1960–1964," *Asian Survey,* 4, no. 11 (November 1964): 1135–1143. The figures on per capita income in this paragraph are in purchasing power parity (PPP) in constant 2005 dollars. The data is 1967, the earliest year available for Mali. Source: World Bank, *World Development Indicators 2014.*

2. Thayer Watkins, "The *Office du Niger* and the Scheme to Irrigate the Sahara Desert," San Jose State University, http://www.sjsu.edu/faculty/watkins/officeduniger.htm, retrieved June 11, 2015.

3. Prybyla, "China's Economic Relations with Africa," p. 1137.

4. Ai Ping, "From Proletarian Internationalism to Mutual Development: China's Cooperation with Tanzania, 1965–95," in *Agencies in Foreign Aid: Comparing China, Sweden and the United States in Tanzania,* ed. Goran Hyden and Rwekaza Mukandala (London: Macmillan Press, 1999), pp. 156–201; Deborah Bräutigam and Xiaoyang Tang, "An Overview of Chinese Agricultural and Rural Engagement in Tanzania," IFPRI Discussion Paper 01214, Development Strategy and Governance Division, Washington, DC, October 2012.

5. FAO AQUASTAT "Uganda," FAO, 2014, http://www.fao.org/nr/water/aquastat/countries_regions/uga/index.stm.

6. Carolyne Muyama, "Rice Improves Life in Doho," *New Vision* (Uganda), February 10, 2010.

7. Xingtu Liu et al., "Regional Development, Environmental Change, and Improved Resource Management in the Sanjiang Plain," in *Land Resources of the People's Republic of China,* ed. Kenneth Ruddle and Wu Chuanjun, (Tokyo: United Nations University Press, 1983).

8. Xiuli Xu, Gubo Qi, and Xiaoyun Li, "'Business Borderlands' China's Overseas State Agribusiness," *IDS Bulletin* 45, no. 4 (July 2014).

9. Chenlie Liu, "Modernizing the Great Northern Wilderness," *China Reconstructs* (February 1985): 50–53; The Yufu Zhao quote in this paragraph comes from Keith Schneider, "Scarcity of Water and Land Shifts Geography of Food Production and Irrigation Networks to China's Northeast," *Circle of Blue: Water News,* November 9, 2012, http://www.circleofblue.org/waternews/2012/world/scarcity-of-water-and-land-shifts-geography-of-food-production-to-chinas-northeast/.

10. Japan Foreign Trade Council, *The 21st Century as an Age of Advancement with the Rest of Asia: New Roles for Japanese Trading Firms* (Tokyo: Japan Foreign Trade Council, 2000), http://www.jftc.or.jp/shosha/publish/asia_shosha_e.pdf.

11. "Business News," Associated Press, Tokyo, October 15, 1979. This paragraph draws as well on these sources: Club of Bologna, "Proceedings of the 15th Members' Meeting," Bologna, Italy, November 12–13, 2004, http://www.clubofbologna.org/ew/documents/num-1.pdf; see also "Chinese, Japanese Official Discuss Cooperation," Xinhua, September 5, 1983; "China's State Farms to Use More Foreign Investment," Xinhua, August 8, 1984; Xiuyun Yang, "The Sanjiang Plain," *China Today* 39, no. 4: 68–72; and World Bank and People's Republic of China, "Loan Agreement: Heilongjiang Land Reclamation Project,"

Loan No. 2261-CHA, May 20, 1983, http://www.worldbank.org/projects/P003412/heilongjiang-land-reclamation-project?lang=en.

12. USDA Economic Research Service, "China Agricultural and Economic Data," USDA, July 11, 2012, http://www.ers.usda.gov/data-products/china-agricultural-and-economic-data/national-and-provincial-data.aspx#P3562ed2e41af429e99970a7283ec81a3_3_oHit0.

13. "China's State Farms to Use More Foreign Investment," Xinhua, August 8, 1984.

14. Dennis Woodward, "A New Direction for China's State Farms," *Pacific Affairs* 55, no. 2 (Summer 1982): 231–251.

15. "Fruitful Agricultural Cooperation," China Internet Information Center, December 10, 2003, http://www.china.org.cn/english/features/China-Africa/82040.htm.

16. Fox Butterfield, "Company Ready to Bring Peasants from China to U.S. for Farm Work," *New York Times*, September 25, 1987, p. A1.

17. "China to Encourage Foreign Investment in Agriculture," AFP, May 31, 1998.

18. CP Group's subsidiary in China is generally known as Chia Tai, but for the sake of simplicity we use CP Group throughout. Unless otherwise noted, all information on the CP Group comes from these sources: Peter Janssen, "Grown from Small Seeds," *Asian Business* 30, no. 2 (Feb. 1994); Rajeswary Ampalavanar-Brown, "Overseas Chinese Investments in China—Patterns of Growth, Diversification and Finance: The Case of Charoen Pokphand," *China Quarterly*, 155 (Sept. 1998): p. 627; and Carl Goldstein, "Not Just Chicken Feed," *Far Eastern Economic Review*, October 21, 1993, p. 70.

19. Gwen Robinson and Jake Maxwell Watts, "Meet Dhanin Chearavanont, the Man Who Swooped in on Ping An," *BeyondBRICs* (blog), *FT*, December 6, 2012, http://blogs.ft.com/beyond-brics/2012/12/06/meet-dhanin-chearavanont-the-man-who-swooped-in-on-ping-an/#axzz2n5m3JTlR. Land figure confirmed by Gwen Robinson, e-mail to author, January 8, 2014.

20. Yingqi Wei and Xiaming Liu, *Foreign Direct Investment in China: Determinants and Impact* (Northhampton, MA: Edward Elgar, 2001), p. 28.

21. Yvan Cohen, "Dhinan Chearavanont: The Integrator," *World Business* 3, no. 1 (Jan/Feb 1997): 47–48.

22. "Nichimen to Form Joint Trading Venture in China," *Asian Economic News*, November 16, 1998, http://www.thefreelibrary.com/Nichimen+to+form+joint+trading+venture+in+China.-a053247543.

23. Jinboa Su, "A Study on the Processing and Sale of Rice in the Context of Xinhua State Farm: An Agribusiness Model for Heilongjiang Province," *Journal of Agricultural Development Studies*, 16, no. 1, (1990).

24. "US Giant to Expand Potato Production in China," *China Daily*, February 4, 2002.

25. This paragraph draws on these sources: "Coastal Areas Boost Export-oriented Agriculture," Xinhua, October 27, 1992; Lou Hui, "Analysis of the Use of Overseas Funds," Xinhua, September 25, 1994; "China-Investment-Agriculture: Foreign Investment Welcomed in Agriculture in Liaoning," Xinhua, March 6, 1995; Jeremy Gordon, "Hungry for Investment," *China Business Review*, 24, no. 5, (Sept./Oct.1997): 26–27.

26. "Case Study: Chinese Frozen Vegetable Exports," in *Meeting Standards, Winning Markets Regional Trade Standards Compliance Report East Asia 2013*, UNIDO and IDE-JETRO (Vienna: November 2013), http://www.ide.go.jp/Japanese/Publish/Download/Collabo/pdf/2013UNIDO_IDE11.pdf.

27. AP, "Del Monte Pact," *New York Times*, January 13, 1983.

28. "PepsiCo: Sustainable Agriculture," PepsiCo, http://www.pepsico.com/Purpose/Environmental-Sustainability/Agriculture, June 16, 2015, retrieved June 12, 2015; "PepsiCo to Partner with China's Ministry of Agriculture to Promote Sustainable Farming," PepsiCo press release, September 19, 2011, http://www.pepsico.com/PressRelease/PepsiCo-to-Partner-with-Chinas-Ministry-of-Agriculture-to-Promote-Sustainable-Fa09192011.html.

29. Tina Helsell, "Turning Farmers into Entrepreneurs," *CBR*, 24, no. 5 (Sept./Oct. 1997): 22–27.

30. "Foreign Investment Boosts China's Agricultural Growth," Xinhua, January 5, 1998.

31. "Sino Europe Agricultural Cooperation Centre Opens in Zhangzhou, Fujian," Xiamen, April 14, 2011, http://whatsonxiamen.com/news18514.html. The Dutch sponsored a hog-breeding center in Beijing, the Sino-European Agricultural Development Center in Fujian, the Sino-Dutch Dairy Demonstration and Training Center in Henan, the Agricultural Demonstration Center for New and Advanced Technologies in Tianjin, and the Sino-Dutch Horticultural Training and Demonstration Center outside Shanghai.

32. "Flower Port a Gardener's Paradise," *China Daily*, December 25, 2006.

33. "Introduction of SIDHOC," Sino-Dutch Horticultural Training and Demonstration Center, http://www.sidhoc.com/en/archives/index_en.php/id-intro.html, retrieved June 11, 2015.

34. J. Li and D. Liu, "The Impact of Foreign Capital Merger and Acquisition on China's Agricultural Enterprises Development and the Countermeasures," *Journal of Agricultural Economic Problems*, 11 (2006): 67–69, as summarized in Licai Lv, Simei Wen, and Qiquan Xiong, "Determinants and Performance Index of Foreign Direct Investment in China's Agriculture," *China Agricultural Economic Review* 2, no. 1 (2010): 45.

35. Robert D. Dennis, "The Countertrade Factor in China's Modernization Plan," *Columbia Journal of World Business* 17, no. 1 (1982): 67–75.

36. Department of Foreign Aid, "China's Economic and Trade Relations with African Countries," in *Almanac of China's Foreign Economic Relations and Trade 1988* (Beijing: Ministry of Foreign Economic Relations and Trade, 1988): 73–74; see also Guo Jianquan, "Friendship and Cooperation to Create 'Win-Win'—Mali Sugar Briefing," China Light Industry Group, December 12, 2010. This paragraph also draws on Wei Hong, "Woguo duiwai yuanzhu fangshi gaige de jingyan yu wenti" [Experiences and issues in the reform of China's method of giving foreign aid], *Guoji Jingji Hezuo*, no. 5 (1999).

37. The COVEC story draws on World Bank, "Implementation Completion and Results Report (IDA-3390, 3393a) on an Adaptable Program Loan in the Amount Of SDR 86.7 Million (US$115.1 million equivalent) to the Republic of Mali for a National Rural Infrastructure Project in Support of the First Phase of the National Rural Infrastructure Program," Report no. ICR0000798, World Bank, June 30, 2008, http://www-wds.worldbank.org/external/default/WDSContentServer/WDSP/IB/2008/08/05/00033 3037_20080805234027/Rendered/PDF/ICR7980ICR0P041closed0August0402008. pdf; Djibril Aw and Geert Diemer, *Making a Large Irrigation Scheme Work: A Case Study from Mali* (Washington, DC: World Bank, 2005), p. 84, http://siteresources.worldbank. org/INTARD/Resources/making_a_large_scale_irrigation_system_work_DID.pdf; Moussa Djiré, Amadou Kéita, and Alfousseyni Diawara, *Current Dynamics of Large-Scale Agricultural Investments and Inclusive Business Models in Mali—Trends and Case Studies, Final Report* (IIED/FAO: Bamako, May 2012), p. 20, http://www.fao.org/fileadmin/templates/tci/pdf/InternationalInvestment/IIED/Mali_-_Final_report_-_June_2012. pdf; Chongfang Zhang and Wei wei, "Shamo li jian qi 'yumizhixiang'" ['Land of plenty' built up in the desert], Xinhua, June 27, 2006, http://news.xinhuanet.com/banyt/2007-06/27/content_6296695.htm; and Isaie Dougnon and Lamissa B. Coulibaly, "Institutional Architecture and Pro-Poor Growth in the Office du Niger," Discussion Paper Series, no. 13, Institutions for Pro-Poor Growth (IPPG), School of Environment and Development, University of Manchester, August 2007, http://www.ippg.org.uk/papers/dp13.pdf.

38. The Farako story comes from these sources: "Usine thé de Farako: Trop vetuste pour resister à la concurrence," *L'Essor* (Mali), April 8, 2009; "Jinhua chaye zhuanjia Mali chadao shizhe," [Tea experts from Jinhua are tea missionaries to Mali], *Africa Windows* (blog), August 26, 2007, http://www.africawindows.com/html/feizhouzixun/renzai-feizhou/20070826/11276.shtml.

39. John W. Bruce, "Options for State Farm Divestiture and the Creation of Secure Tenure," report to USAID/Mozambique, Land Tenure Center, December 28, 1989, http://pdf. usaid.gov/pdf_docs/PNABI037.pdf.

40. The farms were Moamba State Farm north of Maputo and Matama State Farm in the Niassa province. "Mosangbike nongye ziyuan, nongye zhengce he xiyin waizi de youhui zhengce" [Mozambique's agricultural resources, agricultural policies and incentives to

attract foreign investment], MOFCOM, Maputo, March 28, 2006, http://mz.mofcom. gov.cn/aarticle/wtojiben/wtojieshao/200603/20060301771650.html, retrieved July 10, 2014; webpage no longer valid. See also Wolfgang Bartke, *The Economic Aid of the PR China to Developing and Socialist Countries*, 2nd ed. (Munich: K. G. Saur, 1989), p. 92. The Chinese also donated farm machinery and sent a team of 26 experts to assist with communal agricultural projects in Maputo's urban "Green Zone" program.

41. This paragraph draws on "China: Li Peng Pledges More Cooperation with Mozambique," Xinhua May 8, 1997; "China: Xinhua 'Roundup' on Sino-Mozambican Economic Ties," Xinhua, March 29, 1998; "Mozambique Wishes to Cooperate with China in Agriculture," Xinhua, March 26, 1999; "Chinese Projects Suitable for Mozambique," Xinhua, April 1, 1999. Emphasis added.

42. Anshan Grain and Oil Export Import Company secured the lease. Sérgio Chichava, "China in Mozambique's Agriculture Sector: Implications and Challenges," Institute of Social and Economic Studies (IESE), Maputo, November 2010, p. 5 http://www. iese.ac.mz/lib/noticias/2010/China%20in%20Mozambique_09.2010_SC.pdf. On the rough start, see "Hezuo jianjie (zhong, mo shuangbian jingmao, jishu hezuo)" [Cooperation Summary (China-Mozambique Bilateral Economic, Trade, and Technical Cooperation)], Commerce and Economic Affairs Bureau, Chinese Embassy in Mozambique, August 1, 2008, http://mz.mofcom.gov.cn/aarticle/zxhz/ hzjj/200203/20020300004293.html.

43. Philippe Asanzi, "Chinese Agricultural Investments in Africa—Interests and Challenges," *China Monitor*, 69, (2012): 4–9.

44. Interview, Chinese economic counselor, Maputo, November 14, 2014.

45. "COFCO Group, China's Largest Food Processer (Company Profile)" ChinaAg, November 11, 2012, http://chinaag.org/2012/11/11/cofco-group-chinas-largest-f ood-processer-company-profile/.

46. "Zhongliang Ning Gaoning: haiwai shougou zu'ai shao wei feizhou zhengzhi bianhua da" [COFCO chairman Ning Gaoning: few impediments for foreign purchases, only that African political landscape is unstable], Ifeng.com (the Internet website of Phoenix satellite television, Hong Kong), January 14, 2013, translation by author and Jyhjong Hwang, http://finance.ifeng.com/hk/sckx/20130114/7554506.shtml.

CHAPTER 4

1. For more details on the "Baoding farmers" story, see Brautigam, *The Dragon's Gift*, pp. 267–270 and 367; see also Susan Ramsay, "China Sees the Continent as an Ideal Source of Raw Materials and Oil—With Farmland Aplenty for Displaced Peasants," *South China Morning Post*, November 25, 2007. The Chongqing story draws on Zhongguo Jinchukou Yinhang, "Chongqing Qing Nonghu ke Qu Feizhou Kai Nongchang," [China Eximbank: Chongqing peasant households may go to Africa to set up farms], September 18, 2007, *Chongqing Ribao* (China); Ramsay, "China Sees the Continent," is the source of the "landlords overseas" quotation. We were unable to find a Chinese language article with this claim. The blog headline is from "China to Dump Its Unemployed Rural Laborers on Africa," *African Agriculture* (blog), September 26, 2007, http://www.africanagriculture-blog.com/search/label/China; website discontinued. The story about the NPC debate can be found at Antoaneta Bezlova, "China: Latest Africa Foray: Altruism or Hegemony?" Inter Press Service, June 9, 2015, http://www.ipsnews.net/2009/11/china-latest-africa-foray-altruism-or-hegemony/.

2. Jamil Anderlini, "China Eyes Overseas Land in Food Push," *FT*, May 8, 2008.

3. This section draws on Duncan Freeman, "China's Outward Investment: Institutions, Constraints and Challenges," *Brussels Institute of Contemporary China Studies, Asia Paper* 7, no. 4 (2013): 22, http://www.vub.ac.be/biccs/site/assets/files/apapers/Asia%20 Paper%207,%204%20-%20Duncan%20Freeman.pdf; and Wenbin Huang and Andreas

Wilkes, "Analysis of China's Overseas Investment Policies," (Bogor, Indonesia: CIFOR Working Paper 79, 2011).

4. Deborah Brautigam, "Doing Well by Doing Good," *CBR* 10, no. 5 (1983): 57–58.

5. Figures in this and the following sentence are from: "Weisheme yao tigao tongchou liyong guoji guonei liang ge shichang, liang zhong ziyuan nengli?" [Why integrate the use of domestic and international market resources and capabilities?], Xinhua, December 24, 2008, http://news.xinhuanet.com/newscenter/2008-12/24/content_10551287.htm.

6. The Ministry of State Farms and Land Reclamation was merged into China's Ministry of Agriculture in 1982. China National Agricultural Development Corporation was founded in October 2004, merging China National Fisheries (Group) Corporation and China Animal Husbandry Group Corporation and annexing other firms including China National Township & Enterprises Corporation, China Feedstuff Corporation and China State Farms Agribusiness Corporation. CNADC is under the supervision of SASAC (State-owned Assets Supervision and Administration Commission). "Profile of the Corporation," CNADC website, http://www.cnadc.com.cn/English/ProfileCorporation/, retrieved June 6, 2015.

7. Communist Party of China and State Council, "Guanyu zuo hao 2001 nian nongye he nongcun gong zuo de yijian" [Opinion on correctly implementing agricultural and rural work in 2001], *People's Daily*, January 11, 2001 (emphasis added), http://www.people.com.cn/GB/jinji/31/179/20010213/394050.html. The quote in this paragraph is from President Hu Jintao, "Speech at the Central Rural Work Conference," January 8, 2003, http://www.reformdata.org/index.php?m=wap&c=index&a=show&catid=359&typeid=0&id=6347&remains=true (emphasis added).

8. "Africa: Top Option for China's Agricultural Investment," Xinhua, September 28, 2002, http://www.chinagate.cn/english/2925.htm. The quotation in this paragraph is from this source (emphasis added).

9. The two positions can be found in "China Can Feed Its Own People: Official," *China Daily*, May 20, 2004, http://english.peopledaily.com.cn/200405/20/eng20040520_143870.html and "China to Lease Overseas Farmland to Solve Food Problem," Xinhua, May 24, 2004, http://english.peopledaily.com.cn/200405/24/eng20040524_144221.html.

10. "Enhance International Cooperation and Promote Common Development," MOFCOM website, June 3, 2004, http://english.mofcom.gov.cn/aarticle/translatorsgarden/famousspeech/200803/20080305440291.html. On the food security report, see Jiao Jian, "Zhongguo liangshi anquan baogao" [China food security report], *Caijing* (China), December 9, 2013, http://finance.sina.com.cn/china/20131209/090817572042.shtml.

11. People's Republic of China, Ministry of Commerce, Ministry of Foreign Affairs, and National Development and Reform Commission, "Duiwai touzi guo bie chanye daoxiang mulu (1)" [Foreign investment industry guidance country catalog (1)], July 8, 2004, http://www.china.com.cn/chinese/PI-c/626171.htm; "Duiwai touzi guo bie changye daoxiang mulu (2)" [Foreign investment industry guidance country catalog (2)], May 12, 2005, http://www.gddoftec.gov.cn/dept_detail.asp?deptid=1049&channalid=1297&contentid=10644; "Duiwai touzi guo bie changye daoxiang mulu (3)" [Foreign investment industry guidance country catalog (3)], January 31, 2007, http://www.fdi.gov.cn/1800000121_23_60729_0_7.html.

12. Ministry of Finance, "Duiwai jingji jishu hezuo zhuanxiang zijin guanli banfa" [Regulations for management of the special fund for foreign economic and technical cooperation], *Cai Qi*, no. 255, Beijing, December 9, 2005, http://qys.mof.gov.cn/czzxzyzf/201112/t20111206_613354.html. The rest of this paragraph draws on Guoqiang Cheng, "Foreign Agricultural Resource Utilization: Current Status and Problems," *China Economic Times*, January 21, 2014; MOFCOM, Department of Outward Investment and Economic

Cooperation, "Guanyu zuo hao 2012 nian duiwai jingji jishu hezuo zhuanxiang zijin shen-bao gongzuo de tongzhi" [Strengthening economic and technical cooperation in 2012: Notice on special funds requirements] *Cai Qi*, no. 141, Beijing, July 12, 2012; and an interview with an MOA consultant, Beijing, March 5, 2015.

13. For an excellent overview of the FOCAC, see Ian Taylor, *The Forum on China–Africa Cooperation (FOCAC)* (Oxford: Routledge, 2011).

14. "Energy Partnership with Africa Based on Equality," *China Daily*, June 22, 2006.

15. "China Agri Ministry, Development Bank Support Agri Projects," *SinoCast China Business Daily News*, November 22, 2006. As of the end of 2010, the balance of the fund was RMB 19.47 billion, with $420 million left for going global projects; "Nongye bu yu guojia kaifa yinhang qianshu guihua hezuo beiwanglu" [Ministry of Agriculture and the State Development Bank signed a memorandum of cooperation plan], MOA, February 18, 2011, http://www.moa.gov.cn/zwllm/zwdt/201102/t20110218_1821730.htm.

16. Chinese currency figures in this paragraph were converted to dollars at the 2009 exchange rate. Xiaomeng Teng, "Haiwai maizudi zhongliang zhengce jianyi fangan shangbao guowuyuan" [Policy recommendation regarding foreign land purchasing and leasing for crop production presented to the State Council], Sina, May 8, 2008, http://finance.sina.com.cn/roll/20080508/01074842380.shtml. The rest of this paragraph also draws on "Woguo nongye 'zou chuqu' xianzhuang, wenti yu duice" [China's agriculture "going out" situation: problems and countermeasures], *Guoji Jingji Hezuo* (China), March 20, 2009, http://ccn.mofcom.gov.cn/spbg/show.php?id=9007&ids=RMB; Foreign Economic Cooperation Center (FECC), "Zhiyue woguo nongye 'zou chuqu' de buli yinsu ji wei-lai fazhan zhanlüe" [Negative factors restricting our agriculture "going out" strategy and recommendations for the future], MOA, June 26, 2009, www.fecc.moa.gov.cn/dwtz/200803/t20080325_2063805.htm.

17. Zesheng Xia, "Quanmian tuijin zhong fei nongye hezuo zhengfengqishi" [It's the right time for comprehensive promotion of agricultural cooperation between China and Africa], *Guoji Shangbao* (MOFCOM), November 20, 2006.

18. Teng, "Haiwai maizudi" [Foreign land purchasing]; "Woguo nongye 'zou chuqu' xian-zhuang," [China's agriculture "going out" situation].

19. "China to Make Unremitting Efforts to Ensure Grain Security: Report," *China Daily*, October 19, 2008.

20. Anderlini, "China Eyes Overseas Land In Food Push."

21. "The 2nd Chinese Enterprises Outbound Investment Conference: Program (draft)," China Council for the Promotion of International Trade, April 11, 2008, http://english.ccpit.org/Contents/Channel_2094/2007/0704/90064/content_90064.htm, retrieved May 5, 2014; website discontinued.

22. Liu Yinghua, "Nongye bu jianyi qiye haiwai 'zu di zhong liang'" [Department of Agriculture recommends that companies overseas 'rent land to grow grain,'], *Beijing Morning Post*, reposted on Xinhua, April 29, 2008, http://news.xinhuanet.com/overseas/2008-04/29/content_8070829.htm.

23. Liu, "Nongye bu jianyi," [Department of Agriculture recommends].

24. Denis D. Gray, "China Farms the World to Feed A Ravenous Economy," AP, May 4, 2008.

25. Teng, "Haiwai maizudi" [Foreign land purchasing].

26. Anderlini, "China Eyes Overseas Land in Food Push."

27. Rowan Callick, "Chinese Firms Eye Aussie Farmland," *Australian*, May 12, 2008,

28. "Chinese Debate Pros and Cons of Overseas Farming Investments," *Guardian*, May 11, 2008.

29. "China to Deepen Rural Reforms," Xinhua, December 24, 2013.

30. Jiao, "Zhongguo liangshi anquan baogao," [China food security report].

31. "China, Outline of China's Medium- to Long-Term Food Security Plan (2008–2020)," International Poverty Reduction Center of China, Beijing, http://www.iprcc.org/front/article/article.action?id=617, retrieved October 14, 2014.

32. "National Framework for Medium-to-Long-Term Grain Security, 2008–2020," Xinhua, November 11, 2008, http://www.gov.cn/jrzg/2008-11/13/content_1148414.htm.

33. "Wu haiwai tuntian jihua jinhou shiyong you jiagong lingyu zhongfang konggu"[No plans for future overseas farming; edible oil processing areas will be controlled by Chinese], JRJ Finance, November 13, 2008, http://finance.jrj.com.cn/2008/11/1311242754114.shtml.

34. Xiang Li, "No End to Soybean Wars," *China Daily,* April 20, 2009; "Guonei: Fagaiwei: Jinhou shiyong you jiagong lingyu zhongfang konggu" [China: NDRC: China Holdings Future Edible Oil Processing Areas]," *Galaxy Futures,* November 13, 2008, http://yhqh.com.cn/index.php?m=content&c=index&a=show&catid=245&id=51018.

35. Sources for this paragraph: "Guanyu jiakuai tuijin hubei nongye 'zou chuqu' de diaoyan baogao" [Research report on accelerating Hubei agriculture 'going out'], Hubei Province Government Affairs Network, April 28, 2010, http://www.hbzyw.gov.cn/News.aspx?id=10267; "About Us," Wanbao Grains and Oil, http://en.wblyjt.com/comcontent_detail1/&FrontComContent_list01-134211484ContId=e5b9b9e7-f4b5-4279-ab90-94da50605e3a&comContentId=e5b9b9e7-f4b5-4279-ab90-94da50605e3a.html, retrieved June 10, 2015; and Yun Chen and Liping Liao, "Xiamen guli qiye dao feizhou zhong liang" [Xiamen encourages companies to grow food in Africa], China Internet Information Center, April 22, 2014, http://finance.china.com.cn/roll/20140422/2353551.shtml.

36. Ministry of Agriculture and China Eximbank, "Guanyu zhengji liyong Zhongguo jin chukou yinhang daikuan shishi nongye duiwai hezou xiangmu de tongzi" [Solicitation letter about the use of China Eximbank loans to implement foreign agricultural cooperation projects], circulated by Hunan Foreign Economic and Technical Cooperation Center on July 13, 2011, http://www.hnagri.gov.cn/web/gjhzc/tzgg/content_77636.html, retrieved June 16, 2015. See also Li Ruogu, "Zou chuqu zhanlüe de licheng yu fazhan," [The history and development of the 'going out' strategy], *China Finance,* December 1, 2011, http://www.cnfinance.cn/magzi/2011-12/01-14016_3.html; China Eximbank, *Annual Report* 2013, p 32.

37. Ministry of Agriculture and China Eximbank, "Guanyu zhengji liyong Zhongguo jin chukou yinhang daikuan shishi nongye duiwai hezuo xiangmu di han" [Solicitation letter about the use of China Eximbank loans to implement foreign agricultural cooperation projects], *Nongwai Zi,* no. 3 (2014); Ministry of Agriculture, circulated by Taizhou Leading Agricultural Enterprises Association, http://www.tznylt.com/xhgk_189508.htm?aid=278331; China Eximbank, *Annual Report* 2013, p. 32.

38. "Guanyu women" [About us], ZhongFei Nongye Touzi Gongsi [China-Africa Agriculture Investment Company], http://www.caaic.com.cn/Article_List.aspx?columnID=1, retrieved June 10, 2015, Ntandoyenkosi Ncube, "Interview: China-Africa Development Fund to Increase Agriculture Investment in Africa," Xinhua, May 20, 2012. This paragraph also draws on CDB, "$57mn Invested in Agriculture by China-Africa Development Fund," press release, May 31, 2012, http://www.cdb.com.cn/english/NewsInfo.asp?NewsId=4159.

39. Ministry of Finance and Economic Development, "Public Sector Debt Bulletin No. 9," Debt Management Directorate, Federal Democratic Republic of Ethiopia, Addis Ababa, Ethiopia, October 2012; "Aisai tangye gongsi yu guojia kaifa yinhang qianshu daikuan xieyi" [Ethiopia Sugar Corporation and China Eximbank sign loan agreement], MOFCOM, September 28, 2012, http://et.mofcom.gov.cn/article/jmxw/201209/20120908364782.shtml.

40. Golden Agri-Resources Ltd, "Miscellaneous: Banking Facility for Golden Veroleum Limited of USD 500 Million," Singapore Stock Exchange, March 13, 2013.

41. In 2011, China's Agricultural Development Bank provided an RMB 30 billion ($4.7 billion) line of credit to allow COFCO to strengthen its global position. In 2013, CDB added another RMB 30 billion line of credit.

42. Brautigam, *The Dragon's Gift,* pp. 267–270 and p. 367; "The Latest on the Baoding Villages," *MQVU* (blog), Aug. 6, 2009, https://mqvu.wordpress.com/tag/yan-hairong/; "Is *Baoding Cun* a Hoax? Or a 'Cultural Phenomenon?' Have You Heard about the Story of the Baoding Village in Africa?" *MQVU* (blog), Feb. 20, 2010, https://mqvu.wordpress.com/2010/02/20/baoding-villages-again/. A PhD candidate in the Netherlands, Josh Maiyo, reported on his efforts to track down a reported (but nonexistent) Baoding investment in

Uganda: "The Political Ecology of Chinese Agricultural Investment in Uganda: The Case of Hanhe Farm," SAIS-CARI Policy Brief No. 1/2014, Washington, DC: Johns Hopkins University School of Advanced International Studies, CARI, October 2014. For a good example of how this story continued to re-emerge, see Clifford Coonan, "China's New Export: Farmers," *Independent*, February 19, 2010. Coonan did not go to Africa to report this story.

43. The original story in the Chinese media can be found at Bin Liu, "Renda daibiao: guojia ying zhichi bai wan nongmin dao feizhou chuangye" [NPC representative: The country should support one million farmers to start ventures in Africa], *Yanzhao Dushibao*, reposted at Wangyi Caijing, March 12, 2009, http://money.163.com/09/0312/10/546SKEFC002537HU. html. See also Deborah Brautigam and Xiaoyang Tang, "An Overview of Chinese Agricultural and Rural Engagement in Ethiopia," IFPRI Discussion Paper 01185, May 2012, p. 12, http://www.ifpri.org/sites/default/files/publications/ifpridp01185.pdf.

44. Chao Wang, "Haiwai zhong liang xu raoguo 'di er dai zhimin zhuyi' menkan" [Overseas grain required to bypass the 'second generation colonialism' obstacle], Sina, May 11, 2011, http://finance.sina.com.cn/roll/20110511/19589826788.shtml; see also Mandy Zuo, "Farm Overseas to Help Nation, Companies Told," *South China Morning Post*, September 7, 2011.

45. Jay Si and Joseph D. Weinstein, "New NDRC Regulatory Measures on Outbound Investment Effective May 8, 2014," Davis Wright Tremaine LLP, May 22, 2014, http://www.dwt.com/New-NDRC-Regulatory-Measures-on-Outbound-Investment-Effective-May-8-2014-05-22-2014/#_ftn4n.

46. Chunfang Sun, "Nongcun gongzuo huiyi ding diao nongye xiandaihua lujing: liangshi anquan weishou wu" [Rural Work Conference establishes the path toward agricultural modernization: Food security is priority], Sina, reposting from *21st Century Business Herald* (China), December 24, 2014, http://finance.sina.com.cn/china/20141224/014621148668.shtml.

47. See, for example, Guoqiang Cheng, "Woguo jingwai nongye ziyuan liyong xianzhuang yu wenti" [Our country's foreign agricultural resource utilization: Current situation and problems], *China Economic Times*, January 21, 2014, http://jjsb.cet.com.cn/show_173908. html.

48. Xuedong Ding, "China Will Profit from Feeding the World's Appetite," *FT*, June 17, 2014.

CHAPTER 5

1. William Ide, "China Supports Global Pariahs, Gets Resources and Criticism in Return," Voice of America, June 27, 2011, http://www.voanews.com/content/china-supports-global-pariahs-gets-resources-and-criticism-in-return-124648814/141455.html.

2. D. Gray, "China Farms the World to Feed a Ravenous Economy," AP, May 4, 2008.

3. "Buying Farmland Abroad: Outsourcing's Third Wave," *Economist*, May 21, 2009; Olivier De Schutter, "Report of the Special Rapporteur on the Right to Food," A/HRC/13/33/Add.2, Human Rights Council, UN General Assembly, December 28, 2009; Stephen Leahy, "Agriculture: Foreigners Lead Global Land Rush," Inter Press Service, May 5, 2009, http://www.ipsnews.net/news.asp?idnews=46724; Lester Brown, *Plan B 4.0: Mobilizing to Save Civilization* (New York: W. W. Norton, 2009), p. 9; Saskia Sassen, "Land Grabs Today: Feeding the Disassembling of National Territory," *Globalizations* 10, no. 1 (2013): 25–46.

4. "Senegal's Wade Reaffirms Support for Chinese Investor," Xinhua, July 23, 2008.

5. Mthuli Ncube, "The Expansion of Chinese Influence in Africa—Opportunities and Risks," *Inclusive Growth* (blog), African Development Bank, August 14, 2012, http://www.afdb.org/en/blogs/afdb-championing-inclusive-growth-across-africa/post/the-expansion-of-chinese-influence-in-africa-opportunities-and-risks-9612/.

6. Ward Anseeuw, Mathieu Boche, Thomas Breu, Markus Giger, Jann Lay, Peter Messerli, and Kerstin Nolte, *Transnational Land Deals for Agriculture in the Global South. Analytical Report Based on the Land Matrix Database*, (Bern/Montpellier/Hamburg: International Land Coalition, Centre de Coopération Internationale en Recherche Agronomique pour le Développement, Centre for Development and Environment, German Institute for Global and Area Studies and Deutsche Gesellschaftfür Internationale Zusammenarbeit, 2012), http://www.oxfam.de/sites/www.oxfam.de/files/20120427_report_land_matrix.pdf.

7. "The Land Matrix: Much Ado About Nothing," *Rural Modernity and Its Discontents* (blog), April 27, 2012, https://ruralmodernity.wordpress.com/2012/04/27/the-land-matrix-m uch-ado-about-nothing/; and *Rural Modernity* blogger, e-mail to author, June 13, 2012. The author of this blog is employed by a large international organization and has chosen to remain anonymous to avoid having his posts cleared in advance by his organization's press office.

8. Carlos Oya, "Methodological Reflections on 'Land Grab' Databases and the 'Land Grab' Literature 'Rush,' " *Journal of Peasant Studies* 40, no. 3 (2013), p. 503–520.

9. Ian Scoones, Ruth Hall, Saturnino M. Borras Jr, Ben White, and Wendy Wolford, "The Politics of Evidence: Methodologies for Understanding the Global Land Rush," *Journal of Peasant Studies*, 40, no. 3 (2013), p. 473.

10. Cotula et al., *Land Grab or Development Opportunity?*

11. Laura German, George Schoneveld, and Esther Mwangi, "Contemporary Processes of Large-Scale Land Acquisition by Investors: Case Studies from sub-Saharan Africa" (Bogor, Indonesia: CIFOR Occasional Paper 68, 2011); George Schoneveld, "The Anatomy of Large-Scale Farmland Acquisitions in sub-Saharan Africa" (Bogor, Indonesia: CIFOR Working Paper 85, 2011).

12. Schoneveld, "Anatomy of Large-Scale Farmland Acquisitions," p. 7.

13. Maria Cristina Rulli, Antonio Saviori, and Paolo D'Odorico, "Global Land and Water Grabbing," *Proceedings of the National Academy of Sciences*, 110, no. 3 (2013). The quote from their study is found on p. 893.

14. "GRAIN Releases Data Set with over 400 Global Land Grabs," GRAIN, February 23, 2012, (emphasis added), http://www.grain.org/article/entries/4479-grain-releases-data -set-with-over-400-global-land-grabs.

15. Matt McGrath, "Database Says Level of Global 'Land Grabs' Exaggerated," BBC News, June 10, 2013, http://www.bbc.com/news/science-environment-22839149.

16. Yan Jia, "Zhongxing toushen zonglu zhongzhi ye boqu xianjin liu" [ZTE enters the oil palm industry to get cash flows], China Information Industry Net, September 5, 2009, http://www.cnii.com.cn/20080623/ca493010.htm. ZTE planned to invest RMB 1.3 billion at an exchange rate of RMB 7.6 to $1.00; this becomes $171 million.

17. Craig Timberg, "Some in Congo Long for the Order Of Late Dictator," *Washington Post*, July 30, 2006.

18. "Un milliard Usd de Pékin pour des palmeraies à huile en République démocratique du Congo," *Digital Congo* (DRC), May 30, 2007, http://www.digitalcongo.net/article/44029#. See also "DR Congo: Chinese Company to Invest $1 Billion In 3 Million Hectare Oil Palm Plantation," Biopact, July, 28, 2007, http://news.mongabay.com/bioenergy/2007/07/dr-congo-chinese-company-to-invest-1.html.

19. "Convention de partenariat entre la RD Congo et la ZTE International Investment Co. Ltd. en vue de l'implantation et de l'exploitation d'une palmaraie industrielle," Ministry of Agriculture, Fisheries and Animal Husbandry, DRC, and ZTE International Investments Co., Ltd., November 1, 2007.

20. This paragraph draws on: Zhongxin nengyuan gufen youxian gongsi jieshao [Zonergy Company Ltd. About Us], ZTE, http://www.zte-i.com/investment/ines_detail.php?infoid=65; "L'ambassadeur Wu Zexian: La Chine n'a pas de vises impérialistes," *Le Potentiel* (DRC), January 14, 2008, posted on the website of the Chinese embassy in the DRC, http://cd.chineseembassy.org/fra/xw/more/t399806.htm; "Chinese

Agribusiness Company in DR Congo to Offer Thousands of Jobs for Locals," Xinhua, July 10, 2009.

21. "Kinshasha's Missing Millions," *Africa-Asia Confidential* 3, no. 4 (Feb. 2010).

22. "Zhanlüe suoding shiyong you" [Strategically targeting edible oils], "Zhongguo-Yinni jingmao hezuo wang" [China-Indonesia Trade Cooperation Network], MOFCOM, May 9, 2008, http://www.cic.mofcom.gov.cn/ciweb/cic/info/Article. jsp?a_no=147479&col_no=459.

23. In 2009, a private arrangement with a customary chief led to a 20-year contract for 246 hectares of relatively degraded land on the Batéké Plateau. ZTE invested $4.4 million to develop a mixed farm. Their corn was certified by the World Food Programme, which bought it to feed refugees fleeing the conflict that still troubles the Congo. "We still have this concession," Wang Kewen told me in 2015, "but we have stopped planting there. We are in court with a legal case. The neighbors claim this land is theirs." This paragraph also draws on Philippe Asanzi, "Understanding the Challenges of Chinese Agricultural Investment in Africa: An Institutional Analysis," *Academic Research Journal of Agricultural Science and Research*. 2, no. 5 (2014): 76–87; Louis Putzel, Samuel Assembe-Mvondo, Laurentine Bilogo Bi Ndong, Reine Patrick Banioguila, Paolo Cerutti, Julius Chupezi Tieguhong, Robinson Djeukam, Noël Kabuyaya, Guillaume Lescuyer, and William Mala, "Chinese Trade and Investment and the Forests of the Congo Basin: Synthesis of Scoping Studies in Cameroon, Democratic Republic of Congo and Gabon" (Bogor, Indonesia: CIFOR Working Paper 67, 2011); and "Agriculture: Les chinois reprennent le site de la N'Sele," *L'Avenir* (DRC), March 3, 2010.

24. "Chinese Firm Given Land Deal in Sudan," *Sudan Tribune*, March 16, 2010, http://www. sudantribune.com/spip.php?iframe&page=imprimable&id_article=34444.

25. Jie Shao, "Zhong Su nongye hezuo qianjing guangming" [Bright Prospects for Cooperation on Agriculture between China and the Soviet Union], Xinhua, May 11, 2010, http:// finance.qq.com/a/20100511/006461.htm.

26. "Chinese Firm Given Land Deal in Sudan," *Sudan Tribune*.

27. This paragraph draws on "Zimbabwe: Minister Moyo Denies Chinese Group Contracted to Farm Nuanetsi Ranch," *Herald* (Zimbabwe), February 14, 2003; and Andrew Meldrum, "Mugabe Hires China to Farm Seized Land," *Guardian*, February 13, 2003.

28. "Zhong shuidian gongsi zhongbiao jinba buwei zui da nongye kaifa xiangmu" [China International Water and Electricity Company wins largest agricultural development project in Zimbabwe], MOFCOM website, February 24, 2003, http://www.mof-com.gov.cn/article/i/jyjl/k/200302/20030200070817.shtml. See also "Zimbabwe Awards Chinese Company Huge Farming Tender," PANA Press (South Africa), February 9, 2003, http://www.panapress.com/Zimbabwe-awards-Chinese-company-h uge-farming-tender—13-472405-18-lang2-index.html; and Dumisani Muleya, "Chinese Win Big Tender to Grow Food for Zimbabwe," *Business Day* (South Africa), February 11, 2003. The rest of this paragraph draws on "Oral Answers to Questions," Parliament of Zimbabwe, August 27, 2003, http://www.parlzim.gov.zw/attachments/ article/117/27_August_2003_30-6.pdf; "Clearing of Land At Ranch Slow—Mudenge," *Herald* (Harare), March 10, 2004; A. Mukaro, "Chinese Firm Abandons Nuanetsi Project," *The Standard* (Zimbabwe), April 8, 2005; Sam Moyo, "Land Concentration and Accumulation after Redistributive Reform in post-Settler Zimbabwe," *Review of African Political Economy* 38, no. 128 (2009): 269. The quotation "negotiated in bad faith" is from Gavin du Venage, "Harare's Ties with Beijing Begin to Falter; China Unhappy as Unpaid Bills Mount Up for Aircraft, Engineering Work and Construction Projects across Zimbabwe," *South China Morning Post*, May 19, 2006. Unless otherwise stated, the figures in this story are US dollars.

29. Robert Rotberg, "China's Trade with Africa at Record High," *Africa Monitor* (blog), *Christian Science Monitor*, March 19, 2014, http://www.csmonitor.com/World/Africa/ Africa-Monitor/2014/0319/China-s-trade-with-Africa-at-record-high.

30. "Convention d'investissement dans le domaine agricole entre La République du Mali et La Grande Jamahiriya arabe Libyenne populaire et socialiste," Republic of Mali and the Great Socialist People's Libyan Arab Jamahiriya, May 2008, http://farmlandgrab.

org/post/view/14150-convention-d-investissement-dans-ie-domaine-agricole-entre
-le-mali-et-la-libye-2008.

31. "Ji-Ma jingli bu qianyue xin xiangmu" [The Guinea-Mali manager of Zhongdi signs new project], China Geo-Engineering Corporation, December 22, 2008, http://www.zdjt.cecep.cn/tabid/1360/sourceId/4064/infoid/2235/Default.aspx.

32. The agreement with the China National Hybrid Rice Research & Development Center to cooperate with CGC and Malibya to set up the Malibya-China Hybrid Rice Research & Production Joint Venture Stock Company, Ltd. is described in this announcement: "Xinshidai jituan lianshou Yuan Longing xiang feizhou tuiguang zajiao shuidao yanfa xiangmu" [China New Era Group Corporation jointly promotes hybrid rice development project in Africa with Yuan Longping], SASAC, May 21, 2009, http://www.sasac.gov.cn/n86114/n326638/c901205/content.html.

33. Oakland Institute, "Understanding Land Investment Deals in Africa: Malibya in Mali," Land Deal Brief, Oakland Institute, June 2011.

34. Neil MacFarquhar, "African Farmers Displaced as Investors Move In," *New York Times*, December 21, 2010. The quotation in the next paragraph is also from this source. Additional information on this project comes from Stéphane Ballong, "Kassoum Denon: 'Nous n'avons jamais bradé des terres à qui que ce soit,'" *Jeune Afrique*, May 31, 2011, http://www.journaldumali.com/article.php?aid=3233; Soumaila T. Diarra, "Mali: Rush For Land Along the Niger," Inter Press Service, April 22, 2010.

35. "About Hunan Dafengyuan," Hunan Dafengyuan Agriculture Co., http://www.dafengyuan.com/about.asp, accessed July 26, 2011, website discontinued.

36. A copy of the land rent contractual agreement made between the Ethiopian Ministry of Agriculture and Hunan Dafengyuan Agriculture is available at "Land Rent Contractual Agreement Made Between Ministry of Agriculture and Hunan Dafengyuan Agriculture Co., LTD," Oakland Institute, July 12, 2010, http://www.oaklandinstitute.org/sites/oaklandinstitute.org/files/HuanaDafengyuanAgriculture-Agreement.pdf.

37. "Waiting Here for Death: Forced Displacement and 'Villagization' in Ethiopia's Gambella Region," Human Rights Watch, January 17, 2012, http://www.hrw.org/fr/node/104305.

38. "Qingsuan gonggao" [Liquidation Announcement], *Hunan Ribao*, March 20, 2012, http://epaper.voc.com.cn/hnrb/html/2012-03/20/content_473746.htm?div=-1; "Touzi feizhou, A mian yangguang B mian bayou" [Investing in Africa, A-side sunny but B-side stormy], *Xiaoxiang Chenbao*, January 7, 2013, http://epaper.xxcb.cn/xxcba/html/2013-01/07/content_2676287.htm.

39. Josh Maiyo, "The Political Ecology of Chinese Agricultural Investment in Uganda: The Case of Hanhe Farm," SAIS-CARI Policy Brief No. 1/2014, Washington, DC: Johns Hopkins University, SAIS-CARI, October 2014.

40. David Lewis, "Chinese Back Africa's Farms but Want Greater Support," Reuters, February 11, 2009. All quotations in this paragraph are from this source.

41. "About Us," Wems Agro website, http://www.wemsagro.com/about.html, accessed June 12, 2015.

42. "History," Juyoung Tech website, http://www.juyoung-tech.com/pcb/eng/01_company/02_history.htm, accessed June 12, 2015.

43. Brautigam and Ekman, "Rumours and Realities," p. 7.

44. Sigrid-Marianella Stensrud Ekman and Filipe Di Matteo, "The Differential Impacts of Emerging Economy Investors in the Agricultural Sector in Mozambique," Bogor, Indonesia: CIFOR, 2014 (draft).

45. See, for example, Philip Seufert, ed. "The Human Rights Impacts of Tree Plantations in Niassa Province, Mozambique," FIAN International, September 2012, http://www.tni.org/sites/www.tni.org/files/download/niassa_report-hi.pdf

46. The block quote is from Wang Bingfei, "Country Rises from Ruins of Strife," *China Daily*, May 9, 2014. See also Loro Horta, "In Seeking to Feed Itself, China Can Make Sure Others Are Well Fed Too," *South China Morning Post*, December 19, 2014.

47. Jinyan Zhou, "Neither 'Friendship Farm' nor 'Land Grabs': Chinese Agricultural Engagement in Angola" SAIS-CARI Policy Brief No. 7/2015, Washington, DC: Johns Hopkins University, SAIS-CARI, March 2015.

48. Eckart Woertz, *Oil for Food: The Global Food Crisis and the Middle East* (Oxford: Oxford University Press, 2013).

49. Eckart Woertz, "The Global Food Crisis and the Gulf's Quest for Africa's Agricultural Potential," in *Handbook of Land and Water Grabs in Africa: Foreign Direct Investment and Food and Water Security*, ed. John Anthony Allan, Martin Keulertz, Suvi Sojamo, and Jeroen Warner (London: Routledge, 2012), pp. 104–119.

50. Harry Verhoeven and Eckart Woertz, "Mirage in the Desert: The Myth of Africa's Land Grab," CNN, July 9, 2012, http://www.cnn.com/2012/07/05/business/op-ed-africa-land-grab/. The quotation in this paragraph is from this source.

51. Eckart Woertz, "A Sheikh, Ethiopia, and Pitfalls of Journalism," *Oil for Food* (blog), June 19, 2014, http://oilforfood.info/?p=652; Frederick Kaufman, "Letter from Gambella: The Man Who Stole the Nile: An Ethiopian Billionaire's Outrageous Land Grab," *Harper's*, July 2014.

52. Hussein Mousa, "Saudi Arabia Grain and Feed Annual," GAIN Report no. SA1402, USDA, Global Agricultural Information Network, February 19, 2014, http://gain.fas. usda.gov/Recent%20GAIN%20Publications/Grain%20and%20Feed%20Annual_ Riyadh_Saudi%20Arabia_2-19-2014.pdf.

53. Interview, Ministry of Agriculture, Beijing, March 4, 2015; Wei Cheng and Yang Li, "Shaanxi nongken jituan zai kamailong qianding nongye kaifa xiangmu xieyi" [Shaanxi State Farm Agribusiness Corporation Signed an Agricultural Development Project Agreement in Cameroon], *Shaanxi Ribao* (China), March 31, 2010, http://news.aweb. com.cn/2010/3/31/117201003310916400.html.

54. Yang Haomin, telephone interview with Hanning Bi, March 26, 2015. Translation by Hanning Bi and the author.

55. Savitri Mohapatra, "Cameroon: Central Africa's Potential Rice Granary," *Rice Today*, October-December 2013, pp. 36–37, http://irri.org/rice-today/cameroon-central-africa-s-potential-rice-granary.

CHAPTER 6

1. The origins story comes partly from the field notes of Solange Guo Chatelard, who interviewed a Chinese expert who had been in Zambia at the time. Solange Guo Chatelard, e-mail message to author, September 15, 2014. CSFAC owns 60 percent and JSFAC owns 40 percent.

2. The story and all quotations are from a television report: "Lost in Translation," by reporter Chris Masters for *Four Corners*, Australian Broadcasting Company, April 12, 2004, http:// www.abc.net.au/4corners/content/2004/s1086375.htm. Data on the state of the farm in 2007 is from China National Agricultural Development Corporation, "Guanyu xiezhu xuan pin haiwai nongye kaifa xiangmu gongzua renyuan de tongzhi" [Notice on the selection of staff to assist overseas agricultural development projects], CNADC, July 23, 2007, www.cnadc.com.cn/rlzy/2007/7/66c9kuu94t.htm.

3. " 'The Engineers and Technicians Sent by Chairman Mao Are Excellent!'—Report on Chinese Agricultural, Land Reclamation and Water Conservancy Engineers and Technicians in Mauritania," *Peking Review*, February 21, 1969, pp. 11–12. Unless otherwise noted, all quotations in the Mauritania story come from this source.

4. "Development of Irrigated Agriculture in Mauritania: General Overview and Prospects, Proposals for a Second Programme 1980–1985," Club du Sahel, October 1979, http:// pdf.usaid.gov/pdf_docs/PNAAP500.pdf.

5. "Zhongguo yu feizhou yi shishi de hezuo xiangmu yilanbiao" [List of China and Africa's cooperation projects implemented], China Internet Information Center, www.china.com. cn/chinese/zhuanti/zf/426895.htm, retrieved June 4, 2015.

6. "Fruitful Agricultural Cooperation," December 10, 2003, China Internet Information Center, http://www.china.org.cn/english/features/China-Africa/82040.htm#.

7. "Guanyu xiezhu xuanpin haiwai nongye kaifa xiangmu gongzhuo renyuan de tongzhi" [Notice regarding assistance in hiring foreign agricultural development project employees], CNADC, July 23, 2007, www.cnadc.com.cn/rlzy/2007/7/66c9kuu94t.htm; "Zhong-Jia hezi hezuo xiangmu jianjie" [China-Gabon joint venture collaboration project summary], MOFCOM, March 14, 2002, http://ga.mofcom.gov.cn/article/zxhz/hzjj/200203/20020300004539.shtml.

8. Unless otherwise noted, the story of CALF Cocoa comes from these sources: "31st December Movement, Chinese Company in Joint Venture," Ghanaweb, July 3, 1997 http://www.ghanaweb.com/GhanaHomePage///NewsArchive/artikel.php?ID=1200;   Dela Tsikata, Ama Pokuaa Fenny, and Ernest Aryeetey, "China—Africa Relations: A Case Study of Ghana," Scoping Study Prepared for the African Economic Research Consortium, Institute of Statistical, Social and Economic Research, University of Ghana, January 2008, (draft), p. 26; "Adding Value to Our Exports without Partisanship," *Statesman* (Ghana), July 24, 2007, http://www.copal-cpa.org/newsletters/No.%20241.pdf; "31 Dec. Women's Movement Asks Government to Release Money to Cocoa Factory," Ghana News Agency, May 18, 2007, http://ghananewsagency.org/economics/31-dec-women-s-movement-asks-government-to-release-money-to-cocoa-factory-2821; Maame Agyeiwaa Agyei "Chinese Bank Refused to Write Off Ghana's Debt ... MOFEP Tells Justice Appau," *The Chronicle* (Ghana), July 28, 2014, http://thechronicle.com.gh/chinese-bank-refused-to-write-off-ghanas-debt-mofep-tells-justice-appau/.

9. Jin Zhu, "China, Africa Forge Farming Ties," *China Daily*, August 12, 2010,

10. Serge Michel and Michel Beuret, *China Safari: On the Trail of Beijing's Expansion in Africa* (New York: Nation Books, 2009), p. 3.

11. Interview, CLETC official, Sinolight, Beijing, December 20, 2013. CLETC also built the factory at Koba Farm and developed the sugarcane fields

12. Edward A. Gargan, "International Report; Tanzania's 'Green Gold' Woes," *New York Times*, June 23, 1986.

13. M. G. Tenga, *Sisal Industry in Tanzania Since Colonial Era* (Xlibris, April 15, 2008), pp. 37–38. Peter Mohamed, "Sisal Board Introduces Mobile Decorticators to Revolutionise Farming," IPP Media, October 19, 2012, http://www.ippmedia.com/frontend/index.php?l=47097.

14. Nicholas Kristof, "The Third World: Back to the Farm," *New York Times*, July 28, 1985.

15. Land Rights Research and Resources Institute (LARRRI), "The State of the Then NAFCO, NARCO and Absentee Landlords' Farms/Ranches in Tanzania," February 14, 2009, p. 9. http://www.hakiardhi.org/index.php?option=com_docman&task=doc_download&gid=75&Itemid=11.

16. Xiaochen Chen, "Ploughing Africa: The Story of a Chinese Sisal Farm in Tanzania," China Africa Reporting Project, University of Witwatersrand, Johannesburg, South Africa, http://china-africa-reporting.co.za/2013/06/ploughing-africa-the-story-of-a-chinese-sisal-farm-in-tanzania/. This article was originally published in *China Business News*, May 21, 2013.

17. "Bright Future for Sisal Cultivation," People's Republic of China, Economic and Commercial Counselor's Office in the United Republic of Tanzania, April 14, 2005, http://tz2.mofcom.gov.cn/aarticle/chinanews/200504/20050400063729.html.

18. Li Zhang, Xiuli Xu, and Xiaoyun Li, "Zou chuqu de zhongguo ziben: wenhua zaoyu yu ronghe—zhendui yijia zhongzi qiye zai tansangniya de tianye guancha" [Chinese capital going global: Cultural encounters and fusion—field observation on Chinese-funded enterprises in Tanzania], *Journal of China Agricultural University* (*Social Science*) 29, no. 4 (Dec. 2012).

19. Xiuli Xu, Gubo Qi, and Xiaoyun Li, "Business Borderlands: China's Overseas State-owned Agribusiness," in *IDS Bulletin, Special Issue: China and International Development: Challenges and Opportunities,* ed. Jing Gu, Xiaoyun Li, Gerald, 45, no. 4 (July 2014): 114–124. A CSR mandate had been imposed in January 2008 by China's SASAC, which provides oversight for all of the 100-plus state-owned enterprises (SOEs) directly under the central

government. "Guidelines to the State-owned Enterprises Directly under the Central Government on Fulfilling Corporate Social Responsibilities," SASAC, Beijing, retrieved June 15, 2015, http://en.sasac.gov.cn/n1408035/c1477196/content.html.

20. Managing director, sisal farm, interview with author, Morogoro, Tanzania, September 20, 2011.

21. Xiaochen Chen, "Gengyun Feizhou: Tansangniya Zhongguo jianma nongchang de chen-shi gushi" [Ploughing Africa: The true story of a Chinese sisal farm in Tanzania], *China Business News*, May 21, 2013, http://finance.sina.com.cn/roll/20130521/012715526584. shtml.

22. Yanrong Zhao, "Sowing the Seeds of Success in Tanzania," *China Daily*, March 26, 2013.

23. Hairong Yan and Barry Sautman, "Chinese Farms in Zambia: From Socialist to 'Agro-Imperialist' Engagement?" *African and Asian Studies* 9 (2010): 307–333.

24. "Africa Feature: Story of Nurse-turned Chinese Farmer in Zambia," *People's Daily*, October 23, 2006.

25. Philip Hsiaopong Liu, "How China's 'Trade Not Aid' Strategy Became Construed as Charitable Help: Deconstructing the 'Touching' Idyll of Li Li's Investment in Africa," *Identité, culture et politique*, 12, no 2 (2011): 1–18, http://www.codesria.org/IMG/pdf/ Philip_Hsiaopong_Liu.pdf.

26. Xiangshan Han, "Great Potential of Agricultural Development in Africa," *West Asia and Africa*, 1 (2003): 62–65.

27. Shenyu Shao and Feng Lu, "Shen nongke zai faizhou ban qi sizuo nongchang" [Provincial State Farm Agribusiness Corporation establishes four farms in Africa], Sina, June 4, 2004, http://news.sina.com.cn/c/2004-06-04/07162713916s.shtml. See also Hairong and Sautman, "Chinese Farms in Zambia," pp. 307–333.

28. Joseph Catanzaro and Fangchao Li, "Success That No One Can Rob Them Of," *China Daily*, July 14, 2014.

29. Zambeef, *Annual Report 2011*, http://www.nedbank.co.za/website/uploads/files/A%20 -%20Zambeef.pdf.

30. "A Record Year for IFC in Sub-Saharan Africa," International Finance Corporation, World Bank Group, http://www.ifc.org/wps/wcm/connect/region__ext_content/regions/ sub-saharan+africa/news/record_year_for_ifc_africa, retrieved June 12, 2015.

31. I appreciate the suggestion of Solange Guo Chatelard that I emphasize this point. Solange Guo Chatelard, e-mail message to author, December 1, 2014.

32. Zhijie Liu, " Zhongken jituan canyu faizhou nongye kaifa jie shuoguo" [Ken Group involved in fruitful African agricultural development], *People's Daily*, October 19, 2000, http://www.people.com.cn/GB/paper39/1716/277533.html.

33. Jin, "China, Africa Forge Farming Ties." The five surviving projects were China–Zambia Friendship Farm (Zambia); Zhongken Estates (Zambia); Koba Farm (Guinea); Zhongken Friendship Farm (Zambia); Rudewa and Kisangata Estates Sisal Farms (Tanzania).

34. "Zimbabwe: China Turns Down Mugabe's Farm Offer," ReliefWeb, October 12, 2005, http://reliefweb.int/report/zimbabwe/zimbabwe-china-turns-down-mugabes-farm-offer.

CHAPTER 7

1. Manoela Borges, "A Spoonful of Chinese Sugar Sours U.S. Investors in Mali," Confidential cable, US Embassy Bamako to Washington, DC, February 23, 2009, Wikileaks 09BAMAKO104, released August 30, 2011.

2. "Mali shangkala tanglian jiangjian disan tangchang" [Mali Sukala to build third sugar refinery], Chinese Embassy in Bamako Commercial Office, March 19, 2006, http:// ml.mofcom.gov.cn/aarticle/jmxw/200603/20060301709328.html.

3. Andrew Anderson-Sprecher and Junyan Jiang, "China, People's Republic Of, Sugar Annual," GAIN Report no. 14020, USDA, Global Agricultural Information Network, April 30, 2014, http://gain.fas.usda.gov/Recent%20GAIN%20Publications/

Sugar%20Annual_Beijing_China%20-%20Peoples%20Republic%20of_4-30-2014. pdf; "EU Sugar Market Developments in 2011," Agritrade.cta.int, May 28, 2012, http://agritrade.cta.int/en/layout/set/print/Agriculture/Commodities/Sugar/EU-sugar-market-developments-in-2011.

4. "Zhong-Duo Aniye zhitang lianhe qiye qianjing anhao" [Good Prospects for China-Togo sugar joint venture in Anié] Xinhua, November 6, 2005, http://news.sina.com. cn/w/p/2005-11-06/13458225159.shtml.

5. "A Very Sticky Situation," *Indian Ocean Newsletter*, May 2, 1998, http://www.africain telligence.com/ION/economics/1998/05/02/a-very-sticky-situation,49237-ART.

6. Joseph Bassay, "Qui sauvera la sucrerie de Lotokila?," *Mongongo* (DRC), July 31, 2011, p. 2, http://www.stanleyville.be/documents/Journal_Mongongo_41.pdf.

7. Unless otherwise stated, information about Anié comes from these sources: Cheng'an Wang, "Five Year's Operation of the Leased Sugar Complex of Togo Brings in Notable Economic Returns," Department of Foreign Aid, Ministry of Foreign Economic Relations and Trade, *Almanac of China's Foreign Economic Relations and Trade 1993/94* (Hong Kong: China Resources Advertising, 1993) pp. 888–889; "Duoge Aniye tanglian de chengzhang zhuangda jianzheng le Zhong-Duo huli gongying de fengshuo chengguo" [The growth and maturation of Togo's Anié sugar complex witnessed the fruitful win-win results of China-Togo cooperation], MOFCOM, February 25, 2012, http://tg.mofcom.gov.cn/ article/a/201202/20120207983340.shtml; "Zhong-Duo Aniye zhitang lianhe qiye qian-jing kanhao" [China-Togo Anié sugar complex outlook promising], Xinhua, November 6, 2005; "Zhongcheng gufen gongsi duoge aniye tanglian—luxing shehui zeren, shixian huli gongying" [Zhongchen Ltd.'s sugar joint venture in Anié—fulfilling social responsi-bility, achieving mutual benefits and win-win scenario], MOFCOM, September 17, 2012, http://www.mofcom.gov.cn/aarticle/i/jyjl/k/201209/20120908343467.html.

8. Interview, senior Complant official George Guo, Sierra Leone, December 2007. In 1997, Complant negotiated a 10-year management lease and signed a new 20-year lease in 2007.

9. "Un complexe sucrier connu de tous au Togo," Xinhua, August 29, 2011.

10. Frédéric Giraut, "La petit ville, un milieu adapté aux paradoxes de l'Afrique de l'Ouest" (Paris: Thèse Université Panthéon-Sorbonne, 1994). The others averaged a ratio of one to two.

11. Symonette Fanjanarivo, "Sucoma de Morondava: l'etat devrait percevoir 1,2 milliard ar en 2012," *La Gazette de la Grande Île* (Madagascar), October 11, 2012.

12. African Development Bank, "Madagascar: Projet Sucriére d'Analaiva, Rapport d'Évaluation de la Performance de Projet," Departement de l'Evaluation des Operations (OPEV), February 5, 1996, http://www.afdb.org/fileadmin/uploads/afdb/Documents/ Evaluation-Reports-_Shared-With-OPEV_/05402243-FR-MADAGASCAR-ANA LAIVA-SUGAR-PROJECT.PDF. This factory and plantation are known variously as Sirinala de Morondava, Sucoma, and Sucriére d'Analaiva. For ease of presentation, the factory and plantation will be referred to as Morondava and the investor company as Sucoma.

13. Unless otherwise indicated, the story of Sucoma and quotations from local officials are from these sources: "État Déplorable de la Sucrèrie de Namakia," *Madagascar Tribune*, December 13, 2010; "Location-gérance de la Siranala 875 à 962 Millions Ar de Loyer Annuel Fixé," *La Gazette de la Grande Île* (Madagascar), September 18, 2013; Symonette Fanjanarivo, "Filière sucre: Plus de 5 000 Squatters Entravent L'Essor de la Sucoma," *La Gazette de la Grande Île*, September 18, 2013; "Sucoma: un Complexe Sucrière en Peril," *La Gazette de la Grande Île*, September 18, 2013; Symonette Fanjanarivo, "Squat à la Siranala: Des Pénalités Élevées en Cas de Départ des Chinois," *La Gazette de la Grande Île*, September 19, 2013. All translations by the author.

14. The Chinese had wanted a longer contract, pledging to invest another $40 million in upgrading the 30-year-old complex. They agreed to a contract with a fixed rent between 875 to 962 million Ariary (about $400,000 to $440,000) per year and a variable rent of

3.5 percent of revenues, rising to 5.5 percent in the fifth year. "Location Gerance de la Siranala 875 à 962 millions ar de Loyer Annuel," *La Gazette de la Grande Île*, September 18, 2013.

15. "Madagascar: La Préférence des Consommateurs Défavorise la Production de Sucre," Xinhua, August 11, 2014.

16. The story of the December riots and their aftermath is drawn from these sources: Seth Andriamarohasina, "Morondava—Émeutes Meurtrières à la Sucoma," *L'Express de Madagascar*, December 12, 2014; Sylvain Ranjalahy, "Arrêtez le Mas . . . Sucre," *L'Express de Madagascar*, December 12, 2014; "Maharante Jean de Dieu: 'Les Chinois doivent changer,'" *La Gazette de la Grande Île*, December 17, 2014; Lantoniaina Razafindramiadana, "Sucoma Morondava—Le Contrat Avec les Opérateurs Chinois Examiné," *L'Express de Madagascar*, February 16, 2015.

17. This story of Magbass draws on Bräutigam, *The Dragon's Gift*, pp. 259–265, where it is told in more detail.

18. "Lease Contract on Magbass Sugar Complex of Sierra Leone," Minister of Agriculture, Forestry and Food Security, Government of Sierra Leone, and China National Complete Plant Import & Export Corporation, Freetown, Sierra Leone, January 23, 2003.

19. "Koroma Challenges Magbass to Expand," *Politico* (Sierra Leone), June 16, 2013, http://politicosl.com/2013/06/koroma-challenges-magbass-to-expand/. All quotations in this paragraph are from this article.

20. Ibrahim Seibure, "Sierra Leone: COMPLANT Magbass Sugar Company Commences 2012/2013 Production," *Concord Times* (Freetown, Sierra Leone), November 22, 2012.

21. Pauletter Nonfodji, "China's Farmland Rush in Benin: Toward a Win-Win Economic Model of Cooperation?" (Paper presented at the International Conference on Global Land Grabbing, April 6 to April 8, 2011, organized by the Land Deals Politics Initiative), http://www.iss.nl/fileadmin/ASSETS/iss/Documents/Conference_papers/LDPI/27_PAULETTE_NONFODJI.pdf.

22. "Sugar Sector," Executive Brief Update 2011, Technical Centre for Agricultural and Rural Cooperation (ACP-EU), July 2011, http://agritrade.cta.int/en/Agriculture/Commodities/Sugar/Executive-Brief-Update-2011-Sugar-sector.

23. United Nations Economic Commission for Africa, "Survey of the Status of Agreed Multinational Core Industrial Projects within the Context of IDDA in the Respective Subregions," ECA/IHSD/CO-OO/011/89, December 29, 1989.

24. Seidi Mulero, "Nigeria: Obasanjo, Kerekou Reconcile," *Tempo* (Nigeria), January 28, 2000.

25. "Bénin: Paralysie des activités de l'ex Société Sucrière de Savè—Roger Dovonou obtient la levée de la grève," *L'Autre Quotidien* (Benin) August 10, 2009.

26. Jean-Jacques Gabas, Frédéric Goulet, Clara Arnaud, and Jimena Duran, "Coopérations Sud-Sud et nouveaux acteurs de l'aide au développement agricole en Afrique de l'Ouest et austral: Le cas de la Chine et du Brésil," Agence Francaise de Developpement, June 2013, p. 52, http://www.afd.fr/webdav/site/afd/shared/PUBLICATIONS/RECHERCHE/Scientifiques/A-savoir/21-A-Savoir.pdf.

27. Clem Khena, "Nigeria: Citizens in Benin Republic Get Severance Benefits Next Month," *Leadership* (Nigeria), November 15, 2008; Gabas et al., "Coopérations Sud-Sud." Unless otherwise noted, all quotations in this paragraph and the next come from this latter source.

28. Gabas et al., "Coopérations Sud-Sud," p. 52.

29. Aaron Pan, "China's Hua Lien International Buys Three African Sugar Growers," *Bloomberg*, February 27, 2008, http://www.bloomberg.com/apps/news?pid=newsarchive&sid=aF8bdvua8mJs&refer=africa; Hua Lien, *Annual Report 2008*, http://202.66.146.82/listco/hk/hualien/annual/2008/ar2008.pdf; Hua Lien, *Annual Report 2010*, http://202.66.146.82/listco/hk/hualien/annual/2010/ar2010.pdf.

30. Eric Ng, "Hua Lien to Invest in African Fuel Venture," *South China Morning Post*, February 2, 2010.

31. This paragraph draws on three sources: Nonfodji, "China's Farmland Rush in Benin," p. 4; Hua Lien, *Annual Report 2011*; and "Zhongcheng jituan yu beining zhengfu qianshu guanyu shengwu ranliao xiangmu di baiwanglu" [Complant and the Benin government

signs memorandum regarding biofuel project], MOFCOM, November, 11, 2014, http://www.mofcom.gov.cn/article/i/jyjl/k/201007/20100707042267.shtml.

32. "Putting Technology to Work to Improve Property Rights in Benin: Poverty Reduction through Secure Land Tenure," Millennium Challenge Corporation, October 23, 2009, http://www.mcc.gov/documents/press/successstory-102309-action-benin.pdf.

33. All quotations in this paragraph are from Hua Lien, *Annual Report 2013*, p. 6 and from "Announcement on the Provision for Impairment Losses on Ethanol Biofuel Business in Benin and Profit Warning," Hua Lien International (Holding) Company Ltd., March 3, 2014, http://www.hkexnews.hk/listedco/listconews/SEHK/2014/0303/LTN201403031856.pdf.

34. *Land Rush*, directed by Hugo Berkeley and Osvalde Lewat, Normal Life Pictures, 2012, http://whypoverty.net/wp-content/uploads/files/Land%20Rush%20transcript.pdf.

35. The project would be organized in two components: the refinery, to be owned 94 percent by Illovo, several private investors and Schaffer, and the plantation, 90 percent of which would be owned by the government of Mali.

36. Shuren Chen, "Mali tang lian youdian 'tian'" [Mali Sugar Alliance is a little bit 'sweet'], Commercial News Network, *Guoji Shangbao* (MOFCOM), June 19, 2012, http://www.shangbao.net.cn/zuhe/special/d/101971.html, retrieved October 23, 2014; webpage no longer valid but reposted at China International Information Center, http://finance.china.com.cn/roll/20120618/810592.shtml.

37. Michael Cohen, "Illovo Pulls out of Mali Sugar Project on Security Concerns," *Bloomberg News*, May 28, 2012, http://www.bloomberg.com/news/2012-05-28/illovo-pulls-out-of-mali-sugar-project-on-security-concerns-1-.html.

38. Nama Ouattara, "Essai sur l'investissement agricole responsable: Une etude de cas de projets d'investissements de la Chine dans le sous-secteur du sucre au Mali" (unpublished paper, Université Paris-Sud, 2014).

39. "Office du Niger: La Prospection d'Opportunites Nouvelles," *L'Essor* (Mali), October 23, 2013, http://www.malijet.com/actualite_economique_du_mali/84528-office-du-niger-%3A-la-prospection-d%E2%80%99opportunites-nouvelles.html.

40. "Key Sugar Projects in Southern Africa," *Annual SADC Sugar Digest 2014*, December 4, 2013, http://sadcsugardigest.com/key-sugar-projects-in-southern-africa.

41. "Kenana Red Sea Sugar Refinery: Agreements on Questions Raised by COMPLANT and CAD-Fund," Baidu Library, November 17, 2011, http://wenku.baidu.com/view/2690e105a6c30c2259019e94.html. A year later, a Sudanese newspaper article on the project made no mention of Chinese involvement but noted that the refinery was now being built by an Italian company, Aradanie. "Minister of Industry Supports Establishment of Sugar Refinery in Port Sudan," *Sudan Vision* (Sudan), October 12, 2012, http://news.sudanvisiondaily.com/details.html?rsnpid=215309.

42. Government of Ethiopia, Ministry of Finance and Economic Development, "Public Sector Debt Statistical Bulletin, No. 9," Debt Management Directorate, October 2012, p. 11.

43. John Gayle, CEO of SCJ Holdings, Jamaica, interview with author, Washington, DC, November 20, 2013; "Sugar War—Major Players Haggle Over 2010 Divestment Process," *Gleaner* (Jamaica), October 21, 2012, http://jamaica-gleaner.com/gleaner/20121021/lead/lead11.html. Mark Titus, "New Pan Caribbean Head Wants to Wipe the Slate Clean . . . Partially," *Gleaner* (Jamaica), October 25, 2013, http://jamaica-gleaner.com/gleaner/20131025/business/business1.html.

CHAPTER 8

1. Muchena Zigomo, "China Asks to Plant 2 mln ha of Jatropha in Zambia," Reuters, March 31, 2009, http://af.reuters.com/article/zambiaNews/idAFLV96195120090331.

2. Joachim von Braun and Ruth Meinzen-Dick, "'Land Grabbing' by Foreign Investors in Developing Countries: Risks and Opportunities," IFPRI Policy Brief 13, 2009, http://www.ifpri.org/sites/default/files/publications/bp013all.pdf.

3. "Outsourcing's Third Wave," *Economist*, May 21, 2009.

4. Professor Thomson Sinkala, interview with the author, Lusaka, Zambia, June 3, 2013. Unless otherwise noted, all Sinkala quotations in this chapter are from this interview.

5. George Christoffel Schoneveld, *The Governance of Large-Scale Farmland Investments in Sub-Saharan Africa* (Delft: Eburon, 2013), pp. 35–36.

6. "Zambia and China Undertaking Feasibility Study in Kawambwa on the Biofuel Project," *Lusaka Times* (Zambia) March 19, 2009.

7. Barry Sautman and Hairong Yan, "Chinese Farms in Zambia: From Socialist to "Agro-Imperialist" Engagement?" *African and Asian Studies* 9 (2010): 324.

8. Anonymous, "Comment," (blog), House of Chiefs, April 2, 2009, http://www.house ofchiefs.com/2009/03/land-is-available.html.

9. "Qinli 'jianshe Feizhou' " [Witnessed "building Africa"], *Beijing Ribao*, November 6, 2006, www.bjd.com.cn/bjxw/mtdd/sbjx/200611/t20061106_113999_2.htm.

10. "A Brief Introduction to the China-aided Agricultural Technology Demonstration Center," Embassy of the People's Republic of China in the Republic of Liberia, http://lr.china-embassy.org/eng/sghdhzxxx/t720776.htm.

11. In 2010, LPHT explored the possibility of setting up an agricultural park in Zambia. "We went to see the Nansanga bloc, where the Zambian government is asking for investment," LPHT vice president Zhou Dan told me. "It was five hours from Lusaka. The roads were terrible. They needed to be paved. We would not have been able to bring the harvest out by truck." In 2011, LPHT was shortlisted for the Nansanga bloc, along with firms from Hungary, the UK, South Africa, Mauritius, and Zambia, but LPHT chose not to submit a final bid. "ZDA, Chinese Firm Seal Agro Deal," *Times of Zambia*, August 21, 2010; Ndinawe Simpelwe, "ZDA Receives Only 2 Bids for Nansanga Bloc," *Zambia Post*, June 26, 2011; Zhou Dan, interview with author, Changsha, Hunan, December 16, 2013. All Zhou Dan quotes are from this interview.

12. In 2006, Hunan Academy of Agricultural Sciences (one of the shareholders in LPHT) was selected to implement one of China's official ATDCs in Madagascar. They began trials for hybrid rice there in November 2006 and opened the Madagascar hybrid rice demonstration center two years later. Yuan International's joint venture with CAAIC in Madagascar is said to be leasing 6,000 hectares of land with plans to grow hybrid rice. "CAAIC and Yuan's International Company Successfully Sign Agreements about Hybrid Rice Project," China Africa Agricultural Investment Company, November 3, 2013, http://www.caaic.com.cn/en/NewsInfo.aspx?NId=11403; "Jiji liyong yuanwai pingtai, cujin wo sheng nongye geng hao de 'zou chuqu' " [Actively use foreign aid as a platform to promote agricultural going out in our province], Foreign Economic Cooperation Office, Ministry of Commerce, Hunan Province, September 20, 2012, http://hzc.hunancom.gov.cn/swdt/342289.htm.

13. Yang Jiao, "Chinese Agricultural Entrepreneurship in Africa: Case Studies in Ghana and Nigeria," SAIS-CARI Policy Brief 05-2015, Washington, DC, January 5, 2015.

14. National Agricultural Seed Council of Nigeria, "Registered Seed Companies," 2012, http://www.seedcouncilngr.org/index.php?option=com_content&view=article&id=46 &Itemid=300.

15. Garba Muhammad, "Landgrab by Foreigners Forces Kebbi Farmers to Move to Niger State," *Daily Trust* (Birnin Kebbi, Nigeria), May 22, 2014. The quotation in the next paragraph is also from this source.

16. For an excellent overview of this topic, see Carlos Oya, "Contract Farming in Sub-Saharan Africa: A Survey of Approaches, Debates and Issues," *Journal of Agrarian Change* 12, no. 1 (January 2012): 1–33.

17. On China-Africa Cotton, see Xiaoyang Tang, "The Impact of Asian Investment on Africa's Textile Industries," Carnegie–Tsinghua Center for Global Policy, Beijing, August 2014, http://carnegieendowment.org/files/china_textile_investment.pdf.

18. The Tianze story draws on Ian Scoones, Nelson Marongwe, Blasio Mavedzenge, Jacob Mahenehene, Felix Murimbarimba, and Chrispen Sukume, *Zimbabwe's Land Reform: Myths and Realities* (Suffolk: James Currey, 2010), p. 6; Langton Mukwereza, "Situating Tian Ze's role in Reviving Zimbabwe's Flue-Cured Tobacco Sector in the Wider

Discourse on Zimbabwe: China Cooperation: Will the Scorecard Remain Win-Win?" (FAC Working Paper No. 115, February 2015); Sean Christie, "Zimbabwe's Forests Are Going Up in Smoke," *Mail & Guardian* (South Africa), November 1, 2013; Samuel Moyo, *Agrarian Reform and Prospects for Recovery*, African Institute for Agrarian Studies, Harare, 2009, cited in Scoones et al. *Zimbabwe's Land Reform*, p. 148; "China Drives Zim Tobacco Recovery," *Zimbabwe Daily News*, Feb. 25, 2011, http://www.zimbabwesituation.org/?p=28826.

19. In 2005, CSFAC visited Zimbabwe to explore agribusiness investment, but with Zimbabwe's economic crisis, nothing came of these discussions. "Zimbabwe—Chinese to Take Over Former White-owned Farms," Zim Online, May 19, 2005, http://www.freerepublic.com/focus/f-news/1406205/posts.

20. Lixin Zhu, "A Dream to Build a New Zimbabwe," *China Daily*, April 7, 2014; Zhu Lixin, "Fields of Dreams and Success," *China Daily*, May 2, 2014. Unless otherwise noted, information on Wanjin's investment comes from these sources and my interviews in Zimbabwe, June–July 2013.

21. SOCFIN, "Sustainability Report 2013," http://www.bollore.com/en-us/our-commitments/publications.

22. Wenjun Ma, "Rough Yet Unlonely Venture into African Continent—Venture Documentary of GMG SUDCAM in Cameroon," Sinochem, July 5, 2013, http://english.sinochem.com/g834/s1775/t8725.aspx.

23. Samuel Assembe-Mvondo, Paolo Cerutti, Louis Putzel, and Richard Eba'a Atyi, "What Happens When Corporate Ownership Shifts to China? A Case Study on Rubber Production in Cameroon," CIFOR slide show, June 20, 2015, http://www.slideshare.net/CIFOR/what-happens-when-corporate-ownership-shifts-to-china-a-case-study-on-rubber-production-in-cameroon.

24. "Hainan xiangjiao changye 'zoujing feizhou'" [Hainan rubber industry 'goes to Africa'], Hainan Rubber Group, July 1, 2013, http://www.hirub.cn/show-1036.html.

25. Ministry of Agriculture official, Beijing, March 4, 2015.

26. Wu, "Zhongguo ren Feizhou chuangye" [Chinese entrepreneurs in Africa].

27. Yu Zhang, "Zhongguo Nongken haiwai tuohuang" [China State Farm Agribusiness Corporation overseas farming], *Oriental Outlook* (China), June 12, 2008, http://www.lwdf.cn/oriental/business/20080612144232666.htm, accessed July 14, 2008; webpage no longer valid. The quotations in this paragraph are from this source.

28. Gaza Province Department of Agriculture and Hubei Province State Farms, "Accordo de Gemelagem Especifica para a Área da Agricultura entre A Direcção Provincial da Agriultura de Gaza e a Direcção Provincial de Administração das Farmas Estatais de Hubei (Hubei Lianfeng ozambique Co, LDA) Para Execução do Projecto de Produção Agrícola Alimentar No Regadio de Xai-Xai," October 20, 2008; Sérgio Chichava, "Chinese Rice Farming in Xai-Xai: A Case of Mozambican Agency?" in *China and Mozambique: From Comrades to Capitalists*, ed. Sérgio Chichava and Chris Alden (Auckland Park, South Africa: Jacana Media, 2014), pp. 129, 133–134.

29. Joel K. Bourne, Jr. "The Next Breadbasket," *National Geographic*, July 2014, p. 34.

30. Baohua Min, Jie Han, and Mingwen Gong, "Goujian mosangbike de guojia liangcang—wanbao liangyou youxian gongsi shishi 'zou chuqu' zhanlüe jishi" [Building Mozambique's national granary: Wanbao Oil Co. "going out" strategy], *Xiangyang Daily* (China), December 18, 2012, http://www.hj.cn/html/201212/18/1843657012.shtml. See also Chao Wang and Andrew Moody, "Harvest Success Puts Rice on Table," *China Daily*, March 7, 2014, p. 9.

31. Min, Han, and Gong, "Goujian mosangbike de guojia liangcang" [Building Mozambique's national granary.]

32. The draft environmental impact study is in Chinese and is on file in Maputo. Sigrid Ekman, personal communication to author, November 18, 2014.

33. Interview, Armando Ussivane, Xai-Xai, Mozambique, November 17, 2014.

34. The two Hubei teams each had about 25 Chinese agricultural workers, and each team was allocated about 650 hectares to manage. The two Heilongjiang teams, each with about 56 Chinese workers, who were more accustomed to vast mechanized farms, were to cover a

total area of about 6,000 hectares. One Hubei team was from a *junken* farm. As chapter 3 noted, *junken* farms were originally set up in the 1950s by the People's Liberation Army (PLA), which organized active and demobilized soldiers to establish self-contained settlements, usually in border areas or virgin territory. At least one of the parents of workers on today's *junken* farms would probably have been a soldier, but their children simply grew up in these communities. Today, the *junken* farms are managed not by the PLA but by provincial branches of CSFAC. They have diversified, developing programs for tourism and "pick your own" orchards and berry farms. However, as Li Shubo, a Chinese scholar, told me later, the military and pioneer roots of *junken* farms created a particular, proud culture of discipline in their work teams. Li Shubo, telephone interview with author, December 22, 2014. This section also benefited from Chuanhong Zhang, Gubo Qi, Yanlei Wang, Xiaoyun Li, "What Dominates China-Africa agricultural Encounters—An Ethnographic Research on a Large-scale Chinese Rice Project in Mozambique" (Working Paper, China Agriculture University, Beijing, 2014, draft).

35. Wang and Moody, "Harvest Success Puts Rice on Table," p. 9.
36. "About Us," Wanbao Grains and Oils, http://en.wblyjt.com/comcontent_ detail1/&FrontComContent_list01-134211484ContId=e5b9b9e7-f4b5-4279- ab90-94da50605e3a&comContentId=e5b9b9e7-f4b5-4279-ab90-94da50605e3a.html, retrieved June 3, 2015.
37. Wang and Moody, "Harvest Success Puts Rice on Table," p. 9.
38. Interview, Anastacio Natavel, FONGA, Xai-Xai, Mozambique, November 17, 2014.
39. Both this and the number of displaced people are from Sérgio Chichava, "Chinese Rice Farming in Xai-Xai: A Case of Mozambican Agency?" in Chichava and Alden, *China and Mozambique*, p. 137.
40. Ibid.
41. Andrew England, "Mozambique Farming Project Launched," *FT*, May 13, 2012.
42. "Mozambique: Mozfoods Optimistic about Rice Production," Mozambique News Agency, November 7, 2011, http://www.mozambiquehighcommission.org.uk/?s=10&g rupa=1&id=447&new=ok.
43. England, "Mozambique Farming Project Launched."
44. Interview, Chinese economic counselor, Maputo, November 19, 2014.
45. Yuefeng Liu and Shuguang Liu, "Xīn shíqí zhōng fēi nóngyè hézuò jìnzhǎn jí qiánjǐng" [Progress and prospects in the new China-Africa agricultural cooperation], *World Agriculture* (China), November 2011, http://e-nw.shac.gov.cn/wmfw/hwzc/ hygl/201204/t20120410_1315842.htm.
46. "Special Report: Brazil," *Economist*, September 28, 2013, p. 7.
47. "Nigeria's Zimbabwean Farmers: Nothing Like Chicken Feed," *Economist*, April 13, 2013, p. 50.

CONCLUSION

1. Richard Munang and Jesica Andrews, "Despite Climate Change, Africa Can Feed Africa," special edition, *Africa Renewal*, 2014, p. 6.
2. Tegegnework Gettu, "Preface," *Africa Human Development Report* (New York: UNDP, 2013).
3. "U.S. Agricultural Trade: Exports," USDA Economic Research Service, March 3, 2015, http://www.ers.usda.gov/topics/international-markets-trade/us-agricultural-trade/ exports.aspx; "Ag and Food Statistics: Agricultural Trade," USDA Economic Research Service, April 6, 2015, www.ers.usda.gov/data-products/ag-and-food-stat istics-charting-the-essentials/agricultural-trade.aspx.
4. World Food Programme, "China Emerges as World's Third Largest Food Aid Donor," July 20, 2006, http://www.wfp.org/node/534.
5. FAO, "The State of Food Insecurity in the World: In Brief," Rome, 2014, http://www.fao. org/3/a-i4037e.pdf; figure includes North Africa.

6. Around "874 million hectares of land in Africa" is "suitable for agricultural produc-tion." FAO, "Extending the Area under Sustainable Land Management and Reliable Water Control Systems," in *Comprehensive Africa Agriculture Development Programme* (Rome: FAO, 2002), http://www.fao.org/docrep/005/y6831e/y6831e-03.htm.

7. The five boroughs of New York City cover 1,214 square kilometers or 121,400 hectares.

8. L. German, G. Schoneveld, and E. Mwangi, "Contemporary Processes of Large-scale Land Acquisition by Investors: Case Studies from sub-Saharan Africa," CIFOR Occasional Paper 68, Bogor, Indonesia, 2011; George Schoeneveld, "The Anatomy of Large-Scale Farmland Acquisitions in sub-Saharan Africa" (CIFOR Working Paper 85, 2011).

9. Joachim von Braun and Ruth Meinzen-Dick, "'Land Grabbing' by Foreign Investors in Developing Countries: Risks and Opportunities," IFPRI Policy Brief 13, 2009, http://www.ifpri.org/publication/land-grabbing-foreign-investors-developing-countries.

10. French, *China's Second Continent*, p. 172.

11. Ekman and Matteo, "Differential Impacts of Emerging Economy Investors," and Sigrid-Marianella Stensrud Ekman, e-mail message to author, June 16, 2015.

12. Brautigam and Ekman, "Rumours and Realities," p. 7.

13. Sigrid-Marianella Stensrud Ekman, e-mail message to author, May 24, 2015. To sum-marize, as of late 2014, there were three operating Chinese farms above 500 hectares in Mozambique: Hubei Gaza Friendship Farm (20,000 ha concession); Hao Shengli (2024 ha); and Lianhe (2000 ha). Two additional farms had stopped operating due to vari-ous problems: Rizao Sunway (500 ha) and Chamei Agrícola in Zambézia province (ha unknown). Wanbao's 6000-hectare Chokwe investment and several other farms had been approved but not yet started. China Africa Cotton also operated a large cotton contract farming project.

14. Ibid. See also Ekman and Matteo, "Differential Impacts of Emerging Economy Investors"; and Sigrid-Marianella Stensrud Ekman and Carmen Stella Macamo, "Brazilian Development Cooperation in Agriculture: A Scoping Study on ProSavana in Mozambique, with Implications for Forests" (CIFOR Working Paper 138, Bogor, Indonesia, 2014).

15. Rubinstein, "China's Eye on African Agriculture."

16. Hong Yang, "Haigui liangshi: Nongye 'z'ou chuqu huhuan guojia zhanlue" [Returnees' food: Agriculture 'going out' needs a national strategy], *China Economic Herald*, July 2, 2013, http://www.ceh.com.cn/cjpd/2013/02/171247.shtml.

17. Ministry of Agriculture and China Eximbank, "Daikuan shishi nongye duiwai hezou xiangmu de tongzi" [Loans to implement foreign agriculture cooperation projects].

18. French, "The Next Empire."

19. CDB, "$57 mn Invested in Agriculture by China-Africa Development Fund," CDB web-site, May 31, 2012.

20. Deutsche Bank, "Innovative Public-Private Financing Structures to Improve Food Security in Africa: The Africa Agriculture and Trade Investment Fund (AATIF)," https://www.db.com/cr/en/concrete-Africa-Agriculture-Trade-and-Investment-Fund.htm.

21. China Africa Agriculture Investment Company official, interview with author, Beijing, December 2013.

22. National Bureau of Statistics of China, *China Statistical Yearbook* (Beijing: China Statistical Press, various years).

23. Joseph Catanzaro, Li Fangchao and Zhang Yuwei, "Chinese Project to Create 100,000 Jobs," *China Daily*, May 30, 2014.

24. UN Comtrade Database, http://comtrade.un.org/data/, retrieved May 25, 2015.

25. Ibid. According to UN Comtrade, between 2004 and 2014, South Africa exported a total of 473 metric tons (mt) and Zimbabwe exported 200 kilograms (kg) of maize to China; Nigeria exported 1,443 mt and Madagascar exported 3 mt of cassava to China; South Africa also exported 30 kg of soybeans to China in 2004.

26. Crusoe Osagie, "Nigeria to Export $272m Worth of Cassava Chips to China," *This Day* (Nigeria) January 22, 2013, http://www.thisdaylive.com/articles/nigeria-to-export-272m-worth-of-cassava-chips-to-china/137119/.

27. Olivia Kumwenda, "South Africa's Maize Farmers Look East," *Mail & Guardian*, June 25, 2012, http://mg.co.za/article/2012-06-25-target-as-safrica-farmers-look-east. See also Nompumelelo Magwaza, "China Deal Amazing News for SA Farmers," *Independent* (South Africa), December 8, 2014, http://www.iol.co.za/business/news/china-deal-amazing-news-for-sa-farmers-1.1791956#. Other data in this paragraph comes from FAOSTAT, Rome, Italy: FAO. For US corn exports of 5.4 million tons in FY 2012, see USDA Foreign Agricultural Services, Export Sales Query System, http://apps.fas.usda.gov/esrquery/esrq.aspx. The USDA quotation is from Fred Gale, James Hansen, and Michael Jewison, "Prospects for China's Corn Yield Growth and Imports," Economic Information Bulletin No. EIB-136, Economic Research Service, USDA, February 2015, p. 22, http://www.ers.usda.gov/media/1389736/fds-14d-01.pdf. The Brazil figure is from Wei Xu, "Brazilian Farm Exports to China expected to Still Rise," *China Daily*, February 17, 2014.

28. See previous note.

29. All data from FAOSTAT, using Zimbabwe's reporting of its exports.

30. Yuxiao Zhu, "Remarks at the Handover Ceremony of the China-aided Agricultural Technology Demonstration Center by H. E. Mr. Yuxiao Zhou, Chinese Ambassador," Embassy of the PRC in the Republic of Liberia, July 22, 2010, http://lr.chineseembassy.org/chn/dszc/jianghua/t719935.htm

31. Chinese embassy official, interview with author, Maputo, Mozambique, November 19, 2014.

32. Bin, "Renda daibiao: bai wan nongmin" [NPC representative: one million farmers].

33. Chatelard and Chu, "Chinese Agricultural Engagements in Zambia."

34. Center for Rural Economy Research Group, "Zhongguo qiye duiwai nongye touzi yanjiu baogao" [Chinese enterprises foreign agricultural investment research report] MOA, Beijing, February 2014 (draft).

35. Wu, "Zhongguo ren Feizhou chuangye" [Chinese entrepreneurs in Africa].

36. Chatelard and Chu, "Chinese Agricultural Engagements in Zambia."

37. Geoffroy Touroumbaye, "La coopération avec la Chine est un modèle de transparence, selon les responsables tchadiens," Xinhua, July 6, 2012.

38. Jiao, "Zhongguo liangshi anquan baogao" [China food security report].

39. The countries are Malawi, Mozambique, Zambia, Zimbabwe, Chad, Togo, and Mali. "About," China-Africa Cotton Development, http://www.ca-cotton.com/Indexe.asp?id=10, retrieved June 16, 2015.

40. "Empire of the Pig," *Economist*, December 20, 2014.

41. Yang, "Haigui liangshi" [Returnees' Food].

42. Karen Harris, "Anti-Sinicism: Roots in Pre-industrial Colonial Southern Africa," *African and Asian Studies*, 9 (2010): 213–231.

43. Philip Snow, *The Star Raft: China's Encounter with Africa* (New York: Weidenfeld & Nicolson, 1988), p. 49.

44. Ibid., p. 99.

45. Feed the Future, "President Obama Announces New Alliance for Food Security & Nutrition to Fight Global Hunger," May 22, 2012, http://feedthefuture.gov/article/president-obama-announces-new-alliance-food-security-nutrition-fight-global-hunger.

46. Dean Mick Sikaenyi Mwala, interview with the author, University of Zambia, June 3, 2013. All quotes are from this interview.

INDEX

Note: Page numbers in *italics* indicate tables and charts.